ID0926409

Governor Reagan, Governor Brown

GOVERNOR REAGAN, GOVERNOR BROWN

A Sociology of Executive Power

Gary G. Hamilton *and*
Nicole Woolsey Biggart

New York / Columbia University Press / 1984

Library of Congress Cataloging in Publication Data

Hamilton, Gary G.
  Governor Reagan, Governor Brown.

  Includes bibliographical references and index.
    1. California—Governors—Staff.   2. Executive
power—California.   3. Reagan, Ronald.   4. Brown, Jerry, 1938–
    I. Biggart, Nicole Woolsey.   II. Title.
JK8753.S8H35 1984   353.979403'1   83-25191
ISBN 0-231-05902-7
ISBN 0-231-05903-5 (pbk.)

Columbia University Press
New York Guildford, Surrey

Printed in the United States of America

Clothbound editions of Columbia University Press books are
Smyth-sewn and printed on permanent and durable acid-free paper.

To Janet *and* Jeff

CONTENTS

PREFACE

THE POLITICAL SOCIOLOGY of recent years includes few close examinations of modern political organizations. Rather, political sociologists have turned overwhelmingly to understanding the structure and influence of the state and its relationship to other major sectors of society. Work on social movements, on stratification, on education, on almost all topics of interest to sociologists has pointed to the centrality of the state in understanding modern society. Particularly important in this regard has been the research of historical sociologists, who show in diverse studies the growing presence and decisive influence of the state in all spheres of human conduct. Despite the excellence of most studies, there has been little investigation on the internal structure of political institutions. If the modern state is strong, is it due only to the structure of the economy or to the dominance of political elites? Or can some of the strength be traced to the structural composition of the modern state apparatus? The purpose of this book is to examine an aspect of this question, the sociological and intraorganizational character of political leadership in today's government.

A topic such as this one would appear to fall within the disciplinary boundaries of political science. In fact the boundaries are unclear. Although political scientists regularly write on closely related subjects, they rarely study the normative structure of government or the influence of organization on the exercise of power. Instead most political scientists interested in executive leaders approach the subject in one of two ways. Many look at a political institution—the presidency or the governorship—and examine the characteristics of the office or of the people elected to the office. Presidential biographies and studies of the imperial presidency are examples of this genre. Others examine executive positions with an emphasis on policy and policy making; they trace how particular decisions were made and perhaps offer suggestions for improving decision-making procedures. Studies about the Cuban missile crisis and the decision to escalate the war in Vietnam are examples of this approach. Despite the purview of political science, the importance and strength of the modern state cannot be understood totally in either great or ignoble leaders, in either momentous decisions or extraordinary events. If the state is strong, part of the explanation must be located in the daily round, in the stuff of normal routine. These routines of executive power are the focus of our analysis.

As our footnotes testify, we have incorporated many conclusions from the works of political scientists in our own research, but the object of our investigation is not exhausted by any of these conclusions. This book inquires into the organization of executive power and into the normative orientation of those charged with executive leadership. This is an empirical study, because the answers we offer about executive power have been supplied by people who actually ran a highly complex, powerful government.

The planning, research, and writing that has led to this book covers almost six years. We owe more debts than acknowledgments can possibly repay. The project itself would not have been launched had it not been for a National Science Foundation research grant (Soc-7806945), which we received with the assistance of Roland Liebert, who was at that time Program Director for Sociology at NSF. The Institute of Governmental Affairs, University of California, Davis Campus administered this grant; Lloyd Musolf, Florence Nelson, and the entire staff of IGA made the research process smooth and entirely enjoyable. Dena Robertson and John Sutton helped us in the research itself, Dena with interviewing and John with the proofreading, coding, and filing. Both contributed their insights, and so helped to shape the final product. John, in addition, insightfully commented on the first draft of most chapters. For the tedious process of transcribing, we thank Carol She, Janis Lopez, and especially Catherine Closson.

The success of our research stems from the willingness, on the part of our interviewees, to answer our questions with candor and in good faith that we would not use their words, in a partisan fashion, to discredit either governor or his appointees. We thank the many who took the time out of busy schedules to be interviewed. Gabrielle Morris, of the Regional Oral History Office, University of California, Berkeley Campus shared with us her work on the California Government History Project. We particularly want to acknowledge the effort of Molly Sturges Tuthill, who is in charge of the Reagan Collection at the Hoover Institution, for her assistance in locating the principals of Reagan's administration, for helping to arrange our interviews with Edwin Meese III, and for her unfailing encouragement of our work even before she had seen any results. Molly also read and commented on large portions of the manuscript in various stages of revision.

Others who commented on one or more chapters of one or more versions of the manuscript include Mitchel Abolafia, Pierre van den Berghe, Larry Berman, Bruce Hackett, Lyn Lofland, John Lofland, Lloyd Musolf, Philippe Nonet, A. Alan Post, and Philip Selznick. Their comments have immeasurably enriched our analysis, even if we elected not always to follow their advice. A special acknowledgement goes to Charles Perrow and Guenther Roth, both of whom gave us such detailed comments on an earlier draft of the manuscript that we suffered through a major revision to get to the present version. We also owe gratitude to Peter M. Detwiler, formerly a Brown appointee in the Office of Planning and Research and now a staff consultant to the California Legislature. Peter's encouragement and detailed reading of much of the manuscript sharpened our insights from the viewpoint of an insider to California government and saved us from many errors.

Finally, for typing and retyping various versions of the book, we acknowledge the assistance of Catherine Closson, Sasha Bessom, Wava Haggard, Josephine Chu, Linda Walters, and Diane Chave.

Chapter One
EXECUTIVE ORGANIZATION

THREE VIEWS

I N 1974 California Governor-elect Jerry Brown sent his new chief-
of-staff, Gray Davis, and his Legal Affairs Secretary, Anthony
Klein, to Sacramento to meet with Edwin Meese III. The agenda
for their meeting was the executive organization of the executive
branch. Meese, Executive Assistant to outgoing Governor Ronald
Reagan, had been at his post for almost six years and, throughout the
period, had been in charge of the organizational details of the Reagan
administration.[1] Moreover, Meese was a devotee of organizational
know-how. "Public management," Meese told us in an interview, "has
been a hobby of mine since I majored in Public Administration back
at Yale . . . and when I was in Sacramento, I spent a lot of time
studying management patterns and the staff organization of everybody
I could get my hands on." Meese was proud of how the Reagan administration had in eight years developed the management and staff
structure of state government, and he wanted to convey this sense of
accomplishment to Davis and Klein. In addition, Meese hoped to
suggest how these improvements of the executive organization could
be adopted and advanced still further by Brown.

Klein, who had been Brown's classmate at Yale Law School and
an activist lawyer before Brown brought him into state government,
remembered the meeting and his initial impression of Reagan's aides.
"I was here [in the Governor's Office] when Meese and the staff were
still [here]. They seemed to me to be very much management [ori-
ented]. They were really organization men." The meeting, Klein recalled, turned out to be more like a briefing than a discussion. "The
first time Gray and I met Ed, he sat us down in his office and he
showed us a chart of state government in 1930.[2] It had a million lines
down to a million agencies. Then he showed us a chart of state government in the last year of Reagan's administration. They had four

lines from the governor to the four main agencies and a fifth to Finance." Amused, Klein saw Meese's presentation as further evidence of the management orientation of Reagan's aides and the organizational character of Reagan's administration. "It was all very impressive," said Klein, "but I don't know whether it worked. I don't know what it all meant." Klein was certain of one thing, however. "I think you really have to suit the personal style of the individual who is the governor. I think that [his organization] probably suited Reagan's style a hell of a lot better than our organization would. I know that Reagan's didn't suit Jerry Brown."

Klein's view of executive organization is a common one, and represents a personalized conception of the roles and functions of the governor's appointed aides and managers. This view implies a belief that *executive organization is an expression of individual goals and personal proclivities*. It is the view that, at the presidential level, the White House organization of FDR or Eisenhower or Kennedy or Nixon blended the personal idiosyncrasies and program preferences of a particular president with the institutional tasks that a chief executive must accomplish. So conceived, executive organizations are without histories; they are manipulable and must be constituted anew with each executive.[3] In this conception executive organization is, like the order on one's desk or the tidiness of one's appearance, a matter of personal style; insofar as it does not detract from one's work, it is a matter of indifference.

Jerry Brown, Klein went on, was largely indifferent to organization. He was policy oriented as opposed to management oriented. Brown believed that too much rigidity in the organizational structure of state government quashed ideas and innovative programs that might help solve some of the serious problems of the day. Pulling the state phonebook from his desk in the Governor's Office and pointing to the organizational chart on the back cover, Klein explained Brown's nonchalance. "We took [this organizational arrangement] from the Reagan administration. We didn't change it. . . . This box here [the Governor's Office] hasn't changed that much. We took the titles. You see, under the Reagan administration things were very formal. If you had the word Secretary after your name, as I do, 'Legal Affairs Secretary' . . . that meant you were at a cabinet level rank within their hierarchy. That's a distinction that doesn't seem to have much meaning here, frankly. But, except for that, we've adopted the titles. But I think that my function is very different than my predecessor's. . . . I think I play a very different role."

This idea, that organization is an expression of personality and that the roles and functions within an organization change with a change in the executive, was a view that Brown and many of his aides and appointees shared. Moreover, as this book shows, it was a view that had some important consequences in how state government ran during Brown's eight years as Governor of California.

Ed Meese, Reagan's Executive Assistant, had a different view of executive organization, the same view, we were told, that Reagan held. "Just like nature supposedly abhors a vacuum," explained Meese, "government abhors a vacuum even more. Where there's a vacuum somebody's going to rush in to jockey for position within that vacuum. The idea [of management during Reagan's term] was to keep as few vacuums as possible by setting out kinds of authority and communications." Meese's goal, he said, was not simply to establish businesslike routines and a businesslike efficiency in government. "The thing about government, particularly when you have a politically elected office holder, is that it's unlike any other business. . . . It's not like stamping out cans. I know how to run an operation stamping out cans: You're going to do the same thing every morning when you come to work. Whereas here [in government] you have a legislature shooting back at you; you've got the press hammering you questions, you've got the opposition political party. . . . Nothing is the same one day from the day before. You've got a constantly dynamic situation." Executive organization, Meese felt, must be flexible, must allow for constant changes in programs and people. At the same time it had to defuse the tensions and fill the vacuums that flexibility created. "My personal management philosophy," stressed Meese, "is that if you have everybody informed, you're going to have a happier crew. A lot of people disagree with this, but I've found in my own experience that it is really the *only* way you can keep people moving together. If you don't have a lot of communication, you then have cliques form or you have power groups, and they are at war with each other."

Meese's idea of organization at the top of government is a version of a widely held view that *organization has an intrinsic purpose and that the purpose is to accomplish goals.*[4] Organization consists of structure and procedures, and should not be personalized, should not be a matter of personal taste or party preference. This view, long held in honor among public administrators, asserts that politics and administration should be kept separate and that administration should be merely the *means* to accomplish political functions and political goals. Like Klein's view, this idea of executive organization is ahistorical. But unlike Klein's view, organization here is a tool, and like any tool, it should differ according to the job to be done, not according to the person doing the job. Hence, executive organization should be designed to accomplish efficiently and well the tasks of the chief executive, regardless of who occupies that position.

During Reagan's eight years as Governor of California, Meese, with Reagan's blessing, pursued what he hoped would be the ideal executive organization for California state government. "We were never satisfied with the organization," says Meese, "just to leave it set in a particular pattern. [We wanted] to improve it, make it more responsive to the governor's needs and the people's needs, and so, as everybody grew in their responsibilities . . . you had an evolving system, not only evolving in the sense of changes in the organizational structure, but better definitions of how we were doing things, processes." At one point early in Reagan's second term, Meese recalled, "I took some paper and, without regard to where they belonged, . . . listed every function in the [Governor's Office] from correspondence, to answering phones, to education decisions. We must have had 100 to 150 different functions. Then we started developing groups of functions, and then we started playing with organizational structure, and finally we evolved this idea of having all of the functions that cut across the office divided under three principal assistants to me." The plan that Meese worked out became the basis of the reorganization of the Governor's Office that Reagan announced publicly in 1971, and that with a few minor additions lasted until the end of Reagan's term. It was also the plan that Gray Davis and Anthony Klein heard about in their meeting with Meese. And because Meese had constructed the organization in order to fulfill the duties of the chief executive, he sincerely believed that his innovations should have suited Brown's needs as well.

But Brown defined the governor's duties differently from the way Reagan had, as Klein recognized. Brown believed that the governor's foremost role was that of problem-solver rather than that of manager. It was the function of executive organization to aid the governor in his task as policy maker in a time of crisis. With this goal in mind, Brown took Reagan's organization chart—four lines to agencies and one to Finance—and ignored all the formality that went with it. Where Reagan had advocated hierarchy, Brown wanted debate among peers; where Reagan had desired a means to accomplish goals, Brown sought a forum to discover what the proper political goals should be. With Brown, titles lost their rank, and procedures their finality. What Reagan and Meese had worked so hard to construct, Brown and his aides laid aside. The artificial, the manufactured character of Reagan's executive organization became an organic, natural, substantive endeavor during Brown's term as governor.

This book contrasts the Reagan and Brown approaches to executive organization, but not simply to judge which is the more effective. Rather, we place the two in the broader context of state government to show that any approach to organizing the executive is altered by the larger and more complex organization of the administrative bureaucracy. We show as well that executive organizations do have consequences upon state government, though not always the ones that governors and aides anticipate.

The executive office is an organization within an organization, and each influences the other. But senior civil servants, who have a third view of all this, downplay the mutual interaction between the executive and state organizations and see instead the limitations that the state bureaucracy places upon any attempt to organize executive power.

The Klein and Meese assessments of the executive are insider views, both showing the bias of one who looks at state government from the inside of the Governor's Office. These assessments emphasize the value of action and decision-making, and rest upon the assumption that how the governor decides to organize will actually make a difference in how the state is run and in what is accomplished.

Many senior state employees, all outsiders to the Governor's Office, disagree with both views. To be sure, they recognized that Brown and Reagan, as well as their respective aides, had divergent ideas about the proper organization for the executive ranks of state government. Moreover, these senior civil servants, Career Executive Assignees, or CEA's as they are known, were divided on which governor's approach they preferred. Some thought Reagan's way was too rigid, too much "business as usual." These people liked Brown's approach because Brown asked for, listened to, and took their ideas seriously. But others, in Brown's term, yearned for a return to Reagan's sense of management, for fixed responsibilities and known procedures.

Although the CEAs certainly knew that Brown and Reagan differed in their approaches to government, many thought that it was a difference that had few long-term consequences. These CEA's subscribed to another view of executive organization. They told us that regardless of who is in power or how they are organized, state government always goes on in much the same way, not merely within the bureaucracy, but at the executive level as well. "Governors, staffers, department directors," said one long-time civil servant, "they all act pretty much the same, year after year, term after term."

This is a view from outside the Governor's Office, a view implying that the governor and his appointees do not actively decide how to organize as much as they react to the cycles of office-holding. In this view *executive organization is more a consequence of events than their cause.* CEA's point, in particular, to two cycles that constrain the governor and in large part determine his organization: the political cycle and the business cycle.

The political cycle consists, typically, of two terms in office—the four years between election and reelection and the four years between reelection and leaving office. Long-time state workers know the pattern because they have seen the cycle repeated several times. The first four years are chaotic, taken up with people learning their jobs and with the governor's attempts to pass a political agenda in order to claim results in time for the reelection campaign. The last four years slide into maintaining routines and programs, keeping up the facade of business as usual, while the governor tries to extend his political career, sometimes by becoming a presidential possibility. Civil servants realize that governors must respond to the political cycle and that, despite all protestations to the contrary, executive organizations must also double as political staffs.

The business cycle is the annual turning of state government, first to budget preparation, then to legislative hearings and bill signings, and then back to budget preparation again. Senior civil servants live by the rhythm of this cycle, and they know that the governor and his appointees keep time by this yearly round as well. Politicians learn that budget and legislative processes are the only effective means they have to gain some control over the executive branch and to get their political programs made into law and implemented. Civil servants know, therefore, that for politicians to be effective they must allow themselves to be drawn into the larger arenas of state government.

This study takes the civil servant view of government as seriously as the other two views. Each view, of course, is partially correct, and were they confronted with the alternatives, Meese, Klein, and the CEAs would readily admit the truth in the other views. In leadership roles, individuals do make a difference, and Meese would be the first to say so, especially about Reagan. But goal-oriented, management organization also counts for a lot, and often itself makes the difference between good and bad policies, which is a point that some Brown appointees could not stress strongly enough. Finally, government organization—the lineup of roles, functions, the cycle of business—precedes any politician who becomes a chief executive. These precedents establish what is organizationally possible, and sometimes, as this study shows, even what is thinkable. That governors and their appointees end up acting much like their predecessors is not for want of imagination or initiative. Rather, as all would acknowledge, executive roles structure the logic and channel the actions of those who, in filling them, try to accomplish their jobs.

Rather than separating the three views of government, we combine them. In particular, we look at the interaction between business routines and politics on the one hand, and Reagan's and Brown's specific ways of organizing their appointees on the other. It is this interplay between politicians and procedures, between temporary officials and permanent administration, that provides the central focus of our study: the organization of executive power.

PROBLEMS AND ANALYSIS

This book is a case study of the California executive branch and has been written so that nonspecialist readers can appreciate the complexity of social life at the top reaches of government. Most references of interest to scholars are in the notes at the back. Unlike many case studies, however, our interest is not descriptive or ethnographic. There are a number of quite good and far more complete descriptions of the working of state government. Rather, our interest is theoretical and we have chosen this case as a vehicle for exploring problems in political sociology, especially the social and organizational sources of power in modern government. The differences and similarities between Reagan's and Brown's administrations provide the individual and organizational data for analysis; the changes in California's governorship during the last hundred years provides an historical context that makes these two governors and their approaches to executive management general phenomena rather than historical accidents. We are concerned, however, with neither the policies of these two politicians, nor the substance of California government. Our interest is an analysis of the organizational character of modern political rule.

Our theoretical focus encompasses three dimensions of executive power: historical, organizational, and individual. Our historical concern is with the growth of an organizational definition of the executive branch and a managerial definition of the governor's power. Both of these definitions are recent, showing up in California only within the last hundred years. Until the end of the nineteenth century executive power in California was split among twelve independently elected officials whose duties overlapped so that no one could wield kingly power. Many other states had a similar division of power, a division that worked against a unified command, and a unity of executive functions.

Today in California, as in other states, the governor's prerogative has grown as the governor has assumed managerial control over state administration. Executive power, however, is still divided among different people, but now the division of power stems from the governor's delegation of authority to his subordinates who, by right of their position, fulfill gubernatorial functions. The governor's personal staff, members of which work in the Governor's Office, act as the governor's advisors on policy and political matters. The governor's appointed managers head the administrative units of the executive branch. And the CEAs, civil servants without tenure rights, serve as professional managers and technical advisors to the governor and his appointees. Government is becoming more systematically an organization and the governor more securely the manager in charge. The historical problem for analysis is to understand this transformation that has occurred in California state government during the past one hundred years, a transformation in which an organizational paradigm has become the taken-for-granted reality of modern political rule.

The mode of analysis for the historical dimension is to show the developmental sequence by which executive power took its modern form, and the underlying organizational logic that has served and continues to serve as justification for such changes. Within the field of historical sociology, this form of analysis is Weberian.[5] Although social and economic factors outside state government (e.g., population growth, inflation, declining industrial core) have certainly been important in causing state government to alter its form, we have limited our analysis to the changing institutions of executive power within state government and to their organizational justification.

The second dimension of our analysis is an examination of the organizational content of executive power. We have chosen not to focus on the formal organization or on the formal institutions of the governor's power, such as the duty to prepare state budgets or the right to veto legislation; the organization at the top of government is more dynamic and more complex than a listing of its formal qualities would suggest. Instead, we explain through an organizational analysis how temporary holders of power—the politician and his appointees—gain and maintain control of the administrative apparatus of modern government.[6] Government today is a highly organized social system whose structure has a profound impact on the activities of its membership. To understand power in modern government one must move beyond equating it with specific people or with formal duties. Instead, because power is an institutionalized, socially organized feature of the executive branch, it may only be understood by knowing how it is articulated through organizational roles. We demonstrate how roles thrust people into unavoidable conflicts over power because of contradictory norms, and argue that power is not simply a matter of more or less resources. Organizational power, including government's, has as its basis a substantively rational, essentially moral character.

An important problem for elected officials is learning the norms and structural underpinnings of this social system so as to control it. We uncover the norms and structure of government through a detailed analysis of top management positions, investigating the interaction between individuals and the roles they occupy. This approach emphasizes the appointees' commitment to serve the governor, the impact of organization upon this commitment, and the tensions that arise between individuals and what they are required to do.

The key roles that we study are the aides in the Governor's Office, the managers of the major administrative units in state government, and civil servant appointees (CEAs). Individuals in these positions number around 1500. These 1500 constitute the political (and temporary) leadership for the permanent administration, which in 1980 amounted to over 130,000 state civil service employees, not counting the people employed at the state supported systems of higher education. These appointees represent extensions of the governor's power, and collectively form what we refer to as executive organization.

We approach this dimension from the viewpoints of appointees, and then analyze their viewpoints in terms of the structural characteristics of the positions they hold. This approach, like that for the historical dimension, draws on the Weberian perspective, but also supplements this perspective with recent developments in role theory. The Weberian perspective in organizational analysis systematically relates the structure of administrative power to the underlying principles of legitimation.[7] Our adaptation of this approach is to relate the divisions of executive roles and functions that have emerged historically to the organizational logic that appointees use to justify their power. To this mode of analysis we add the insights into social psychology made by role theorists and symbolic interactionists.[8] They argue that socially constructed roles suggest not only a full range of human behavior, but also prescriptions for self-images and for the standards of "authentic" human conduct. We use these insights in our analysis of the tensions between appointees and the requirements of their role.

The third dimension of executive power is an analysis of individual leadership strategies in specific organizational contexts. Strategies of leadership are not equivalent. Their success varies according to the individuals who use them and the contexts in which they are tried. Not every person is an equally effective leader, and a person who is effective in one context may be ineffective in another. For instance, people's gender or ethnicity or education or any one of dozens of other factors will influence the strategies they choose and the success of those strategies. That the success of leaders and strategies vary emphasizes the importance of the social contexts of leadership. Different kinds of groups have an affinity for different kinds of leaders and leadership strategies. For instance, a collectivity of equals, such as Congress, values different qualities of leadership than does a group with a rigid chain of command, such as the military. Similarly, some groups place a premium on leaders with technical competence or with negotiating skills or with demonstrated moral character. In this study of California the underlying theoretical problem is what characteristics of leaders and what strategies of leadership appear successful in the context of modern organizational government.

We contrast the leadership of Governor Reagan and Governor Brown, two governors who developed in the same organization nearly opposite approaches to wielding executive power.[9] Ronald Reagan, who was governor between 1967 and 1975, delegated most executive functions and powers to his subordinates. Jerry Brown, who was governor between 1975 and 1983, retained a great deal of discretion over which functions he would perform and which powers he would exercise. We show that both strategies had anticipated as well as unanticipated consequences upon the governors' ability to use the powers of their office and upon the routine operation of state government. In our conclusion, we evaluate the merger of strategy and structure for each governor.

Our approach to this dimension is an analysis of differences. Most sociological studies take the opposite approach, analyzing a number of cases to locate points of similarity so as to make generalizable propositions. But in sociological fields where numerous examples of a phenomenon are not available, most notably in historical sociology, analysts may examine the differences between a limited number of cases.[10] The logic of this approach is quasi-experimental, in which each case is a control for the others.[11] In our study, we discuss similar structural problems that both governors faced, such as soliciting the loyalty of subordinates, and then systematically contrast the strategies of each governor to deal with that problem.

Our analysis is drawn from a variety of material. The historical analysis is based largely on archival and documentary sources. The analysis of the Reagan and Brown administrations primarily comes from information gained from interviews, which has been checked against and supplemented with newspaper, magazine, and book-length accounts of the two governors and their administrations. We interviewed 110 people and the interviews ranged from slightly less than an hour to over six hours. We recorded all but three interviews and transcribed all we recorded; the quotations that we use throughout the book are drawn verbatim from over 3,000 pages of transcriptions. We interviewed most of the top aides and many agency secretaries and departmental directors in both administrations. In addition, we interviewed a number of CEAs who served under both governors. With the exception of this and the final chapters, we have elected not to identify the names of our respondents, for some because anonymity was the condition under which they agreed to talk with us, but primarily because we want to emphasize the theoretical rather than topical nature of our subject. A description and a statistical summary of our interviews are in the appendix.

ORGANIZATION OF THE STUDY

The three dimensions of our analysis comprise major sections of the following chapters. In the next four chapters (chapters 2–5) we examine the three main types of appointees who serve as extensions of the governor's power: staff aides, administrative appointees, and CEAs. We describe the historical emergence of the three roles, showing how they came out of changing notions of the proper form of government. Each role created in turn a distinctive type of executive authority, each resting on a different legitimating principle. These principles, which are a type of moral precept, both justify the exercise of power by incumbents and limit the normative ways in which that power may be exercised. We describe through the words of our informants the often difficult task of living up to role prescriptions, particularly the prescribed emotional attachments that are important aspects of some positions.

In chapter 6 we look at how these executive roles interrelate in the routine business of government. Because each role binds individuals to different sets of norms, some of which are in contradiction with the norms of others, we examine the procedure by which differences are bridged so that everyone's commitments may be upheld and activity continue. We argue that decision-making processes in government, because they rest on role performances, conform with what Weber described as substantive—not economic—rationality.

In the final chapter we show the constraints that government as an organization places on individual leaders by comparing the very different styles of exercising power of Reagan and Brown. We argue that the structure of government limits the possible successful approaches to governing and, further, the nature of policies that may be successfully implemented. We find that Reagan was administratively more effective than Brown, not because he was a more capable individual or because his style was abstractly "better," but because his management practices did not threaten organizational routines. In contrast, Brown's concern with substantive issues and innovative processes could not be accommodated by the existing government organization.

Chapter Two
THE GOVERNOR'S PERSONAL STAFF

THE HANDFUL OF TOP AIDES that surround important political executives are today among the most well-known figures in American politics. Presidential aides such as Sherman Adams, Clark Clifford, Bill Moyers, H. R. Haldeman, and Hamilton Jordan have been at least as famous, and perhaps as powerful, as the leading senators of their day. This is no less true of the top aides that surrounded Governors Reagan and Brown. The background, lifestyles, and every word of aides such as William P. Clark, Edwin Meese III, Gray Davis, and B. T. Collins were important intelligence in the corridors of Sacramento. These men were regularly quoted in the press and studied seriously by political analysts.

Why did the actions of these and other previously obscure persons take on such interest when they arrived in office with the governor? Because personal staff are rightfully seen as *extensions* of the chief, the closest possible reflection of the ideas and inclinations of the governor himself. The staff shares the governor's view of the executive as a whole in a way that even cabinet members do not. Staff members are privy to the governor's most private thoughts and may even be their source. Unlike any other position in government the staff has no constituency to serve but the governor; they work only for him and work only in his name. In a word, personal staff are the governor's *surrogates*.

Being a surrogate, that is, assuming the role of another, is a difficult position to sustain in a society that values individualism and "thinking for yourself." But the staff role demands that its occupants submerge themselves in the person of the one they serve. They must put his desires before their own, substitute his political needs for their ideas, and represent every act they take as an act in his name. The reward for such self-denial, of course, can be great power and a measure of fame.

In fact, however, few people that we interviewed saw this sacrifice of self as a sacrifice at all; it was what they *wanted* to do. They successfully merged themselves into the considerable demands of the staff role. The social structure of the staff organization predisposes this self-role merger and makes it seem "natural," "inevitable." The construction of the staff world, as we demonstrate in this chapter, makes any orientation other than subordination and personal loyalty to the governor self-defeating and even unthinkable. This is not to suggest that all persons assume the staff role with equal ease. In fact, some people act selfless and devoted while never feeling the emotional bond that makes devotion a meaningful posture: we discuss the dilemmas of such persons at the end of this chapter.

Although it is difficult to imagine contemporary political executives in this country without a coterie of aides surrounding their every move, personal staffs are an historically recent phenomenon. Staffs arose in Washington during Franklin Roosevelt's administration, and in California a few years later during Governor Earl Warren's incumbency. As we demonstrate in the next section, staffs did not emerge simply as the self-aggrandizing tactics of political figures, but were *organizational* responses to larger changes in the demands on government.

THE GROWTH OF THE GOVERNOR'S OFFICE

The Governor's Office, in its present institutional form, did not exist fifty years ago. In 1931 it was simply an office with five people on the payroll—the governor, a private secretary, an executive secretary, a stenographer, and a messenger.[1] Their salaries, including the governor's, totaled $22,100 and their office expenses for the 1930–31 fiscal year added up to $38,388.[2] That fiscal year had been an expensive one, up about $15,000 from the year before because 1930 was an election year. Travel expenses for the governor ran $10,000 over the previous year. The Governor's Office had purchased an automobile for $5,000. The Governor in 1931, James Rolph, Jr., Sunny Jim as he was known, proposed in his budget request to the state legislature for the following two years to more than double the size of the

Governor's Office.[3] He wanted to increase the staff from five to eleven positions by adding an assistant secretary, three stenographer-clerks, a stenographer-reporter, and a chauffeur. He justified the increase by noting that "the practice of borrowing clerical assistance and other help from various branches of State government will be discontinued, as the personnel recommended is deemed sufficient for the increased duties which are required of this office."[4]

By 1981, the Governor's Office was no longer an office. It had become an organization, a separately budgeted unit within the executive branch that included the Office of Citizen Initiative and Voluntary Action, the Office of Planning and Research, and the Office of Emergency Services.[5] The Governor's budget contained the allocation for his executive office, but also the allocations for the offices of the five agency secretaries that sat on the cabinet.[6] For the 1980–81 fiscal year the governor's operating expenses, paying salaries for about 500 people, amounted to over $18,500,000 with $4,495,083 of that set aside for the governor's executive office.

Of the 500 people, the governor's executive office only employed 86.6 of them.[7] This figure remained fairly constant during the entirety of both Ronald Reagan's and Jerry Brown's administrations.[8] Fiscal restraint, however, is not the reason for the lack of growth. There was simply no more room. As the governor's budget increased and the number of people being paid from that budget increased, the Governor's Office repeatedly overflowed the space provided for it.[9] With each overflow the reigning governor would create a new office with an assigned function and space of its own, without removing it from his payroll.[10] The 85-plus who remained in the executive suite were the closest aides, who provided the most critical or most sensitive services for the governor, and a small number of clerical workers who supported them.

The changes in the Governor's Office between 1931 and 1981 were more than ones of size and expense. During this interval, there were comprehensive transformations in the nature of the Governor's Office and in the jobs that members of that office performed.[11] In 1931 the office staff provided the Governor with personal services. They answered his mail, delivered his messages, scheduled his appointments, and served as his aides de camp. They were either menials or confidants, and performed no essential services in the routine operation of state government. By 1981, the Governor's Office was the center of state government, just as the presidential office is the center of the federal government.[12] The modern staff consists of a corps of aides who act as assistants to the governor, and who are crucial to the routine operation of all aspects of governing the state.[13] These aides plan, direct, and coordinate the activities of the executive branch. They select candidates for judgeships, and supervise the relations among local, state, and federal governmental units. They formulate legislation and make policy decisions that influence the state, and sometimes the nation. These aides made up the Governor's personal staff.

Some people might like to think of the members of the Governor's personal staff as clerks or as merely the governor's lackeys, suggesting that personal staffs are political leftovers from an earlier era.[14] But to view them this way is to confuse them with personal servants, which they are not. The Governor's personal staff fills an organizational role within the executive branch, and its members perform organizational duties that are integral to the conduct of state government. In official business they represent the governor. They serve as the Governor's surrogate in lobbying legislators and in interviewing candidates for gubernatorial appointments; they aid in assessing policy recommendations from departments and agencies. Their job, in performing these and many other tasks, is to act as the governor himself would act. As we will show in this chapter, staff members do view their service to the governor in personal terms, but their jobs serve the overall organization of state government and not simply the governor's person, as they did in 1931.

Recent Staff Organizations

In California, the change in the staff role from personal to organizational functions began in the 1940s during the administration of Earl Warren (1943 to 1953).[15] Warren presided over an era of rapid growth in the state's population, in social services provided by state and federal governments, and in the size of the executive branch.[16] In keeping with the management ideas of his day, Warren reorga-

nized the Governor's Office in order to gain greater control over the
conduct of state business.[17] To accomplish this, he divided the Governor's Office into ten functional units and hired nine aides to supervise the units as well as to accomplish a variety of other tasks.[18] Besides an executive secretary and a private secretary, both of which were
positions he had inherited from previous administrations, Warren recruited seven other positions: a press secretary to handle public relations, a legislative secretary to work on legislative programs and to be
the governor's lobbyist, a secretary to the Governor's Council to coordinate "all the work between the Governor's Office and various state
departments, agencies, boards, and commissions," a "Secretary in
charge of Extradition and Executive Clemency and Appointment to
State Office" to serve as legal advisor in matters of extradition and
pardons and to process and advise on applications for appointment to
public office, a "Secretary in charge of Research" to collect "factual
and statistical data . . . [in] collaboration with [the] Governor," a
Secretary to the Disaster Council, and an Office Supervisor to oversee administrative matters in the office itself.[19] During his ten years
as governor he increased the number of positions in the Governor's
Office from 21 in 1943 to 56 in 1953. In the same period the budget
grew to $338,907.[20] More importantly, however, Warren rethought
the scope of the governorship and the responsibilities of those working within the Governor's Office. The Governor, thought Warren,
needed to manage the executive branch, and accordingly, he needed
the personnel that was required to do the job.[21] Warren set into motion a process of defining, systematizing, and extending those duties
that continues today.

Ronald Reagan and Jerry Brown inherited the organizational focus
of the Governor's Office that Warren first developed. The office had
grown slightly between 1953, when Warren resigned his governorship
to become Chief Justice of the Supreme Court, and 1967, when
Reagan took office.[22] In 1967, the executive office contained 87.4
authorized positions with an allocation of $1,450,461 for salaries and
operating expenses.[23] In the same year ten other units were listed under the Governor's Office budget, which added another 178.1 personnel years and $1,763,949 to the Governor's budget.[24] By 1975,
when Jerry Brown became Governor, the executive office had the same

number of people on the payroll as when Reagan took office, 87.7 authorized positions and an annual budget of $2.7 million. But the rest of the Governor's Office had grown; the budget provided for another 230 positions and for an additional $4.2 million allocation.[25]

Despite the overall increase in the Governor's Office, the functional divisions and duties of the governor's personal staff were essentially those of the Warren era. It is Warren who first conceptualized the personal staff as having an organizational role and structured the duties of the staff accordingly.[26] On becoming governors, Ronald Reagan and Jerry Brown assumed control of staff positions whose duties had become institutionalized and had increasingly been brought into the center of the routine operation of state government. Both governors accepted and further developed the staff organization of their predecessors.

THE STAFF-GOVERNOR RELATIONSHIP: PERSONAL LOYALTY

The governor's personal staff has developed over time, and its routines have become institutionalized features of executive organization. The staff organization structures the possibilities for social action by presenting to people who fill the staff role sets of constraints and opportunities.[27] These constraints and opportunities are shaped by the staff's commitment to the governor, a relationship defined in terms of *personal loyalty*. Personal loyalty defines an obligation to the governor but it is also the source of staff power. In this section we present the staff members' descriptions of their commitment to the two governors. In the next sections we show that the source and continuity of this commitment are located in the organizational context of the governorship, not in the person of the governor himself.

Commitment to the Person of the Governor

Members of the governor's personal staff during both Reagan's and Brown's administrations said that the quality defining their relationship with the governor was a commitment to the governor as an individual and not simply to the governor's position or to the governor as a spokesman of a philosophy that they themselves espoused.[28] As if to emphasize this point, staff members constantly used in interviews words connoting emotion and personality to speak about their relationship with the governor. Love, affection, inspiration, awe, commitment, charisma, charm, genius—these were typical expressions staff members used to characterize their attachment to Reagan or Brown. Some staff members were at a loss for words. Most, we judged, were genuinely moved in their attempt to express their relationship with the governor and a few even wept.

Almost in embarassment, a senior aide on Brown's staff, who is widely known for his outspokenness, remarked, "I hate to admit it, and I would never admit it to his face, but he has a way of inspiring us. It's weird how he does it, because I think he does everything wrong, and it is not as if your job is on the line or if you're going to get chewed out. But somehow he inspires you to want to do what is right. I don't know how to articulate it, but I can feel it." One of Reagan's top staff advisors stated this feeling more directly: "You can't be around somebody day in and day out for years without having a great deal of affection for him. Affection is probably a better term than loyalty, because you would be loyal to anyone you have a great deal of affection for. But this was not a respect for his office. Although we respected his accomplishments, we had affection for the man. He had an iron determination; he was the most optimistic person I ever saw in my life."

When describing the governor, staff members consistently concentrated on his personal characteristics. Such attributes as the governor's "command over situations," "his Socratic style of inquiry," and "his genuine concern for others" were traits staff members singled out to justify a personal commitment. This comment made about Jerry Brown was typical: "His honesty is inspirational to me. I really respect his intellect and his searching, his questioning, and his looking for other answers. Even when I disagree with him, I really respect that in him. And that is inspirational." So strong and obviously emotional were many of these statements that it seemed that the governor's personal qualities embodied the office.[29] Such characteristics of the governor had become magnified, infusing into his personality the power of the office, which itself inspired awe: "[Reagan's] the greatest persuader I've ever met in the world." "Something exciting happens when [Brown] walks in the room." "There's just something *there* that just makes [Brown] *the governor.*"

Even for his former and closest associates, the assumption of the governorship created a dilemma in the perception of his identity.[30] One of Brown's top aides had known the governor since his days as an undergraduate; indeed, the aide had been Brown's dormitory monitor and they had continued to have a friendly relationship over the years. But during the first week of the administration, the aide recalled being overwhelmed and speechless in the presence of his longtime friend. He was no longer just Jerry Brown; he was "*the Governor.*" Other friends who were soon to be appointees felt the same way: "[Brown] was in another office, and we were sitting around. Somehow or other the subject came up: 'What shall we call him?' I don't know who spoke first from there. [A recent friend] said that she felt uncomfortable calling him Governor, but didn't feel right calling him Jerry, and she didn't know him that well, so she decided to call him 'Boss.' " [Another friend] who had known him eighteen years said she would call him "Governor." The person and the previous relationship became transformed upon the assumption of a new and powerful role.

This bond of personal loyalty transcended previous friendships, personal philosophies, and career aspirations, but did not necessarily result in sycophancy. One of Brown's closest aides insisted that members of the Governor's Office felt a "sense of personal commitment" to Brown. "By that I mean, the people here are reasonably discreet; they won't talk out of school; they respect the privacy of the Governor; they are committed to most of his policies. But I don't think it means that there are no disagreements. There is a real divergence of opinion around here. . . . I don't think loyalty to the Governor has a chilling effect on the willingness of people to disagree with him. . . . In fact, sometimes I think [governor/staff] relationships could principally be characterized as ones of argumentation." That Brown encouraged disagreement among his aides in matters of policymaking was independently verified many times.

Reagan, too, relied upon his top aides, not for flattery, but for candid advice even though, unlike Brown, he did not encourage open arguments among staff members. [31]

THE ORGANIZATION OF THE STAFF ROLE

That the defining quality of the staff role is personal loyalty does not mean that the role lacks an organizational grounding or that personal loyalty itself has no organizational source. Both the role and the relationship derive from the organization of state government. [32] Both are now institutionalized features of executive government, and have built up around them structural conditions that predispose staff members towards viewing personal loyalty as a necessary component of the staff role. What staff members say in a public forum does not imply that they actually or always feel this sort of attachment to the governor. [33] But whatever the match between public expressions and private opinions, staff members in both administrations nonetheless defined their loyalty so similarly among themselves and so differently from other appointees and career bureaucrats as to require an organizational explanation. The sources of these patterned responses can be attributed, in the main, to the organizational features that we describe below, features that lead individuals who differ by position and motivation to respond in similar ways.

Selective Recruitment

The first support for a bond of personal loyalty is selective recruitment, the predisposition to select people who will develop a genuine personal commitment to the governor and accordingly who will define their behavior in terms of this commitment. [34] The individuals charged with recruiting staff members in both administrations noted that staff work requires people capable of making such a commitment. In the words of one individual so charged, "There isn't as high a premium on expertise [in recruiting people] for [the Governor's] Office as there is for many other appointments, such as for departments and agency [people]. A Director of Health has to know something about the health problems and the health area. In this office, you need somebody who is a lawyer for the Legal Affairs Secretary, but beyond that, there is a lot of room." What is needed, he said, is a basis for "trust." "There is a heavy personal reliance on a day-to-day basis on the staff. [The governor] must have confidence in them. Not only does he interrelate with them on a daily basis, but they are privy to things. He has got to be free to say something outrageous. . . . There must be some privacy [in this office] and there has got to be an understanding that is hard to develop with a person that you haven't known for some time."

Personal friends and acquaintances of both governors provided an important source of candidates for staff positions, especially at the beginning of their administrations.[35] With such individuals, governor-staff interactions were built upon *a pre-existing foundation of trust.* For example, in his initial appointments to the Governor's Office, Brown selected many of his closest aides from among his personal friends, primarily people he met during his undergraduate and law school years.[36] Reagan was unable to do this because most of his friends were from the entertainment industry and would not have been seen as appropriate advisors.[37] Instead, he initially chose people from among his campaign workers, as did Brown to a lesser extent. But within several years after each administration had been established, friends (in the case of Brown) and campaign workers (in the case of Reagan) left the staff and were replaced by people with whom the governor had little, if any, previous relations before assuming the governorship. Most of these new staff members, however, were recommended by one of the governor's top advisors.[38]

Although a pre-existing relationship helped assure a personal commitment, other recruitment factors were more important, and in the long run, seemed decisive for an individual's continuation on the staff as well as his feelings of personal loyalty.[39] The most important factor was *the absence of competing commitments and obligations.*[40] Said one former Brown aide and friend who left after a year, "The difference [between whether or not one stays on the staff] is how much you had other commitments that were going to pull you back from Sacramento." Those remaining on the staff after the first two years of an administration as well as newer staff members were typically young, and either single or willing to put aside family obligations, and without established careers that required their attention. In addition, none had firm roots in an intragovernment or extragovernment constituency; nor were they recognized representatives of some public or private interest group.

When first appointed Reagan's staff appointees were young, 31 years old on the average, and when some of their numbers left, they were mostly replaced by people also in their early to middle 30s. Because Brown drew upon friends and acquaintances, early staff members were about the same age as Brown (36) when elected. Within two years most of these friends had returned to their former jobs and to their families and were replaced by individuals in their 20s and early 30s. Many of the staff members in both administrations were single when first taking a staff job, and those who were married found it difficult to meet the demands of a spouse and the job. One of Reagan's married assistants who was required to travel extensively with the Governor said, "Nancy [Reagan] and the Governor came first, my children came second, and my wife third." This ordering was also expected of Brown staff members: "The fact that Jerry Brown is single and does a lot of his effective work late in the day and at night and on weekends makes it difficult for some people to adjust to staff work. So people leave [the Governor's Office] because of personal demands—wife and family; that is understandable." Marriages were strained by the long hours and draining work often required of staff members.[41] Just as important, the intense commitment to the governor and to the governor's work made it difficult to divide that commitment with another personal relationship. *In the long run, people who remained on the staff were those who had no competing ties or commitments or who were able successfully to subordinate or to defer them.*

Another factor in the selection of staff members was the choice of people for individual traits that indicated their *willingness to mesh their personality with the needs of the office.* Individuals with strong personalities that demanded individual recognition and who refused to be submerged under the influence of the Governor were not selected, or if they had been, they left voluntarily.[42] This situation became, of course, mutually reinforcing: compatible personalities able to put the needs of the governor first came to occupy staff positions, and the situation these staff members were placed in blocked other alternatives.

Coming as they did from inconspicuous positions, staff members were suddenly and without much preparation thrust into positions of considerable importance, responsibility, and power. They said that "despite the work and the pressure" the Governor's Office was the most exciting place they had ever worked, or had ever hoped to work: "It gets in your blood. It is a very heady thing, a great ego trip. It is very hard to leave it and go back to working for a living." Another former staff member said, "I feel like an over-the-hill athlete, selling cookies [for a living]." "I expect withdrawal pains when I leave," anticipated another. In making such assessments as these, they attributed their swift elevation to prominence to the governor himself, for without his intervention in their fate, they would never have had the opportunity. The temporary nature of the appointment, the swift rise in fortune, the excitement of the work, the lack of competing ties—these and other factors created a bond of dependency that joined the staff members to the governor, thereby creating conditions favorable to the development of personal loyalty. This pattern of recruitment was less to please the governor than to serve the organizational purpose of their being the governor's surrogate.

Organizational Supports

Selective recruitment enhanced the likelihood that a bond of personal loyalty would form, and organizational supports within the Governor's Office contributed to this probability by directing and then buttressing the norms of loyalty, making it seem that no alternative form of loyalty would be permitted. There were four such organizational supports that helped ensure that the staff were personally loyal to the governor. Each of these minimized the opportunity and possibility that staff members would seek ties or rewards outside their relationship with the governor. These organizational supports were isolation, uncertainty, vicarious power, and access.

Isolation: The isolation of the staff—physically, organizationally, and psychologically—was an important factor in turning its attention

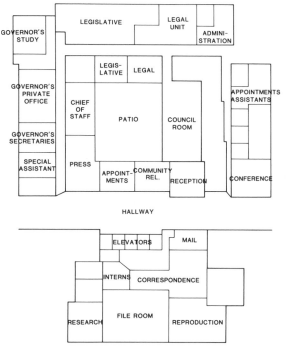

Figure 2.1. The Governor's Office Layout

inward to the person of the governor. While other members of the executive branch were aware that at some level they were responsible to the governor, only Reagan's and Brown's personal staffs, by virtue of their proximity (in all of the above respects), were reminded of it almost daily by the governor's presence.[43] Physical proximity is high in comparison with the other units of the executive branch. The Governor's Executive Office is a small unit, housed with other elected state officials in the State Capitol Building; it is separated from the offices of the executive bureaucracy; for security reasons all entrances into the Office are closely monitored. Once inside the Office, individual offices, including the Governor's private office, surround a courtyard and a conference room. Spatially, the governor's aides formed indeed an inner circle.[44]

What was observed in space could be confirmed as well by the organization of the office. In both administrations the office was orga-

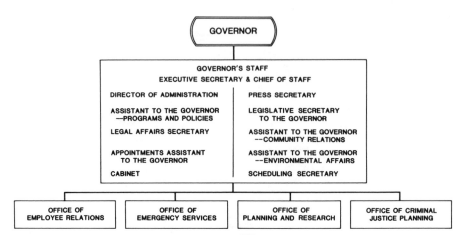

Figure 2.2. The Governor's Office Organization (1977)

nized in a very similar manner.[45] Unlike other governmental units the office had no constituency beside the governor himself, no legislative programs to implement, and no civil servants to guide. Outside the Office staff members possessed no line responsibilities, no statutory duties, and no signatory rights. Within the Office both governors maintained a minimal chain of command, dividing the Office primarily between junior and senior staff. Staff members concentrated on their respective functions, and worked at an equivalent level in the hierarchy. Each aide reported personally to the governor or to his chief of staff or to a senior staff member who in turn was directly responsible to the governor. Most of the routine clerical work, such as letter answering, filing, sorting, typing, was handled by what staff members referred to as "the business end of the office," that part farthest from the governor's private suite. The rest of the Office was divided into small rooms for the governor's advisors, who supervised at most two or three assistants and one or two secretaries/receptionists. The chief aides, their assistants, the clerical pool—all worked only for the governor, each in his own way, as the governor willed. In theory and to a large degree in fact, all lines of organizational authority led up to the governor before they descended into the rest of state government.

Combined with the physical and organizational isolation was a psychological isolation as well. Staff members in both administrations perceived themselves as outsiders, as individuals and as a group distinct from and often in opposition to the rest of the executive branch, including the governor's administrative appointees. Suggesting that the staff belonged to the governor whereas the appointees belonged to the bureaucracy, one of Brown's top aides stated, "I can't imagine [taking an administrative appointment]. It's tough out there and you're in a jungle; you're fighting a lot of people from a lot of different perspectives. [As an administrative appointee] you have the authority to make decisions. We don't have any authority here. We do a lot on [the governor's] behalf and we represent him on a lot of issues. But he makes the decisions." The same aide noted a psychological distance between staff and civil service employees. "There was a real problem that I perceived in the first few years of [the staff's] not having any respect for the civil servant. It was like there was this big body of monsters out there that was just waiting for the next administration, that see governors come and go, [that says] 'I'll be godamned if I'm going to pay any attention to those little whippersnappers,' and that they were out there to screw up whatever it was we wanted. . . . There were a lot of people who came in [to the Governor's Office] and had a lot of new ideas. They were just going to *change the world*." In a similar fashion, a Reagan staff member said, "We [in the Office] were loyalists and we were highly enthused and eager, almost a bit zealous, I think, about our cause and our mission to clean out the Augean stables of [the executive branch]." "As the new administrations came in," recalled another Reagan aide, "there was tremendous distrust of the institutions of state government. And because of that distrust—not trusting what was being recommended by the departments or even by the agencies, your own appointees, and not trusting those civil service guys—we made all the decisions ourselves." Particularly in the early years of both administrations, but continuing throughout, staff members saw themselves as forming an enclave and as working there in isolation from, and sometimes in opposition to, the rest of the executive branch.[46] Whether or not Reagan and Brown enjoyed this centrality they remained, in all respects, at the heart of this enclave.

Uncertainty: Staff members in both administrations operated in an atmosphere of uncertainty that was in direct opposition to the stability of the executive bureaucracy. Unlike career bureaucrats, the governor's appointees to his staff, as well as those serving as heads of the bureaucratic offices, hold "exempt" positions.[47] Exempt positions do not require that appointees fulfill any of the qualifications for civil service, but exempt positions also have no tenure. As one Brown aide put it, "We have no security here. And I don't think you can protect yourself [from the uncertainty]. I think when you take this kind of job, you should take it with the recognition that you serve at the pleasure of the person who appoints you and there is nothing in the world you can or should want to do about it. I wouldn't want to hire anybody, if I were governor, who as soon as he got here was going to start building little protective nets under him. I think some people do, but they shouldn't. The idea is they have to take this position with the understanding that you won't be here long. Nobody is here long. [A few] will stay with the governor for eight years. Most won't stay for four, because they will volunteer to leave. The pressure gets to be more than they want to put up with for the money."

Added to the uncertainty of tenure in the early stages of one's career was the uncertainty of having to define one's own job. Positions in the Governor's Office were designed to be flexible, so that positions could be easily adapted to a governor's style of leadership.[48] Unlike civil service positions, they had no written job descriptions, no guidelines as to how duties were to be performed, and no continuing programs against which one's performance could be measured. The governor, however, did have a number of constitutional responsibilities that were carried out by his staff and that were very technical.[49] What, for example, are the procedures for granting clemency or for requesting extradition? What steps should be followed when appointing someone to a board or commission? How does one analyze and lobby for legislation? Each of these duties, among many others performed in the Governor's Office, have largely unwritten but generally acknowledged procedures. Added to these duties that continued from one administration to another were, of course, many others that Reagan and Brown developed and assigned on their own. These included policy development, long-range planning, and public relations projects.[50] For all these duties staff members had little, if any, previous training, and once they were assigned a task they received little, if any, instruction in how to do it. Much was left to their own initiative.

Everyone in the Governor's Office, including both governors, learned

their roles through on-the-job training. Transitions between administrations were abrupt, and incoming staff members, even if they knew
their assignment, had little time to learn the techniques of doing it.
Sometimes the outgoing staff members (often of the opposing party)
were less than willing to instruct them.[51] In some cases, the clerical
staff instructed newcomers in their duties, but just as often secretaries
departed with their old bosses or were distrusted for being part of the
old order. As a Reagan aide said, staff members learned their jobs
through a process of "self-definition," each person trying to define his
own role in relation and sometimes in opposition to others in the office. A Reagan aide recalled what this process was like: "Chaotic. . . .
Well, you got to remember that here you had a governor, a new governor with no prior experience, who put together a staff, a cabinet,
of people who with one or two exceptions had no prior experience in
politics. . . . And nobody had ever sat down and put together a plan
on how we run the government. Maybe there's no way to do that.
. . . But when I say chaos, I don't mean they were a bunch of in-
competents up there, it means that they were a bunch of guys learning jobs that they had never been in before, without a hell of a lot of
instructions from anybody." Another Reagan aide noted that by the
end of the first year in office, "people began to know their jobs pretty
well." "A nightmare," "total chaos" were how most Brown aides described their first year. "No one knew what to do or how to do it."

The uncertainty about what was expected of them and what was a
good job when there were no measurable programs to manage, and
the knowledge that they could be removed for failing to please, put
the office staff in a position of constantly looking for signs of favor, a
signal that the governor was pleased with their work. Small nods from
the governor, an invitation to a staff meeting, an office a few feet closer
to the chief executive all took on inordinate significance in this environment of uncertainty. Laughing at himself in retrospect, one
Reagan aide told of the consequences of the uncertainty he felt: "Me
and my assistant were in Los Angeles on business, and I got a panic
call from my secretary who said she had heard through the grapevine
that our office was going to be moved. I had a very nice office right
on the courtyard within about 50 yards of the governor's corner office. I said, 'Oh, my God.' I knew I had to drop what I was doing. I
got on a plane and raced back to Sacramento to check that out. Of

course, that was a lot of nonsense, and it was an incorrect rumor. But immediately you perceive that if someone was going to move you out from that office across the hall or someplace else—no matter what your salary, no matter if the organization chart remained the same— you were demoted." Without humor, shortly after he had resigned from the staff, one Brown aide told us of his experiences: "If you're going to wait for answers [from the Governor or his top aide], it is very, very difficult. But if you're going to move on things and make up your own mind and make your own decisions and move on it . . . you're really taking some heavy risks. So you do what you can up to a certain point, then if you go further than that, then you're in trouble. . . . That's why my boxes are packed."

For some, the uncertainty of working in the Governor's Office proved too much and they left. But for the majority, who valued the excitement of the Office and the possibility of future rewards, uncertainty drove their commitment to greater intensity. Possessing the assurance of youth, they remained confident in their intelligence and in their ability to master anything. Knowing that much rode on what they accomplished in a short span of time, they redoubled their efforts to please the governor, who was himself usually too busy to notice. Finding the sustenance to continue this pace in small rewards, they sought the ultimate security—the governor's pleasure, the comfort that he knew and liked what they were doing. Whether or not he wanted that role, only the reigning governor could have provided security. Only he, through his approval, was able to certify a person's performance and sanctify the routines that were being established. But both Reagan and Brown received no training for their jobs, and found upon assuming office that they had unbelievable demands placed upon their time. Neither governor had the time to oversee the establishment of staff routine and to ease the uncertainty of staff members.

VICARIOUS AUTHORITY: THE DUTY TO REPRESENT

The isolation and uncertainty of their work predisposed Reagan's and Brown's staff members to frame their behavior in a way that put the interests of the governors first. But an even more important fea-

ture in the formation and continuity of the staff role was the justification for the authority routinely exercised by staff members. In this
regard, there was always an interplay between power and obedience.
For a person to accomplish the routine business required of staff
members, the act of obeying the governor as a person became the
chief source, and one might argue the only source, of staff authority.[52] This authority is not defined in statute; nor is it authoritative.
Staff authority is best described as *vicarious authority*.

In both administrations staff members exercised little or no authority in their own right. Although they helped formulate policy and draft
memos, regulations, and bills, the governor was the only individual
in the Governor's Office with signatory authority and statutory responsibilities. The power possessed by staff members was, as a Brown
aide put it, "entirely derivative." "Department and agency heads,"
explained another Brown aide, "have their authority spelled out by
law. The law says that the director does this and the director does
that. My only authority is that which flows directly from the Governor." Said a Reagan aide, "No staff member has authority. The only
authority he has is the governor's authority, and you can't separate
that out [from your own]."[53] Not only did staff advisors depend on
the governor for their authority, but they also had no means to gain
extraorganizational support or legitimation. Unlike most government
bureaucracies, which have statutory power and public constituencies
that will come to their aid in legislative and budgetary battles, the
governors' personal staffs have neither an outside constituent nor statutory recognition.

The absence of formal authority, however, does not mean that
Reagan's and Brown's staffs lacked power. Quite the reverse was true.
By their being able to speak on behalf of the governor and to invoke
his name in their relations within and outside of state government,
staff members exercised considerable power, more perhaps than any
other group of state workers. Theirs was the governor's power, and in
wielding this power they took on the mask of the governor. They represented him in public; they used his authority to control the state
bureaucracy; they did his bidding before the legislature. It was their
job to become extensions of the governor—to become, in fact, his
surrogates.

Acting as the governor's surrogate allowed staff members access to the considerable powers possessed by the governor himself, but, at the same time, obligated them to merge their interests (perhaps their persons) with his. By virtue of their jobs and the expectations placed upon them by others, staff members were forced constantly to identify with the governor as a person. This identification undermined any other source of independent stature and power. A former legislative aide in Brown's office explained it this way: "It's not really true [that one can establish one's own power base]. You see, it's really the other way around, because your power only comes from Jerry Brown. That is what is perceived. It is perceived that you are with Jerry Brown or that you can talk to Jerry Brown. Actually your [own] power base atrophies. . . . You are converted in other people's eyes; you are now a way through to Jerry Brown."

The perceptions of others compelled staff members to realize that they did, in fact, speak for the governor. With feelings of uneasiness, they constructed the governor in their minds in order to act as his substitute. Every day the legislative assistant had to decide how the governor would react to a given piece of legislation; the press secretary had to imagine what the governor would consider the appropriate response to the questions of a reporter. Each staff person knew that their every public word could and likely would be taken as the govenor's word. But the governor had time to approve only the most important statements in advance of their being issued. "When I'm talking to other people on business," said one Brown aide, "they always feel I'm saying what the governor wants me to say, which I hopefully am. But what I think he really wants is less explicit sometimes than at other times." "In your trying to approach the thing with honesty," said a Reagan aide, "first you have a natural instinct to protect your boss . . . and you don't want to burden him with every small decision. So you have to use a fine-tuned sense of judgment as to how much power you exercise. . . . Managing the governor's time is a very, very difficult thing, because the demands on his time are absolutely unbelievable. You have to manage his time and your opinion as to whether he had time to do a job is just a matter of judgment. Either you are a good staff person and have those feelings and are sensitive and can make effective judgments, or you don't stay there long."

Because staff aides were constantly required to make judgments without certain knowledge that the positions they took were in fact the correct ones, they had to draw upon their knowledge of the governor, as well as to subordinate their own predilections. Accordingly they fixed upon those things about which they knew best—the governor's personal characteristics, his idiosyncrasies, his predispositions. To do their job well, staff members had to simulate being the governor—*the person*—not the philosophy or the position. They had to attempt to know him well enough to act as he would act. "Every day," recalled a Reagan aide, "I would imagine myself in the place of the governor and think 'What would Reagan do?' " Or as one of Brown's aides said, "I always try to put myself in his shoes, in his mind. I don't know if I'm always successful and he's not going to tell me."

Individuals are unequal in their ability and willingness to exercise vicarious authority. Some staff members in both administrations found that the lack of personal independence was overbearing. As one aide noted, being a "derivative person" is more difficult for some than for others, and it was a factor in the decision of some individuals to leave the Governor's Office.

Many, of course, remained and those who most inclined towards remaining were also those most capable of subordinating themselves to the needs of the governor, if only for a time. This capability helped to reinforce, if not to create, a bond of dependence between the staff member and the governor. The isolation of the Office, the uncertainty of working there, the power derived from dependence—all these gradually transformed the staff members' physical closeness to the governor into a psychological closeness as well, and gave normative status to an emotional bond of personal loyalty. The bond, in turn, provided shape for the standards of inner motivations that one was supposed to feel. Some undoubtedly did embrace them, but many did not or could not, at least not fully.

Access

Because Reagan and Brown staff members only exercised the governor's power, the question was always open whether or not and to what extent staff members were acting on the governor's behalf and with his permission.[54] People within as well as outside of the Governor's Office assumed that the greater a person's access to the governor was or was believed to be, the greater became his or her ability to act as the governor's representative and to use the governor's power. Each aide in the governor's staff, however, had some type of personalized relationship with the governor, either one that was face-to-face or one that was mediated through someone who met with him personally. Each relationship differed slightly from any other. The individual nature of these relationships, as well as the presumption that they were all built upon personal loyalty, provided the platform for competition among staff members, a competition for access that occasionally divided the office into what one Reagan aide called "loyalty factions."

"Access" and "closeness" are terms that staff members and others in state government used to describe an individual's ability to meet with the governor. In both administrations the governor's "close" aides met with him several times a day, often without needing to make an appointment. Other aides met with the governor at regularly scheduled times or as the need arose. Lesser aides never met with the governor other than in exceptional circumstances, and did not presume to do otherwise. But even junior aides were seen as having greater or lesser degrees of access depending upon their connections to senior aides.

Besides these differences between aides, access to the governor also differed between the two administrations. During Reagan's administration, particularly his last term (1970–74), the procedures for seeing the Governor were well established and generally respected.[55] Only three or four aides could see the Governor on routine business without an appointment, and only one aide, Reagan's chief of staff, had unlimited access. Other members of the Governor's Office occasionally met with Reagan, but only rarely without one of the top four aides being present. Such meetings were usually formal, such as in the twice-weekly cabinet sessions. In contrast, a wider range of individuals had access to Governor Brown, but except for his top aides, most had difficulty arranging a meeting: "You never make an appointment to see Jerry Brown. You're crazy if you do, unless you have all day or maybe two days to spend. Not only does he not have a schedule, he doesn't come close to keeping one." While some of

Brown's top aides were with him a large part of the day, lesser staff members tried to catch him between meetings or late at night. But despite differences in both administrations personal access was difficult or time-consuming for all but a few top staff aides.

Individuals on the staff, as well as other government workers, knew the identity of these top aides and their relative importance to the governor. In fact, such "inside" information was of considerable interest to local newspapers, which frequently published detailed accounts of intrastaff pecking orders and rivalries.[56] The speculation about who was rising or falling in favor also circulated through the executive branch, where it was considered to be vital information. To administrative appointees, whose access was practically nonexistent, knowledge about the "magic circle," as Brown's group of close advisors was called, was important in the management of their units. One of Brown's department directors explained it in this way: "I have, in my mind, a hierarchy of calls. If there is going to be a major political flap and I figure it is going to be on the front page of the L.A. *Times*, I'll call [one aide]. If it's a major philosophical issue, I would call [another aide]. If it was a call to find out what the Governor's Office position was on a general bill I would call [yet another aide]. If it has something to do with, I don't like to say image things, but there are some things that I know that I call [still another aide] about. The governor depends on him for certain things and I make a decision when these things come up that I'm either going to call him or I'm not going to call him based on just some feelings that this is something that he would be handling for the governor. And generally that's the way it works out. I would call [these people] because I know that is where the 'plug in,' so to speak, is. I just have to make that kind of a decision. I'm looking for who can help me or who will get the word into the system over there most expeditiously." Such a hierarchy of calls was a chart of those close to the governor, "plug-ins" to the governor and to his opinions on particular issues.

Closeness to the governor, or at least a reputation of closeness, was the source of power and recognition for staff members. It was a commodity that some struggled to gain, and that all who gained it justified with protestations of personal loyalty. Reagan's legislative aide explained the competition by saying that in Reagan's staff, there were "a lot of people who were ambitious, who had not made it yet, and who were in a situation they had no conception of. . . . They had to play the game of how do you get to be the closest to Ronald Reagan. And anyone else who seemed like they were getting close, the obvious thing to do is try to cut him out." One of Brown's top advisors made substantially the same point: "When [staff members] know they are no longer in favor, what is the good of having this job? If you don't have the ear of the Governor, why would you want to put up with this crap?" The motivation to have the ear of the governor sometimes led to what Brown staffers called, among other things, "mau-mauing" and "ego tripping." They said that these were actions in which one must engage if one is to have any influence at all.

In both administrations competition was usually subtle and sub-merged in daily routine. Individuals generally knew where, in the ranking of closeness, they and others were located, and were willing to work within that framework. "Everyone," explained a junior member of Brown's staff, "has a job to do. . . . It's a question that some need to have more access than others. That doesn't necessarily engender any jealousy. . . . When I need to have access to the Governor I have access to the Governor. I would put myself in the second circle. There are people that definitely have more access than I do, but I have more access than others. I have all that I need to get my job done." The same person admitted, however, that "To some people the access to the Governor—the ability to stand in the same room with him—is very, very important. Certainly you can't get away from that." Noted another junior Brown aide, "Within the magic circle the jockeying for position continues continuously."

Occasionally, however, the competition grew intense and led to factional disputes within the staff over who was the most loyal and who had the best interests of the governor at heart. But in times when factionalism was not apparent, there was still a tendency for those with relatively little access to the governor to align themselves with someone who did. In part this was a result of the second and third rounds of recruitment, in which close aides recommended that individuals known to them but relatively unknown to the governor be placed on the staff. When competition, usually between two or more close aides, became intense the office began to divide along lines of previous patronage. Frequently these lines overlapped with an ideological cleavage as well. In both administrations such factionalism emerged at crucial junctures in the governor's political career, for example, when each was running for reelection and was contemplating a run at the White House. In Reagan's Office the split occurred between those on the campaign trail and those remaining in the Governor's Office, between the "politicians" and the "administrators." One of Reagan's political aides said, "It was a continuing battle [between those who left the staff for the campaign and those remaining in the office]. Everybody running the state thinks that they should be running the campaign, and everyone running the campaign thinks they should be [in Sacramento] to keep the old man out of trouble. . . . After the election everything shakes out." After Reagan won reelection, one of the outcomes of this split was the elimination of a special think-tank unit, the Office of Program Development (OPD), a unit within the Governor's Office. According to one aide, the head of OPD "had more integrity with regard to conservative philosophy than the rest of the office did. There was that drive . . . [to see] that particular segment (OPD) impact everything. . . . He felt the ideas were more important than Reagan himself." Similar splits between the campaign staff and the Governor's Office staff, as well as splits within the campaign staff, also occurred when Brown ran for reelection.[57] All these disputes reflected the importance of personal loyalty in the battle for access.

Competition and the occasional factional disputes did not lessen the feeling of personal loyalty; rather they exacerbated it by making the person of the governor the only possible focus of commitment. In this competition, espousal of the governor's publicly known philosophy became less important than the more intimate knowledge of what the governor *really* believed and did. Because this intimate knowledge of the governor became the focus for personal loyalty, those with greater access were presumed also to be the most loyal, as well as the ones most able to speak for the governor; they had a greater measure of vicarious authority.

Despite the correspondence between access and loyalty, there was a constant tension between the two. On one hand, the need for access was, quite simply, rooted in the nature of staff work and staff responsibility. To be effective, simply to do a good job as the governor's representative, demanded that one be seen as having a degree of closeness to the governor, for without such a reputation one need not to be listened to. In other words, access was the source of a staff member's legitimacy. Hence, access was important and worth fighting for, whether or not one actually felt personal loyalty to the governor. On the other hand, having access required a demonstration, outwardly at least, of a personal commitment to the governor; otherwise a staff member would not have been trusted with the sensitive information about the governor, as well as about his management of the state. Because access imputed an inner motivation that staff members knew might or might not actually be there, any dispute that occurred elicited accusations about the lack of a "real" commitment to the governor. Thus, staff members typically interpreted disputes and overt competition as open shows of personality at the governor's expense: "He's got his ego problem." "He had a driving ambition to fight his way to the top of the heap." "He's off on an ego-trip." "[He was] an opportunist." "It was a fight between personalities." In an atmosphere charged with personal loyalty to the governor, all staff actions could be interpreted as self-aggrandizing. Either one was personally loyal or one was not, and because loyalty implied an inner motivation as well as observable actions, one could never be certain about what another actually felt.

This tension between access and personal loyalty was of course paradoxical. Effective staff work required legitimacy; legitimacy required access; access required conspicuous displays of loyalty. The conspicuousness of the displays, however, were always open to a cynical interpretation, as having personal ambitions as their motivation. Hence, the paradox: the harder one tried to be loyal, the more vulnerable one became to charges of self-aggrandizement.

THE LIMITS OF PERSONAL LOYALTY

We have singled out five overlapping dimensions that characterized the staff role during both administrations. These dimensions—selective recruitment, isolation, uncertainty, vicarious power, and access—are common in most other governmental and nongovernmental staff situations as well. We have interpreted our interviews with members of the two personal staffs in light of these dimensions and have found that each dimension organizationally contributed to a situation in which all involved perceived that a personal commitment to the governor was the defining criterion of the staff role. Other state employees, including other staff members, judged the governor's aides according to standards implied by such a commitment, whether or not they actually felt this sort of emotional bond.

The presumption of personal loyalty was an integral feature of the staff role but not necessarily of the persons who occupied that role. Accordingly, we now examine the difficulty that staff members *as people* had in living up to the prescriptions of being a member of the governor's personal staff.

In this section we look at two situations that help to define the tensions that staff members felt in both administrations. First we examine resignations from the staff, a common occurence in both administrations, in order to explore these tensions at their breaking point. Then we investigate at a social-psychological level the implications of routine staff work upon an individual's self identity.

Breach Between Action and Role Obligations: Departure and Protest

People left the Governor's staff for many different reasons, including better financial opportunities, lack of power in a lame duck administration, conflicts, and the inability or unwillingness to meet the demands of the job.[58] But despite the many reasons for leaving, there were normative forms of departure, acceptable ways to abandon the staff role. Whether acceptable or not, all departures were shaped by the personal commitment that people were supposed to feel. Departure usually occurred in ways characteristic of this type of commitment, either by upholding the expected standards or by drawing out its antithesis. The antithesis of personal loyalty is betrayal.

The expected standards of loyalty in the Governor's Office were those requiring a deep commitment to the person of the governor. As normative prescription, this form of loyalty represented a source of inner motivation—the emotional attachment to the governor—that guided and constrained the actions of staff members and kept them, as individuals, aligned with the position they occupied and the functions they performed. As a moral checkpoint, this form of loyalty implied a vocabulary of motives and justifications and created standards by which one could judge the actions of others and of oneself.[59]

Although a defining aspect of the staff role, personal commitment encumbers the individual who would be a staff member. If a person is sincere on the job, such a commitment should continue after working hours as well as when the job is over. Among those on Brown's staff, working late into the night, which was the time Brown often worked himself, became a sign of one's personal commitment to the Governor. For Reagan, years after the end of his administration and before he began his successful run for the presidency, his former staff members and some appointees continued to meet regularly two or three times a year. These "alumni meetings," as they were called by the participants, kept the commitment to Reagan alive and served eventually as the core of the political organization that helped put Reagan into the White House.[60] In both administrations personal loyalty was a demanding form of commitment, both to those who received it and to those who supplied it; it was a commitment that, once made, could not be easily broken. Because it was so demanding relatively few staff members were able to live up to its full prescriptions. Thus, there existed a vocabulary of graceful exits. When individuals desired to leave the Governor's Office gracefully for whatever reason, they phrased their motives for departure in words that upheld the standards of the ideal.

There were two appropriate ways for an individual to break out of a staff role. One was to appeal to a competing personal tie. As a Brown aide said, it is "understandable" that "people leave because of *other* personal demands—wife and family." In fact, when staff members left government service, they almost always cited reasons of family obligation, personal career needs, or health. The other normative way to leave the staff was to be appointed to another post. In this way, someone who had performed well and loyally was rewarded with a position of prestige that did not carry the intense demands of a top staff position. Both Brown and Reagan appointed favorites to state commissions and the bench. Sometimes, though, reappointments served as a way of removing people who did not fit well into the staff but who had desirable qualities, or occasionally, were politically "untouchable" because they represented a voter constituency, such as a minority group.

There were compelling reasons to give a normative reason for leaving the governor's staff, despite the fact that the true reason was quite different. Membership in the governor's staff, while it could have given great personal satisfaction and prestige during its tenure, was usually even more valuable after the term in office. Said one aide, "The prestige of having this job leads to other job offers that are good . . . so once you have had this job for a while the chances are that that puts you in the kinds of position where you can get a better job." Leaving in breach of norms of personal loyalty tarnished one's credentials, revealing one's opportunism or, worse, one's disloyalty and others' suspicions that one had been disloyal all along.

Public reasons, therefore, obscured many private motivations for abandoning the staff role, even when the attachment to the governor continued. "Jerry Brown," said one former close advisor who is still a supporter, "is exhausting to work with. It burns people out. I, for one, was feeling a little burned out. It would have passed, I suppose, but I also think that if I had stayed I would have become dependent on the Governor in terms of my own career." Another Brown aide, a friend whom he had called to work in Sacramento, recalled that "The down side of the job was not just the hours; they were there. And it wasn't like Jerry was a slave-driver; you could see the hours were going to lessen. It's just that you had so much to do and you had to fill a derivative job. If you've been as I was, a person pretty much on his own, it's very difficult to worry about whether what you say is going to be attributed as a signal from Jerry Brown. I had never been faced with that problem—just being a derivative person. There are some people who that problem reaches earlier. It reached me early on. I know it weighs on [others] a bit—this derivative problem. It's tough to be in that situation; it's a consequence of working for a governor in the Governor's Office." Both of these individuals left the Governor's Office for "understandable" reasons, citing the pull of family and career commitments. Because they left appropriately, they remained available to Jerry Brown as candidates for future appointment and as sources of advice. One in fact received a judgeship. The facade, and probably the fact, of their continuing commitment to him remained even though they could not or would not define their lives by the obligations of the staff role.

Betrayal

But a staff person can depart from the role in breach of norms, too. This rarely happened, but when it did, it was also shaped by the standards of personal loyalty. To breach those norms publicly, in protest, was seen as a betrayal. The breach typically took the form of a personal attack, an assault on the very characteristics that were ideally the object of loyalty, the governor's person. At the federal level, such an attack has often appeared as an exposé, as a violation of the sanctity of the personal relationship.[61] Because the personal staff is in a position to know damaging information about the personal habits and failings of a leader, a dissatisfied staff member can reveal much that can hurt him. As the series of books by Nixon staff members attest, such exposés are not so much statements calculated to make public certain criticisms of policy as they are exercises in disenchantment, whose cathartic value is to break asunder the bonds of dependence.

Although he did not write an exposé, a former Reagan aide broke from Reagan in an equally dramatic fashion. The break occurred during the Republican primary in California in 1975, when Reagan was making his bid for the presidency against the incumbent, Gerald Ford. At the time of the break, the former aide was the chairman of the California Republican party organization and in a position to cause considerable damage to Reagan's personal image and campaign chances. At a decisive moment the former aide publicly declared his support for Ford. Despite the fact that Reagan was no longer governor, other Reagan staff members saw this as betrayal, an act of broken faith. The former aide also recognized that his act was a breach of loyalty—a breach that allowed him to break permanently with Reagan. Among the reasons he gave for supporting Ford, which included the power of Ford's incumbency and his belief that Ford could better handle foreign affairs, was the following: "The Ford thing came

on as a 'free, free, free at last' [opportunity]. There is some other ban-
ner that I could rally to, [in order] to, in effect, free myself from the
autocracy that Reagan had allowed to grow up around him. . . . In
all candor, a lot of it, maybe as much as a third of the motivation,
was, 'Ah-ha, we can strike a vote for freedom.' "

To breach a bond of personal loyalty requires an *act of the person*.[62] Because personal loyalty places such demands on an individual
who would occupy a role requiring it, forcing in effect a person's self
to become submerged in the role, a breach acts to supply distance
between the role and the person. This distance places the person in
full view in such a way as to say "*I* am not the role; this breach is *my
act* to proclaim *my freedom*" from those demands." The internal logic
of personal loyalty requires that such a breach be a confrontation between people, and not their roles, a duel between personalities and
not positions. The result is a sense of disaffection, bitterness, and betrayal. It is an outcome that only a very few would pick.

THE DILEMMA OF PERSONAL LOYALTY: BREACH BETWEEN
SELF AND ROLE

We have been describing situations where one's commitment to the
governor did not hold a person in a staff role. In some cases people
had other opportunities or found the conditions of dependence and
isolated work too difficult to live with, regardless of their feelings for
the governor. In such situations most people left gracefully, in a normative fashion. Occasionally, however, someone left in protest, for-
ever declaring that he or she was no longer the governor's person.

Some staff people, conversely, enjoyed or accepted the staff role
but were unable to feel the personal loyalty that gave the position
meaning. In such cases, the loyal actions of the aide were not matched
by the inner emotions those actions implied. For some, this was
painful, especially when they were sensitive to other staff members
who apparently took great pleasure in their selfless commitment to
the governor; the inability to feel what others supposedly felt was dis-
tressing and made them appear hypocritical in their own eyes. This
was sometimes an intense dilemma: although the rewards of working

in the Governor's Office were great, one's personal sacrifice—in terms of one's feeling towards oneself—was also great. For most, however, the circumstances surrounding work in the Governor's Office was enough to pull their inner motivations into line, merging their interests and, in a sociological sense, their selves into the role of personally serving the governor.

Despite these similarities between the two administrations in the normative status of personal loyalty, Governors Reagan and Brown greatly differed in their manner of nurturing commitment in their staffs. These differences between the two men led in turn to some differences in the dilemma of personal loyalty faced by staff members.[63]

Disaffection in the Reagan Staff

Reagan took the loyalty of his staff members seriously. He cultivated their loyalty and used it as a means to hold the Governor's Office together. He charmed his staff. Whenever he returned from an extended stay out of town, he habitually went from one end of the office to the other asking after everyone's welfare. He insisted that everyone's birthdays, especially those of the clerical staff, be celebrated during office hours, and he always attended the party whenever he was in Sacramento. He distributed jelly beans as a means to set people at ease. He passed out acknowledgments of appreciation—his own doodles, pens used to sign bills, autographed pictures—to those who worked with him. He told jokes in cabinet meetings, in staff meetings, in press conferences, wherever he was, and all agreed that no one could tell more jokes or could tell them better than Reagan. He made himself visible and could always be counted on to be in good humor and to be optimistic about the future. By appealing to that which united people—common journeys, good humor, shared happiness—Reagan mastered the ability to become the emotional center of his organization, to become a genuine object of people's affection.

Moreover, Reagan protected this image by providing no alternative interpretation. He took part in none of the office squabbles. Staff and cabinet members made special efforts to avoid any open show of animosity because everyone knew he did not like such conflict. As a consequence, Reagan's closest aides were the ones who did the dirty work of disciplining people, of discharging the worst offenders and sanctioning the rest. Just as important, Reagan had no close personal friends among his aides. He appeared to have no confidants working for him and to give no one special favors. His closest aides were more managerial assistants than friends, though the facade of friendship was certainly there. Friendly and casual, his demeanor remained nonetheless ceremonious and businesslike. Always maintaining good form in public, he then insisted upon personal and family privacy, and upon extended periods away from the Governor's Office. He tried to leave work at five and told others to leave when he did. He took holidays and long weekends at his home in Southern California. The staff in the Governor's Office identified with and loved what they held in common with Reagan, in part because they knew little else about him.

While Reagan was in office, as far as we can determine, the affection and commitment of his top staff members never flagged. But Reagan's style of management produced, nonetheless, its own crisis in commitment. Though they felt loyal, some of Reagan's staff members believed they lacked a means to express that loyalty. They felt shunned and unappreciated. They had no access to Reagan, except through the barrier that Reagan's closest aides had erected, in part to protect his privacy. In the end, bureaucratic ritual and increasing organizational as well as personal distance from Reagan produced considerable animosity among some of Reagan's aides, while at the same time allowing each to remain genuinely loyal to Reagan himself.

Disaffection on Reagan's staff became most apparent on the part of his political advisors who were blocked, or thought they were blocked, by his administrative aides. Staff members who handled Reagan's party duties and campaigns urged the Governor to become more active in his own behalf and to make decisions based on conservative Republican philosophy, as he had promised his voters in his bid for office. The other faction urged Reagan to rise above politics and administer the state according to sound management practices on behalf of all interests. The office politicians saw the administrative faction as naive and afraid to take bold action in the name of the cause; they called them, pejoratively, "the clerks" and saw them suffocating Reagan with timid advice. Although he maintained friendly ties with his campaign leaders and political liaisons, Reagan clearly favored the more cautious advice of his administrative staff, much to the consternation of his political aides. This caused a great deal of anguish for them because they felt they had a better understanding of political reality than Reagan's closest aides. They often accused those aides of loyal incompetence and of limiting their access to Reagan, and access was, of course, critical. The political staff was loyal to Reagan, but Reagan, by delegating everything to his administrative staff, prevented them from acting out this loyalty as they understood it. According to one staff member, who usually sided with the political aides, morale was chronically damaged by this delegation. "Everybody loved him. The staff would have fallen apart without him. We didn't like each other. . . . There was just no friendship there. . . . As a human being, I love Reagan. He's one of the finest men I have ever met and I would have done anything for him. If he came to me today [before the 1980 Presidential campaign]—and I can say this because I know I don't have to worry about that happening—and asked me to do something for him, I'd do it. But he was not an administrator. . . . Ronald Reagan never did anything about anything. [He delegated everything.] The morale problem was created by the competent knowing that the incompetent were always going to stay there."

Even though these political aides were frustrated by Reagan they blamed their dissatisfaction on other staff members rather than on him. Even frustrated and unhappy, they resisted attacking Reagan himself. This same theme was elaborated by another former political aide: "No one who has ever worked for Ronald Reagan has disliked him personally, but he is not a person you really know, no matter how close. . . . He was a delegator and the 'clerks' maintained themselves [in the Governor's Office]. They were dependents. There was an umbrella, and Reagan was the great big giant umbrella, who protected them from having to go out and compete for something else in life. [Other people who have been loyal] are shunned and pushed out. . . . They have feelings too. They like to be consulted and immediately the doors slammed on them and they are excluded from things. Their resentments start building up."

This same aide, a Republican Party loyalist, found the layers of staff around Reagan stifling because of their intense commitment to him. According to him, Reagan, by allowing his staff to represent him, prevented other Republicans from emerging as independent forces in the party. This aide eventually chose party loyalty over personal loyalty. Before Reagan had announced his intention to run for president in 1980, this aide said, "One of the terrible aspects of the [Republican] Party in California is the fact that you have this giant oak tree sitting down there in Santa Barbara, Ronald Reagan. And nothing grows in that shadow, nothing whatsoever, because there's still that mentality, not of Reagan personally, but of the acquiescence of people around him who presumably speak in his name. And he gives them the authority to speak in his name: 'Who's going to do what, and who's going to grab this post in the Party? ' So nothing grows. [The up-and-coming young Republicans] can't get anywhere around here, because everybody that matters is sitting there looking over his shoulders, [saying] 'What is Ronald going to do next? ' "

As a consequence of Reagan's manner, the ambitious junior aides felt dissatisfied but blamed their dissatisfaction upon the senior aides rather than upon Reagan himself. This produced some turnover in personnel at the second level, but did not greatly influence the routine operation of the Governor's Office. In fact, as turnover occurred, the gap between the senior and more junior levels of aides widened and the distinction became firmly established, converting staff tasks into routine bureaucratic work for all except the very top aides.

Disaffection in the Brown Staff

Unlike Reagan, Jerry Brown always seemed slightly embarrassed by all the folderal that went with being governor. He did not like the fact of people fawning over him or those who did the fawning. Almost ritually he avoided situations in which he had to act the part of governor. For instance, he refused to live in the Governor's mansion, to ride in the Governor's limousine, and to give the gubernatorial receptions and parties that his predecessors had. He saw official ceremonies as being beside the point of doing the work required of him as governor. He approached this work seriously, spending long hours debating policy, trying to instill into each decision a sense of moral responsibility that he brought with him to the job. But he did not take part in office parties.[64] He did not joke around with his top aides. He rarely noted the presence, not to mention the work, of anyone except his closest aides. He seldom expressed his appreciation, even to those with whom he worked daily, and he could not be counted upon to attend prescheduled meetings or to be available to answer questions. Brown tried to maintain a distance from the Office of the Governor, in order to accomplish the tasks at hand. He wanted to be seen less as a governor doing governor's work as an intellectual force tackling and solving the problems of our time.

In contrast with Reagan, Jerry Brown did not see the need for a personal commitment from his staff and did much to downplay its importance during his term in office. But even if Jerry Brown did not demand personal loyalty from his aides, and did nothing to nurture such a commitment, the organization and operation of the Governor's Office rested, nonetheless, upon the normative assumption that staff members had made such a commitment. The power of staff members remained tied to the presumption of their having access to Brown. Signs of staff power were important, even more than was the case in Reagan's term, because those outside the Governor's Office were often simply unable to ascertain Brown's position on issues. The organization of government required that staff members personally represent the governor and that they maintain the commitment that goes with this function. But in a situation where a personal commitment went unappreciated and unnoticed, and where seemingly unlimited demands were being placed upon one's time and energy, loyalty became a difficult emotion to feel sincerely. The result was widespread disaffection among Brown's staff, as well as a suspicion that each staff member was working for his own personal gain instead of for Brown or for the public good. A number of people among the senior and junior aides, as well as the clerical staff, told us of the inner conflict they felt as a consequence of their work in the Governor's Office. The following statement of a moral dilemma is among the most reflective we heard.

"I am convinced that people here [in a unit in the Governor's Office] do very, very good work. But no matter how good a job we do, it doesn't amount to anything unless we have access. From one point of view it is a necessary evil to be at the Governor's beck and call, but like the lady who wanted to ride the back of a tiger, you can be swallowed by it. Maybe another analogy is the moth and the candle. It is very seductive. It is very attractive to be right up there with the big kids, preparing position papers that you know not only that the Governor will read this afternoon, but that he's going to use tomorrow. And that is very seductive. On the other hand you will spend all of your time doing that and in the end you will not have made a substantial contribution to the public that I think I want to serve. It's a conflict clearly. You see me dancing around the topic, because I haven't resolved it in my own mind. Access, power, influence—they're seductive. I've seen marriages go bust here. The reason people will give up a marriage, family, is because they are that seductive. Maybe those marriages weren't very good. Maybe those people weren't brought up in a family life. But it is a very deep commitment. Why that commitment works for Jerry Brown, I don't know. I know why it worked for Gene McCarthy; I know why it worked for McGovern; I know why it worked for Bobby Kennedy. It was a sense of intense personal loyalty. I don't think anyone here believes in Jerry Brown. I really don't think so. It's an opportunity to carry out some personal ideology—that's about the best I can describe it. It's selfish in that sense. It's not personal ambition, although [there are exceptions]. It's an opportunity to take a quantum leap in one's career, to have your thoughts used, to have access to decision makers. And that means power and power is seductive. . . . He is the Governor. But I don't think there is very much personal loyalty. I don't burn for Jerry Brown the way I burned for Gene McCarthy. I'll never be 'Clean for Jerry'. . . . Here is a chance to see my thoughts taken seriously, not to have them filtered through fourteen levels of bureaucracy. I would be a terrible civil servant. I would be terribly frustrated. . . . That's why I like working here. It's access. . . . But there's a question between having access and being sucked dry."

In both administrations work in the Governor's Office was seductive. It pulled on one's inner emotions to force a personal commitment. If this commitment was to attach anywhere, it had to attach to the person of the governor, for the man and the position became, for staff members, inseparable. To be unable to feel that loyalty, for whatever reason, produced resentment and dissatisfaction, and opened the way for betrayal. For many staff members being unable to supply genuine personal commitment created not simply a feeling of betrayal, but a moral crisis in governing. This is a condition that Jerry Brown faced more than once during his eight years as Governor of California.

CONCLUSION: MANIPULATIONS OF THE STAFF ROLE

Roles are always flexible, and the staff role is no exception. Ronald Reagan and Jerry Brown both served as the head of the same personal staff organization, the Governor's Office. For each administration staff members performed the same functions in relation to the rest of state government, tended most of the same tasks within the Governor's Office, and faced similar constraints in accomplishing their jobs. The similar experience of both staffs grew out of the features of the staff role—isolation, uncertainty, vicarious power, and access to the governor. Moreover, they felt similar frustrations in being a staff member. These similarities resulted not from the personalities of the two governors or from the particular characteristics of the people they hired. Instead they resulted from the manner in which the role of the governor's personal staff was organized internally and in relation to other units of state government. But even though in charge of the same organization, Governors Reagan and Brown bent the staff role in different directions, which in turn shaped the course of each administration.

The last chapter, Chapter 7, assesses the consequences of Reagan's and Brown's styles of running the executive branch, which includes an analysis of the difference between the two personal staffs. But it is appropriate to suggest here that staff organizations are not rigid and that the influence of an individual executive upon such an organization is considerable.

Among political analysts, it is commonplace to contrast Reagan and Brown according to their patterns of delegation. Analysts view Reagan as an example of one who delegates most all decisions to subordinates and Brown as one who delegates very little. Although the contrast is superficially correct, the consequences of these differing styles upon the staff role is not immediately apparent, and in fact turns out contrary to what on the surface might be expected.

Reagan's pattern of delegating authority led to a highly centralized form of governing. Reagan's style of management built on establishing routines, for himself as well as for others. Everything related to the Governor's Office and beyond to the executive branch—people, jobs, interrelationships—became defined in terms of their function to the smooth running of the whole. Everything was made workaday. Within the first year of the administration, Reagan's top aides had defined as precisely as possible the duties of each staff member, had assigned appropriate personnel titles according to the task and to the level of responsibility required for the task, and had started to systematize the manner in which aides accomplished their assigned functions. Once they had fixed the positions and duties, Reagan and his top aides perpetuated the overall organization in a relatively unchanging form throughout both terms in office.

Delegation of authority in this context meant that specific positions had specific duties attached to them and that the holders of positions had the authority necessary to carry out those duties and no more. Anything exceeding the defined task went, according to preestablished procedures, to the next higher level. *Reagan did not delegate authority as much as he stereotyped the positions of his subordinates.*[65] *This strategy, founded upon the rationale that government ought to be an efficient organization, had the consequence of turning political and social issues into problems of management.* All judgments, including those made by Reagan himself, fell within set routines in which the problems rose to the level of responsibility required to resolve them. Reagan, two or three members of this personal staff, and cabinet officers made all the important decisions during Reagan's entire term in office. Under Reagan's direction, the Governor's Office centralized the duties for which the governor had responsibility and made the performance of those duties routine.

Reagan centralized power by delegating authority. *In contrast, Brown decentralized power by refusing to delegate authority systematically.* Unlike Reagan, Brown believed that administrative procedures did not solve economic problems or social injustices. These required political judgments based upon principles instead of administrative judgments based upon technical knowledge. Brown said he would serve not as a functionary or as a figurehead, but rather as a moral agent elected to put principles into action. Accordingly, Brown conserved his right to make decisions concerning all matters and attempted to spread throughout government a more self-conscious, self-critical approach to making decisions.

This attempt, along with Brown's desire to direct personally the course of state government, had the effect of challenging and often of breaking up administrative routines. Brown had selected his aides to be activists, not bureaucrats, in order to carry moral principles into lobbying for legislation, into appointing judges, into coordinating state agencies, into whatever pursuit Brown's aides seized as goals in their respective jobs. Brown invited, and more often through his reluctance to make timely decisions, forced his aides to appropriate gubernatorial powers. They made the decisions themselves, or at least established the means by which a decision on an issue could be made. Much of this appropriation of gubernatorial powers occurred among junior instead of senior aides. Brown made his top aides colleagues, people with whom he could debate and agonize over moral issues. These aides remained in effect on call, and followed Brown through the day as well as through the issues to which Brown turned his attention. Daily administrative tasks of the Governor's Office, such as making appointments and checking department positions on pending legislation fell to junior aides. These aides had to develop procedures to handle tasks, had to pick out what issues might become important, had to decide their own level of responsibility. As a consequence of simply doing their jobs, Brown's junior aides became important figures in the Brown administration. Brown's conservation of the authority to make decisions led (in comparison with Reagan) to a decentralization of the Governor's Office.

In their management of their personal staffs governors are constrained by the abilities of the people they hire, by the choices of their predecessors, and by the issues of the day. Although these limit the possibilities for managerial choice, governors still have latitude in what they can choose. But whatever they choose, as the governorships of Reagan and Brown reveal, the choices shape not only the conduct of the staff role, but also the course of government.

Chapter Three
THE GOVERNOR'S ADMINISTRATORS

PERSONAL STAFFS have received a lot of bad press in the years since Watergate. In the public consciousness staff members seem too young or too inexperienced for the powerful roles they assume. Even if aides are well chosen as individuals, the public has come to view the staff enclave as a politicized hotbed of gamesmanship and sycophancy. Staffs appear to be annoying if necessary accompaniments to the modern executive. Cabinet officers, on the other hand, rarely have those unfortunate traits of youth and inexperience. Cabinet officials are usually accomplished, even prominent figures. Their appointments are confirmed by ritual tests of knowledge before the Senate (in California as well as Washington), and with today's media coverage, before the public as well. In significant ways appointees to the cabinet and to other high bureaucratic posts are equals of the governor, at least in their fields of appointment. While there is the occasional untalented or unscrupulous appointee, there is nothing about the cabinet organization *per se* that invites suspicion. Rather, in the public mind the cabinet is a gathering of statesmen and if cabinet officers become powerful, they appear to deserve their power.

In fact as well as in appearance, the role of administrative appointees demands a relationship of relative equality with the governor, not the subordinate role assumed by staffs. Perhaps surprisingly, this egalitarian relationship serves the governor's interests: if appointees were not seen as independently powerful and relatively autonomous, they would be ineffective managers of the huge bureacratic empires that they run. Civil servants and constituents would ignore them and look only to the governor for direction, a feat he could not hope to perform effectively alone. Maintaining the impression and the fact of equality, and not subordination, was an important factor in appointees' lives.

This egalitarian relationship, however, required a delicate act of balance, one that was constantly tuned by the governors. Top administrators must be sufficiently independent so that they are effective managers, but they must not be so independent that they run off on their own and become embarrassments or challengers to the governor. The governors attempted to loosen and tighten the tether as they required, but never so much as to destroy the independence of the appointee, or so little as to lose control.

The normative basis of this collegial governor-appointee relationship was loyalty, but unlike the personal loyalty that bound the staff to the person of the governor, appointees expressed *the loyalty of allegiance*. Allegiance is a commitment to the philosophy and ideas of the governor. As long as they acted independently, but within the framework of the governor's philosophy, the collegial relationship was maintained and appointees served the governors' ends.

But this balancing of autonomy and allegiance, as well as the collegial relationship, was often difficult to sustain, both for the appointees and for the governor. In this chapter we describe the structural conditions that tended to maintain the commitment to allegiance. In the next, we look at the bases of the appointees' independent power, the distinctive type of conflicts in which appointees became embroiled, and finally, the frustrations that are inherent to a role with the contradictions of freedom and constraint.

THE ORGANIZATIONAL ORIGINS OF THE GOVERNOR'S ADMINISTRATORS

In California in 1911, the idea of administrative appointees who served at the pleasure of the governor took hold, if only in a small way. In the last decades of the nineteenth century, when reformers pushed for a more professional government and for more state controls over the private sector, appointee status smacked of political patronage, of being the spoils of a victorious party. In those years, in the 1880s and 1890s, only a few people in all of California state government served at the governor's pleasure. The Trustees of the State Burial Ground and The Guardian of Marshall's Monument were two of these;[1] both positions disappeared by the 1920s, when administrative appointees became the rule.

Boards and Commissions

It was not until the turn of the century that the executive branch began to change in a significant way.[2] At first changes came as a rapid increase in the number of boards and commissions.[3] Boards and commissions were legislative creations that put laymen and experts in governmental positions designed to supervise an area of citizen concern and were the preferred manner of arranging executive power from the time of California's statehood in 1850.[4] By constitutional requirement, the governor and eight other elected executive officers (e.g., Lieutenant Governor and the Attorney General), served, often jointly, as *ex officio* members of many boards and commissions, such as the Board of Education and the Board of Examiners. In addition, the governor had the responsibility to appoint those board members whose appointment process was not otherwise specified in the constitution. But he could only appoint people for fixed terms and did not have the power to remove them or to control their decisions, except by persuasion.[5]

When a problem arose that required governmental supervision, the legislature typically responded by creating a board or commission to deal with the situation, so that the number of these agencies gradually increased over time. In 1850 there were three such agencies, and until 1895 they increased every decade thereafter by about ten.[6] In 1895, when the total number of statutory agencies stood at 51, Governor James H. Budd said in his Inaugural Address:

> If the Governor is to be held responsible for the conduct of the departments whose incumbents he names, he should be given control of these functionaries. In this state we should either have a system of continuous tenure during good behavior . . . or else the appointing power . . . should be vested with authority to remove the appointee.[7]

The bills that Governor Budd introduced to accomplish these ends failed to make it out of the committee in either house of the Legislature.

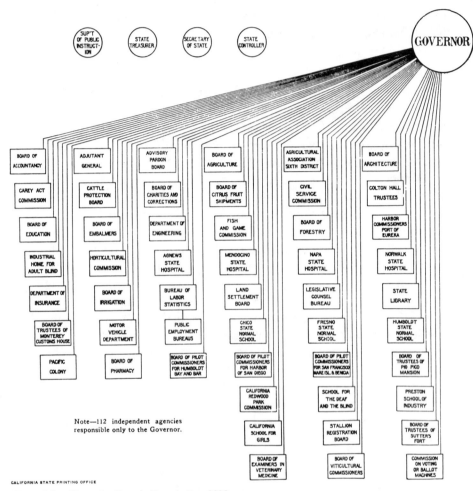

Figure 3.1.   Executive Branch Organization 1919

The proliferation of statutory agencies without gubernatorial control continued for the next two decades. After 1897 the legislature began to respond to voter demands to regulate private spheres of activity and provide more public services, by creating more boards and commissions—the State Board of Pharmacy, the Stallion Registration Board, the Industrial Accident Commission, the State Commission in Lunacy. Between 1897 and 1907 the legislature added 28 agencies, and in the following decade, between 1907 and 1917, they added another

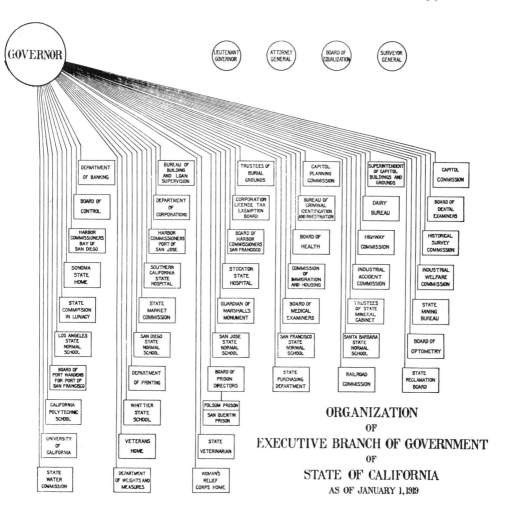

ORGANIZATION
OF
EXECUTIVE BRANCH OF GOVERNMENT
OF
STATE OF CALIFORNIA
AS OF JANUARY 1, 1919

56.[8] By 1919, as the executive organization chart drawn by the Department of Finance shows, there were 112 independent agencies in state government, all of which were responsible only to the governor.[9]

Of these 112 units, only eleven were managed by administrative appointees serving at the governor's pleasure.[10] All of these eleven date from, or come after, the famous 1911 session of the state legislature, which was given over almost entirely to Progressive reforms.[11] A few of these eleven units, such as the State Banking Department, began earlier as boards and only later became departments headed by appointed managers.[12] But most of the eleven, such as the Superintendent of Capital Buildings and Grounds, began as an administrative unit designed to accomplish a task.[13] With the 1911 session, the "bureau" concept grew as a model of executive organization, and in fact a number received that name, such as the State Mining Bureau.[14] But the first bureaus retained a characteristic feature of boards and commissions: their focus was narrow, restricted to specific jobs, to well-defined tasks, and the appointees selected to accomplish these were more like technicians than administrators. This image was captured in most of their titles: State Printer, State Engineer, Superintendent of Banking.

Unifying the Executive Branch

To state politicians and Sacramento watchers, it soon became apparent that substituting bureaus for boards, appointees for board members, would not solve the Governor's problem of supervision and control. In 1915, attuned to the recently developed theories of organization and management, David P. Barrows, Professor of Political Science and later President of the University of California, recommended a comprehensive reorganization of California state government. Preferring bureaus to boards, he wrote, however, that while bureaus fix responsibility in an appointed head and allow for quick decisions, they have "a disposition to routine, to the establishment of unduly rigid methods, and the development of over-conservative ideas."[15] Given this disposition, Barrow argued that "a superior administrative control" is "requisite for the successful conduct of bureau administration," and in the current condition of the executive, the governor "does not have . . . what is essential to close supervision, a department secretary or staff colleague through whom oversight can be exercised."[16] Drawing a sharp distinction between politics and administration, Barrows saw that the Governor of State was "an impressive political figure," "directly elected by the people, necessarily representative of the prevailing will of the commonwealth, in close touch with public opinion. Administratively, however, he continues to be weak. Charged with the duties of seeing that laws are executed, he ordinarily has no control over the officers who must carry out this execution."[17]

Barrow's plan for state reorganization called for the governor's authority to be "centralized and unified" in order to make "the administrative power of the state governor . . . commensurate to his political importance, his public position, and his responsibility to public will."[18] The plan recommended the introduction into California of two features of government present at the federal level: departmental division and an advisory cabinet.

> What the governor really needs is an administrative council of at least six members appointed by him from men who possess his confidence, who will serve both as the directing heads of so many departments of state government, and as an advisory council for the consideration of the numerous political and administrative cares which constantly arise.[19]

Barrows grouped the 112 independent agencies into six departments which he identified according to the function each served to the unity of the executive. And with considerable insight he described the role of administrative appointees as an aspect of an organizational whole.

> It is essential that the closest advisors of a chief executive should be not merely men who are loyal adherents of his party and policies, but, like the chief executive himself, vested with the moderating responsibilities of public office, who are known to the public as those particularly charged with the state's affairs, and who, both by the governor and by the people, can be held to account for their success or mismanagement.[20]

Between 1919 and today, governors and legislators have enacted and re-enacted this vision of executive organization. And time after time, this vision of executive rule has given way to the exigencies of practical politics. As Barrows clearly saw, the role of the administrative appointee is balanced between loyalty to the governor's policies and programs, on the one hand, and freedom of and autonomy in administrative command, on the other. The balance is difficult to maintain and most often tips in favor of administrative autonomy. Accordingly, the role of the governor's administrator must be continually reined in by the governor and occasionally reinforced through executive reorganization.

The first reorganization occurred in 1919, when the legislature initially adopted the concept of departmental structure as the administrative plan for state government. The logic of this plan was clearly organizational in nature, and was stated in detail in the report from the committee assigned to draft the proposal for the reorganization.[21] This group, named appropriately the Committee on Efficiency and Economy of California, recommended that organizational principles of centralization and coordination be put into practice by the following steps:

(1) The creation of a Governor's cabinet, composed of a departmental executive appointed by him.
(2) Insuring co-operation of various departments by bringing their administrative officers together in an executive council.
(3) Placing in departments, under one executive head, those agencies which perform similar or allied functions.[22]

The plan called for the creation of ten departments, and hence for "the centering of larger responsibilities in the departmental executive." This emphasis upon administrative appointees, noted the Committee, "should be accompanied by the creation of a Governor's cabinet, composed of those executives."[23]

The Legislature implemented the plan piecemeal, so that by 1925 there were only five departments and many boards and commissions that remained outside of departmental control.[24] But just as the number of boards and commissions had proliferated, the number of departments kept increasing, and grew beyond the size of effective gubernatorial control. In 1929, there were nine departments; and in 1936, fourteen.[25] By 1959, the number of departments, as well as the number of people on the Governor's Council had reached 21.[26] In that year, Edmund G. Brown Sr., then Governor of California, appointed another committee to recommend a plan for executive reorganization. In its report to the Governor, the committee found that "the Governorship in California has been weakened by diffusion of authority."[27] The governor was unable to supervise the department directors and the department directors "did not have adequate communication with each other."[28] The Governor's Council had grown too large to be an "effective forum at which . . . to discuss major state policies."[29] Although the report did not put it so straightfor-

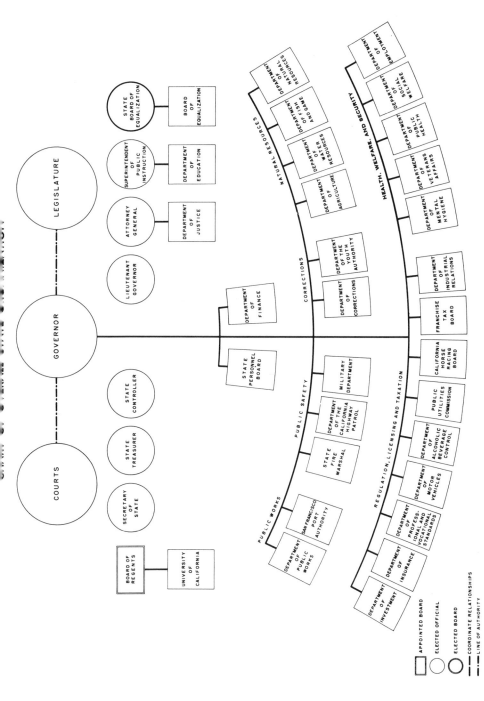

Figure 3.2. Brown, Sr., Administration 1959

wardly, Brown Sr. and one of his top aides, Frank Mesple, both recalled that departmental directors acted more like bureaucrats than
appointees.[30] Recognizing that the balance between gubernatorial
control and managerial autonomy was out of line, the committee
recommended that the departments be consolidated into eight agencies, and that both the agency secretaries and the departmental directors be "appointed by and serve at the pleasure of the Governor."[31]
Agency secretaries would become the Governor's Cabinet, thus re-
placing the Governor's Council composed of department directors.

The legislature also implemented this proposal, "The Agency Plan,"
in a piecemeal fashion. When Reagan took office in 1967, there were
four agencies and 40 departments, boards, and commissions. Although Reagan reorganized several departments during his term in
office, when Jerry Brown became governor in 1975 there were still
the same number of agencies and subordinate units. During his eight
years in office, Jerry Brown added one agency and reorganized two
others, so that there were five agencies, four departmentlike units not
under any agency control, and 50 subordinate departments, boards,
and commissions.

After successive reorganizations and in spite of the tremendous
growth in the size of the executive branch, the role of administrative
appointees during Reagan's and Brown's administrations remained
conceptually the same as it had been in 1919, when it was introduced into state government. It was a role that encompassed a contradiction between freedom and constraint; governors and legislators
built this tension into the role as they developed the structure of state
government, where it has become an object of experience to those
individuals who occupied the role. As Barrows stated in 1915 the role
rests upon those "who are loyal adherents of [the governor's] party and
policies" as well as those "who are known to the public as those particularly charged with the state's affairs."[32] This specific combination
of loyalty and command favors the type of loyalty that we call "allegiance."

APPOINTEE-GOVERNOR RELATIONSHIP: ALLEGIANCE

During the administration of Ronald Reagan and Jerry Brown, administrative appointees, who often said they were loyal to the gover-

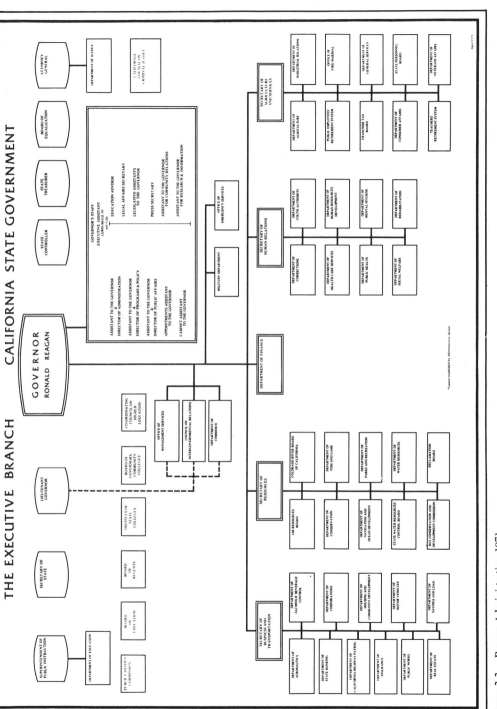

Figure 3.3.   Reagan Administration 1971

nor, did not describe their loyalty in the same manner as did staff members. Loyalty to them was directed not to the governor as a person, but rather to the governor as the chief spokesman of a philosophy, a philosophy to which the appointees themselves subscribed. *Instead of attaching to the person of the governor, this loyalty built on what the governor stood for: his programs, his philosophy, and his goals.*

This type of commitment, allegiance, called upon the administrative appointees to align themselves as a group behind the principles and symbols of the governor's administration.[33] Allegiance represented the obligation to adhere to a shared vision of the purposes and proper execution of the function of government.[34] It was loyalty based on duty owed to principles rather than to people, to ideas rather than personalities. In recalling the appeal that brought him to Sacramento, one of Reagan's agency secretaries phrased this sense of obligation as follows: "I repeated to [one of Reagan's political backers] all the reasons I did not want [an appointment]. But two or three days later [he] called me and said, 'Son, it's your duty. We've spent a lot of time and money getting this guy elected. He has to have people around him who will follow his principles. It's your duty.' So the trumpet blew." Or as one Brown appointee said, "I think I live by Brown's philosophy. [It has] no explicit guidelines but you do have some sense about what policy should be implemented, considered; and what one would be alien to 'The New Spirit.' "

Unlike interviews with staff members, those with administrative appointees showed a marked absence of references to the personal qualities of the governor. The references that did occur were typically made by individuals who considered themselves to be friends of the governor. But even these references were subdued and stripped of emotion. One of Reagan's highest appointees and a close friend noted that he was "keen on the governor." Another Reagan appointee who also knew the governor well remarked that Reagan had around him "a certain aura of ego." But in the same breath he also said that, although a "hanger-on," he shared in that aura and that made him "part of a big team."

Similarly, a number of Brown's appointees with whom the governor was friends before the election expressed their admiration for Brown, but qualified it as well. To these appointees, as well as other

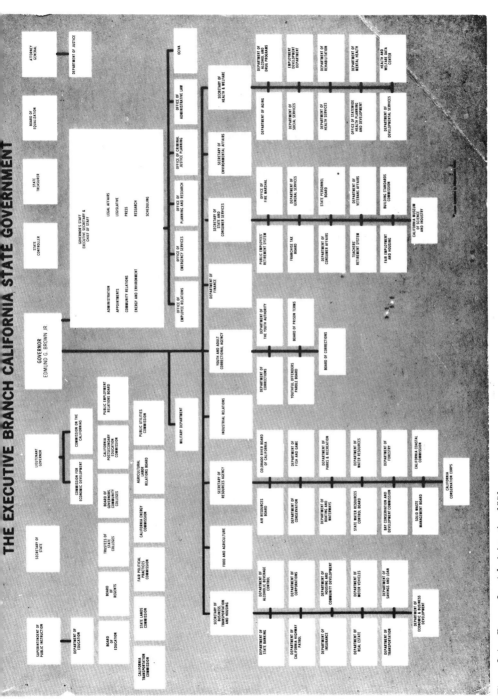

Figure 3.4. Brown, Jr., Administration 1981

appointees who did not know Brown personally, many of Brown's personal characteristics, cited as objects of personal loyalty among staff members, were unfortunate traits from an administrative point of view. Such traits, they suggested, should be ignored insofar as they did not interfere with the articulation of the governor's philosophy or the running of state government. One of Brown's agency secretaries and a friend said, "I think we all felt a certain degree of frustration dealing with Jerry, because he has very little sense of government as something that needs to be managed. . . . That's frustrating to a department director or agency head, because you had something that had to be managed and the only way that you could deal with that problem was that you had pretty much to ignore Jerry except on the major issues. So that's what I did and that's what [another cabinet level appointee] does." At the same time, this same individual holds Brown in high regard. "He is very idealistic and very bright . . . He is an unusual kind of guy." As these comments illustrate, allegiance to the governor's philosophy did not preclude a personal relationship with the governor. But becoming an administrative appointee maintained that personal relationship as a friendship or a colleagueship, a relationship that rested on equality.

Rather than emphasizing the governor's personal qualities, administrative appointees stressed their participation in a cooperative venture. They described themselves as part of the Brown or Reagan "team." As members of this team, they had been given the mandate to carry out the governor's programs in their assigned areas. They expressed this feeling of shared commitment and responsibility with cooperation metaphors, usually from sailing and sports, which they often mixed. "Coming on board" or "on line," "doing my part of the total effort," "running interference for his programs," "we had a good crew"—this was the language of the department director and agency secretary in both administrations. And in this language was expressed the standards of loyalty expected of administrative appointees, standards that differed from those of personal staffs. "I consider myself very much a part of Jerry Brown's team," said one department director. "I don't consider myself a part of his personal staff. A personal staff to me connotes intimate daily staff relationships. I don't do staff work for the Governor. I run one of his big departments. . . . I would say that the team concept is [the appropriate one]."

Administrative appointees invoked a language which articulated a far more collegial relationship with the governor than that which existed in the Governor's Office. Appointees used the vocabulary of allegiance and cooperation to locate the obligations that they were expected to fulfill: while the governor was in charge of the executive branch as a whole, appointees were in charge of particular spheres within it. To be loyal as his appointees, they felt they should govern their respective spheres with the same principles in mind as the governor did over the whole. Given this vision of their responsibility, they saw their loyalty to the governor in terms of team play—a cooperative venture to put shared principles into practice. The collegial ethic of allegiance elevated their efforts to serve the governor and gave meaning to them.

RECRUITING APPOINTEES

The structural factors that operated among appointees supported a more philosophical loyalty than that expressed by the personal staff. Allegiance was felt as acutely by administrative appointees as personal loyalty was felt by staff members, and allegiance also defined obedient actions. But it was qualitatively different and was expressed and maintained in its own characteristic manner. Like personal loyalty, the factors that maintained a bond of allegiance relied on the placement of particular types of people into particular types of organizational structures.

Selective Recruitment

Selecting people for administrative posts posed a two-sided problem for both governors.[35] First, each governor had to choose people who had the administrative experience and the functional expertise necessary to carry out his programs in bureaucratic departments, many of which had thousands of employees and budgets of millions of dollars. Second, each had to select people who he felt confident would be willing to follow faithfully his general policy guidelines. The necessity of combining the needed expertise and experience with the willingness to follow the governor's program made administrative appointees very different from staff members.

The most immediate source of difference arose from the procedures of selection. Staff members were typically recruited informally, through the governor's network of friends and acquaintances or through those of close advisors. Staff members did not require Senate confirmation. Administrative appointments, however, required confirmation, as did the governor's appointments to the numerous boards and commissions and judgeships; accordingly, the recruitment for such positions assumed a more formal appearance. This formality called for procedures and for a staff to carry them out.[36]

The recruitment procedures differed slightly between the Reagan and Brown administrations. In both, however, the appointments section in the Governor's Office bore the responsibility to select qualified individuals for each position.[37] This was not an easy task, for the meaning of "qualified" varied between administrations, and within each administration from position to position, from person to person. A Superintendent of Banks had to know banking. A Secretary of the Resources Agency had to be acceptable to the environmentalists, without being unacceptable to businessmen. The Director of the Department of Health Services, besides knowing about health, had to be an administrator of the first order.[38] Each position carried its own peculiar qualifications. With these qualifications, appointment personnel tried to match individuals who possessed their own special sources of fitness. Appointments had to appear balanced between sexes, ethnic groups, and political factions.[39] Some appointees had to be Northern and others Southern Californians; some had to come from urban and others from rural counties. And in both administrations, there was a list of individuals—campaign workers, defeated candidates—for whom positions had to be found. Yet, despite considerable variation between administrations, between positions, and between persons, the determination of appropriate qualifications always rested on some combination of the expertise needed to perform a specific job and compatibility with the governor's philosophy.

Just locating names of people who were qualified and willing to serve might seem the most difficult part of recruiting appointees. In fact, it was typically the easiest part. Early in both administrations, when there were many vacancies, the appointments section was inundated with applications by people looking for jobs. Besides these applications, the names of hundreds of individuals entered the pool of possibilities, as legislators, party supporters, interest groups, and campaign workers began lobbying for their favorites. In addition, both governors-elect put together an appointments task force to solicit applications from those who, though well-qualified, might not otherwise apply. The efforts of the applicants, supporters, and appointments task forces netted what one Brown aide called an "incredible flood of resumes for all the various appointments."

Knowing that the positions had to be filled quickly, the appointments personnel faced the difficult task, not of finding possible candidates, but of sorting through all the applications in order to locate the "best" one for the job. "You almost reached the point," said a Reagan aide, "where a person's qualifications to fill a position was in inverse proportion to the amount of paper accumulated on his behalf. Those people that really needed the work would just bombard you with letters and bombard you with all kinds of stuff, and the phone would ring." Too much lobbying by anyone seeking to place themselves or someone they knew in a position of importance created doubt about the person's qualifications. "If a legislator, for example," continued Reagan's aide, "started pushing a name at us, we were immediately suspicious." The process of wading through so many applications created its own dynamic, producing criteria of selection that appointments personnel could use to justify their list of finalists for each position. The criteria always included both *expertise* and *philosophic compatibility* with the governor.

Judging Expertise

Even in the best of circumstances, determining a person's expertise was difficult. For appointments personnel working under the weight of deadlines and applications, it was impossible. Nonetheless, we were assured, expertise was essential, the *"sine qua non."* And to judge expertise they relied heavily, as one Brown aide put it, upon a person's "track record, proven experience in an area." The measure of exper-

tise was the size and shape of a person's *past accomplishments*, a fact
that influenced the type of person chosen to be an appointee.[40]

Appointments personnel used an implicit rule of thumb when
judging expertise: some, but not too much. This rule applied equally
to the three different ways expertise was normally assessed: technical
knowledge, administrative skills, and constituency links. For some
positions, technical knowledge was the essential qualification: "In order to be a Director of the Department of Savings and Loans, you've
got to know something about savings and loan laws, or else you can't
do it." But too much technical knowledge was a disadvantage, because "that locks [a person] into doing things in a traditional way and
that can act as a barrier to [change]." For other positions administrative ability was the decisive criterion of selection: "For the Department of Health, you require somebody who has a high knowledge in
the health area and an *enormous* ability to administer." But being seen
as too much a manager was grounds for disqualification: "It is important to put in people who won't just sit in a chair and push paper
from point A to point B to point C; government is more than that."
For a few positions good links to the constituencies served by a department was an important factor in selecting its director. But were
these links seen as too strong, a candidate would be dropped: "[A per-
son] had to be acceptable to the profession," recalled one Reagan aide,
"[but when] the California 'ump-ti-ump' association would come in
with their recommendations, we would consider them, but they would
be at the bottom of the stack, because we felt they were just people
who were in league with the establishment."

Expertise was, said one Brown aide, "a hard thing to quantify," but
"so important." Both Reagan and Brown felt themselves called by the
electorate to change the direction and goals of government from those
of the previous administration. Each wanted capable, talented appointees who could grasp the governor's thoughts, take the initiative
in their own departments, and implement the governor's policies fully
and faithfully. Administrative appointees with too much or too little
expertise could be worse than useless; they could become obstacles.
But possessing only the right kind of expertise in the right amount
was insufficient to become a governor's appointee. Expertise had to

be supplemented with a known commitment to the basic tenets of the governor's philosophy.

Philosophical Compatibility

As one Brown aide noted, the appointments personnel looked for administrative appointees who "seemed to be philosophically in tune with what [the governor was] about. That adds to the likelihood they're going to be loyal, because *they're going down the same path, the same direction, [as the governor]*" (emphasis added). Reagan's appointments secretary said much the same thing: "We tended to shunt the hurley-burley process [of weeding through all the applications] aside. What we tended to do was to bring in those people we felt were both philosophically behind Reagan, loyal to him, and had demonstrated that in the campaign. We tended to go seek out our own type."

Selecting people for their philosophical leanings, like selecting them for expertise, was an art, not a science. How does one determine a candidate's compatibility with the governor's philosophy? The major difference in the recruitment procedures between the two administrations centered on the manner of measuring the likelihood of allegiance. Whereas Reagan delegated this task to his appointments personnel, Brown handled it personally.

In his 1966 gubernatorial campaign, Reagan styled himself as the chief spokesman of orthodox Republicanism. His political philosophy closely corresponded with the Republican Party platform, and had as its core the attempt to carry the ethos of private enterprise into state government.[41] Easily understood and widely publicized, Reagan's political philosophy offered a sharp contrast with that of his Democratic opponent, Edmund Brown, Sr., who was running for a third term in office. Therefore, when Reagan assumed the governorship his appointment aides felt themselves able to interpret accurately the likelihood of an appointee's political compatibility, simply by checking his party registration and his activity in the campaign. The Republicans had been out of power for eight years, and voter registration favored the Democrats at about 2 to 1. Reagan's aides reasoned that a candidate's Republican registration indicated his probable allegiance to Reagan's political goals; working for Reagan in the campaign proved it.

Because of the ease with which allegiance could be determined, Reagan delegated all aspects of selecting appointees to his aides. "He established standards," said one Reagan aide. "To his credit, he told us—he didn't repeat it, he just told us—basically what he wanted. He wanted to avoid the charges of packing [the administration] with hacks and cronies." In establishing criteria, the appointments staff looked for "political acceptability, activity in the governor's campaign, background in the subject field . . . and standing in the community. . . . Political loyalty was a primary consideration, but in the practical course of the thing, was not overriding." When the appointments personnel had screened the finalists for a position, they would personally interview the candidates for administrative posts. They would then make their recommendations to Reagan for his approval. "We always brought in [the recommendations] in memorandum form, a couple of pages at most, usually one page. It summarized the candidates and identified our recommendations by name, age, address, background, and who their principal recommenders were, who their tail wind was, and strongly recommended by X, Y, and Z. That was usually enough for him. He would put his initials 'OK RR' down in the right hand corner. And that was that."

Selecting candidates for their political compatibility was more difficult for Jerry Brown's staff, but was no less important than it was in the Reagan administration. Even to his close aides, Brown's political philosophy was something of an enigma.[42] Reagan's philosophy shared much with the official Republican platform. Brown's philosophy, however, departed from party orthodoxy; it was a personal philosophy, less tangible and more difficult for others to interpret accurately. Whereas Reagan aides were able to distribute to department heads a single page outline of the general tenets of Reagan's philosophy,[43] Brown aides themselves could not always piece together what Brown was thinking. As a consequence, Brown was the sole interpreter of his own philosophy; only he was able to judge the philosophical compatibility of candidates for administrative positions.

Brown's appointment aides, of course, had a general idea of the type of people whose philosophic leanings Brown found acceptable. Said one aide, "[We look for] the human factors, if you will. That is obviously an intangible, but it is very, very important. We really look for people who have a little vision, people that have a sense of what they would be doing if they were appointed to the position. Vision is very important. . . . We need people who question very, very basic assumptions [about government]." In selecting people for their vision, Brown aides largely ignored party registration and sought out community activists, public interest lawyers, and known advocates of controversial points of view. Such individuals had strongly held personal philosophies in their own right, and to the extent that these philosophies seemed to mesh with Brown's, they were deemed appropriate candidates.

For important posts, the appointments personnel often met with Brown before the recruitment process began to discuss what type of person might best fill the position. "Brown," said one aide, "takes appointments very, very seriously. When we discuss appointments, he goes into tremendous depth. I mean just tremendous depth." Based on these discussions, the aides attempted to locate a number of candidates with the appropriate qualifications. From a list of possible candidates, they then interviewed the most likely ones. Based upon these interviews, they made their recommendations to Brown, who in turn personally interviewed, at some length, one or more of the candidates. On a number of occasions, Brown rejected these nominees and asked to interview others.

Administrative appointees typically recalled their interviews with Brown as "an exchange of ideas." The interviews usually lasted between one and three hours, and on several occasions Brown interviewed a person more than once. Said one departmental director, "I got the feeling that mostly what he was doing was feeling me out on his agenda. He asked me questions. The Governor is a good listener. The interview was basically him asking me lots of questions about what would I do with certain parts of the program, and him identifying problems for me to explain the kinds of solutions I would work out and the different ideas I had. That was it for the hour and a half or two hours we talked." Another department director recalled that he "walked away [from the interview] with the impression, 'Wow, what an inquiring mind.' It was such a broad discussion. I felt, 'Here was an extremely intelligent person.' I didn't walk away with any impression that he knew exactly what he wanted to do in any of these areas. It was just that I felt he had a good mind and was responsive to the discussion of ideas and that was about it."

Most of his aides and appointees agreed that Brown used his interview to determine, not whether a candidate was able to subordinate himself to Brown's philosophy, but whether a candidate's own philosophy fit Brown's closely enough. Interviews were not an occasion for receiving instructions about what Brown had in mind for a particular position, as one department director discovered. "I remember saying [to Brown], 'What is it that you want me to do?' His reply was, 'If I have to tell you that, then I've picked the wrong guy.' I said, 'I'll never ask you that question again.' And that was the end of the conversation." Instead, Brown's interviews were directed towards determining the congruence of ideas. As one department director put it, "[Brown] insisted that he felt comfortable with me and that we thought enough alike about [department] issues that I would be able to do the job that needed to be done."

Results of Appointee Recruitment Process

Reagan delegated and Brown conserved the responsibility to assess a candidate's loyalty. But this difference points to an underlying similarity between the two administrations: The loyalty expected from the governor's appointees was to be of a different order from that expected of personal staffs. Neither governor expressed a desire that his appointee be either loyal to his person or, more importantly, subservient to his own individual way of thinking. Instead, each governor wanted individuals who had known commitments that were compatible with his own. There was no evidence in any of our interviews that a candidate, as a condition of his appointment, agreed to downplay his views in favor of the governor's. On the contrary, because of the correctness of their vision and the excellence of their skills, appointees regarded themselves as *chosen*. Their abilities judged, their ideas tested, they began to see in themselves those special qualities that made them particularly fit to serve in this or that administration. *The act of appointing someone to an administrative post became the act of certifying that person—his ideas, his skills, his whole being.*

The effect of recruiting people for their experience and their commitments lent support to this process of certification. The first effect was the appearance, at least, of an absence of patronage.[44] Most appointees had no previous relationship with the governor before their recruitment. This was particularly true of Reagan's administration. Because Reagan's gubernatorial campaign was his first attempt at public office, he did not personally know most of the Republican Party activists, some of whom later became his appointees. As a result, Reagan knew only two or three of his top administrators before appointing them. Although Brown had held public office before being elected governor, he was not a party regular, and in fact he appointed very few of his acquaintances and friends to top positions. But even counting these individuals, Brown personally knew four of the twelve individuals who held cabinet level appointments during his first term in office. Of his 39 department heads, Brown knew well only three or four. By far the majority of the appointees in both administrations had had no previous personal relationship with the governor who appointed them. All, of course, knew something about the governor's campaign and about his political philosophy as it was represented to the public. Most appointees were acquainted with the governor's philosophy but not the governor, a fact both reinforcing the impression of being among the chosen few and favoring allegiance rather than personal loyalty.

The second effect of this recruitment process was the selection of a different type of person to an administrative post than the type appointed to the Office staff. Because appointees were recruited for their past accomplishments and known commitments they were usually people who had considerable experience in a profession, who had standing in their community, or who were prominent among the constituents served by a department or agency. As a result, they were in the middle to late stages of their careers. On the average, they were older than staff members.

The differences in the profile of staff and administrative appointees point to a more important distinction between the two, their differing motivations for accepting a temporary position in state government. Staff members often viewed their work in the Governor's Office as a means to improve their careers. Appointees usually did not view it this way. Some appointees took time off from their already successful careers to work for a while in state government, often at some financial sacrifice. Others, nearing retirement age, saw an appointment as an opportunity to cap off their careers with public service.

One of Reagan's agency secretaries explained his motivation as follows: "It was a very exciting offer. . . . It was just challenging. I had a very difficult decision, of course. [It would be] terribly hard on the family, but my five children were all away or grown, and so I just decided it would be an exciting termination to my public life. I was 55 years old then, and I was happy in my occupation, but I doubted that I would rise much higher in the company that I was with. Although I knew it would be a financial sacrifice to go there, I felt like I could afford it. I just thought it was challenging." One of Brown's agency secretaries noted much the same rationale: "I'd been in a place for 28 years and was approaching retirement [as a vice president with an insurance company]. When I was asked to join the group, one of my concerns was, 'What are you going to do that for?' . . . Personally I was intrigued by the whole idea. It's not often that the Governor invites you to join his staff. Sooner or later, I said to myself, 'It is an interesting opportunity, go ahead and give it a shot.' I felt I could do it, whatever it was. It was a challenge."

Although often implicit in their explanations, one of the most important reasons for accepting appointments was the prestige of having a governor ask for their assistance. The fact of being asked elevated their past accomplishments and present commitments. Past works in their professions and in their communities came into focus and took on a new meaning as they were viewed by a wider circle of people. Their efforts became validated and their pride in them justified. Appointees accepted their call to high public position as an honor, troublesome perhaps, but well-merited. Recognizing the hassles involved in public administration, they regarded public service as a challenge that was worthy of their skills and commitments. Accepting their appointment, they met the governor as an equal, as someone who asked for and needed their help. One of Brown's appointees summarized this motivation as follows: "I didn't *go to work* for Brown. I did him a *favor.*" A departmental director of Reagan's administration made this point even more strongly. "I didn't seek the job. They came after me. . . . They wanted me; I didn't want them. That gave me a certain ego strength all the time I was there."

The process of selective recruitment began subtly to mold the ambiguousness of loyalty into the shape of allegiance. People were appointed because their ideas were correct and their skills adequate for the job at hand. By virtue of their appointment, they had the role obligation to use those ideas and skills in the service of the governor. They did not need to wait for the governor to take the lead in regard to their department or agencies; that was their job. They did not need to ask the governor's permission to begin making most changes; that was what they had been appointed to do. Even those who were uncertain of their skills and who sometimes lacked confidence in their opinions had to rise to the level of being the governor's administrator. They had been confirmed. They had to take the initiative. Most appointees desired this challenge and responsibility, and accordingly would find working in the Governor's Office a poor use of their talents and ideas. As one appointee who had declined an opportunity to work in the Governor's Office said, "I decided I wouldn't work for [Brown]. I don't like to work for people, because I'm not a good soldier, and I have my own views and commitments. I have to have some independence."

This sense of being obliged to take charge was given substance by the process of recruitment. They had not only the obligation but also the right to act on their own behalf. After all, their ideas had standing, for by implication they were the governor's ideas as well. They could determine their own direction, for by implication their direction was also the governor's. They were not appointed to follow the governor, but rather to parallel him—to be leaders in their own spheres just as the governor was the leader of the whole. Their image of their relationship with the governor, as well as with other appointees, was thus not one of dependence or even interdependence. Rather, it was one of *autonomy in unison.*

ORGANIZATIONAL SUPPORTS

Autonomy in unison became less an image and more a reality as appointees faced the demands of their positions. Unlike members of the Governor's Office, administrative appointees often brought with them a prominence independent of the governor. Accordingly, appointees could never be expected to submerge themselves as totally into serving the governor as could members of the Governor's Office. And when appointees took their posts, the gap between the two widened. Facing the demands of their jobs, staff members were drawn into a structure demanding personal loyalty. At the same time appointees were finding that the conditions of their work blocked the viability of personal loyalty but gave substance to the principles of allegiance. They discovered that being the governor's administrator limited the ways they were able to justify their actions, forcing them into a role with which many felt uncomfortable but which they could do little to alter. Their understandings of their managerial role in government grew, in part, from the organizational supports of the role, especially their separation from the governor and the uncertainty of direction that that produced.

Separation

Just as the isolation of the staff *with* the governor helped support the value of a personal commitment, so too did the separation of appointees *from* the governor contribute to the norms of allegiance.[45] This separation occured along four dimensions: physical, organizational, psychological, and legal. The legal dimension will be discussed in the following chapter, when we discuss the power of appointees.

With the exception of the Director of Finance, whose office was in the Capitol building, all agency secretaries and departmental directors had their offices in the buildings occupied by the bureaucratic units they headed. These buildings were physically removed from the Governor's Office by as little as a block and by as much as 400 miles, the distance from Sacramento to Los Angeles. Unlike the offices of the governor's personal staff, appointees' offices revealed rank and importance. They were large and often contained overstuffed chairs, couches, coffee tables, and bookshelves. The walls were sprinkled with works of art, with mementos, with degrees, with symbols of status. In the corner was often an American flag. Despite other attractions, the desk was usually the most prominent feature in the room—solid wood, large, imposing. The office itself was usually on the top floor of the part of the building held by the unit, or if a large unit, on the top floor of the building. If the building was so located, the office was strategically placed in order that its occupant might view the domed Capitol building. Unlike the governor, who shared the Capitol Building with the State Legislature, a unit he could not control, administrative appointees were located in the units over which they had jurisdiction. They were separated from the governor, but ensconced in their own domains.

Separation in space matched separation in the conduct of state government. A glance at an organizational chart of state government suggests a direct relationship between the governor and his agency secretaries, who in turn had a direct relationship with the departmental directors. What is apparent in the chart was less than real in practice. Direct relationships between a governor and his appointees were rare, and if they occurred they were seldom personal and private, but rather formal and in the company of others.

Reagan and Brown differed greatly in their interaction with appointees. Reagan's administration was highly structured with well-established protocol for channeling communication between levels of state government. The centerpiece was the cabinet meeting, around which all else functioned. The cabinet—consisting of four agency secretaries, the Director of Finance, and Reagan's Executive Assistant—met once or twice a week in the Governor's Office. If he was in Sacramento, Reagan always attended the meetings. Reagan delegated to the cabinet the responsibility of debating all the important matters facing state government and of making recommendations on the desired courses of action, and he usually followed their advice. Members of Reagan's administration likened this forum to a corporation's board of directors or to the military's Joint-Chiefs-of-Staff.[46] The top aides in Reagan's personal staff sat in on these deliberations and would occasionally comment on issues in their area of expertise. Departmental directors, however, never attended the meetings unless they were invited to make a presentation, and once they had made their presentation, they left. The director of one of the largest departments in state government noted that, "There's quite a gap between the cabinet and the departmental heads. The cabinet sees the governor [regularly]. The department heads, under Reagan, did not see him very often. I got to the cabinet meeting about three or four times in my two years to present different ideas. I was invited in, made my speech, answered questions, and was invited out."

Besides occasional cabinet meetings, departmental appointees saw Reagan about once a month in what was called the "Management Forum." On this occasion Reagan presided over the meeting of all the department directors. He would answer their questions and present his views on the running of state government. It was an opportunity for them to receive lessons in the governor's philosophy, as well as for building and maintaining team spirit.

Although they met with Reagan frequently in some capacity, Reagan's cabinet secretaries were also separated from the governor, though more subtly than were his department heads. Through the efforts of Reagan's chiefs-of-staff, the cabinet system was designed so that "no one would be able to buttonhole the governor on an issue before it had been discussed in the cabinet meeting." This rule, known to all, applied to all. With few exceptions, agency secretaries did not have private meetings with the governor to discuss issues to be addressed in the cabinet sessions. After receiving some complaints about the difficulties of gaining private access to the governor, Reagan had direct telephone lines installed to each secretary in the third year of his administration, but the telephones were rarely used by either party. The cabinet session, whether at the formal meeting or at a weekly luncheon, became the only appropriate forum for interaction with the governor. It was a group endeavor, with Reagan being one of the group. It was a debate among people who saw themselves as separate but equal.

Brown used the same line-up of administrative appointees very differently. In the first months of his administration, Brown presided over nightly cabinet meetings. Like Reagan's sessions, Brown's included agency secretaries, Brown's Chief of Staff and the Director of Finance, but many others as well. The nighttime cabinet meetings disbanded after a few months, and the cabinet members began to meet, in theory, once a week during the working day. Brown occasionally sat in on these meetings. One member estimated that Brown, in his first term, attended one in four, and fewer than that in the second. Even if he were in attendance, Brown did not use his cabinet as a forum for reaching decisions. Described one member, "Brown deliberately stirs controversy in his pot. He prefers to have [the cabinet] rage, quite often did not make any decision there, and would make the decision in his own mind later. Perhaps that night he'd sleep on it, and he would come back and know what he would want to do. But nobody else would know. . . . So Brown uses his cabinet for informational purposes, for policy guidance and dissemination. He makes it a two-way thing. He doesn't do all the talking. In fact, many times he'd rather listen to the talk and just throw in enough of the needles to keep things not only lively, but see all the sides of an issue, all issues." Another member described the meetings as "discussion sessions." "There is sometimes specific items [sic] that have to be finalized, but it's more of a sounding board for the cabinet secretaries and for the governor, and for the executive secretary. We talk about issues, rather than resolutions.[Therefore] most decisions are made without cabinet input as a cabinet, but may reflect [the opinion] of individual cabinet members."

Unlike Reagan's cabinet, Brown's cabinet had no delegation of power, and the recommendations of cabinet members carried little weight beyond the influence individual members had with Brown. This pattern of using his top appointees was largely structured by the fact that Brown acted as a problem solver; he shouldered the responsibility to see that the alternative solutions for each problem he addressed were explored and discussed by a wide variety of individuals. Accordingly, he did not delegate, in a clear fashion, the responsibility for making decisions on important matters. He reserved the right to make all such decisions himself. He sought advice from people whose opinions he valued as well as from those who were knowledgeable on a specific issue. It was common for him to seek out the individuals who best knew a program and its problems, even if this meant bypassing his appointees to talk to the civil servants in charge.

Because he did not meet regularly with his cabinet or with his departmental heads, most communications between the Governor and his appointees were initiated by the Governor himself, usually over the phone. Brown's appointees at all levels expressed reluctance to contact Brown on anything but the most urgent and serious matters, and only a few had done so. Said one departmental director, "The Governor is rarely contacted by anyone below an agency secretary level. I don't attempt to contact the Governor. He contacts me from time to time, but I don't call him; that would be a breach of protocol." Although agency secretaries had more contact with Brown, most communication was initiated by Brown himself: "I don't get a lot of calls from [Brown]. The phone rings occasionally. It varies as to what he's doing. If he's focusing on something that's going on in this agency, I may hear from him relatively often. . . . You never know [when he will contact you]. It's not daily and to try to put a number on it is difficult. I would say it is moderate contact." "I never bother the Governor or the Governor's staff," said another agency secretary, "unless I have a problem or an issue that they should be aware of."

Despite the difference between the two administrations, the position of the administrative appointees was similar in each. *Appointees were organizationally separate from the governor.* At all levels they were reluctant to contact the governor personally on anything except the most crucial matters. In all routine business in which the Governor's Office had to be involved, such as legislative analysis, appointees dealt with the governor's personal staff, and not the governor himself. All other contacts with the governor were typically formal and in a group setting, as in Reagan's and Brown's cabinet meetings, or by telephone. A frequent, one-to-one relationship with the governor, which was common with staff members, only rarely occurred with appointees. In the conduct of the state's business, administrative appointees accepted, at times unwillingly, this separation from the governor as inevitable, as part of the job. Explained one departmental director, "If every chief executive officer picked up the phone once a week to call the governor, there would be 60 or 70 calls right there. He doesn't have time to deal with that. Then he's got all the legislation to deal with and he is developing new policies. When you look at it from his perspective, he really doesn't want to hear from departmental directors unless it is really vital. I think that is generally understood."[47]

The physical and organizational separation produced a psychological separation as well. Appointees did not see the governor regularly. They came to know their own units thoroughly and made plans based on that knowledge. But they did not know the state government as a whole. They did not know for sure what other department directors were doing, especially those in departments outside their agency. Often they did not understand how the governor made some of his important decisions, and some of these decisions, such as budget formation, affected them directly. What was the role of the cabinet, and of the governor's personal staff? Most important, how did the governor fit into all of this? Said a Reagan appointee who had been first a departmental director and then a cabinet member, "Department heads are not close [to the governor]. They can't take their problems to him. They can't get the personal interplay or even understand the forces that make the governor do what he does." Such nagging doubts existed in both administrations, even in their best moments, and often became a source of tension and, at times, open conflict. As one Brown appointee said, "One of the things that worries me is that when [Brown] gets to a decision, even though I know he's talked to a lot of people, . . . I don't know *who* he's been talking to. Did he get the full impact of the people closest to him, the cabinet and staff? . . . There's a general complaint that 'When a decision is made, I wasn't there and should have been.' "

Uncertainty and the Need to Rely on Philosophy

The physical, organizational, and psychological dimensions of separation from the governor combined to preclude attachment to the governor as a person, and instead produced in many a strong reliance on the governor's philosophy. This reliance stemmed, in part, from the element of uncertainty that arose from the obligation to take charge of and guide the executive bureaucracy. As administrators with the authority and the responsibility to manage large bureaucratic units, appointees had to devote most of their time and energy to manage-

ment and to the formulation and implementation of policies that related to those units. These were matters that required skill and considerable judgment, and being conscientious administrators, they had
to develop some rules about when to inform the governor about the
actions they were taking. In general they knew protocol: for direction
in routine matters, do not ask the assistance of the governor or his
aides. In critical or potentially controversial matters, inform the governor personally or through his chief-of-staff. For those matters that
fall between two extremes, exercise judgment. The limitations imposed by protocol lent an element of uncertainty to the job of being
the governor's administrator. They desired, as a number of appointees phrased it, occasionally "to touch base" with the governor,
because those things they most wanted to accomplish in their short
tenure as appointees were neither routine nor critical. "I periodically
check [with the Governor]," said one Brown department head, "to
make sure I'm going in the right direction." Yet they hesitated to call
the governor or his close aides frequently to check if their plans and
actions accorded with what the governor wanted. And to call one of
the lesser aides was beneath their station.

Rather than contacting the Governor's Office, they relied on what
they knew of the governor's philosophy. They constantly measured
their own ideas and plans against their knowledge of the governor's.
A number of Brown's appointees remarked that they closely followed
the newspapers and broadcast media for statements about Brown's goals
and programs for state government. "The thing we try to do," said
one agency secretary, "is to determine what the governor's policy is.
He tends to articulate it in general terms. Then you have to take those
general terms and try to rate them as to what your responsibility is."
Said one of Brown's departmental directors, "I am trying to take his
policies, concepts, and approaches, and apply them in this [depart-
ment]. For example, when he was running [for governor] in '74, he
said, 'We're going to bring people into state government who have
been excluded from the governmental process. . . . ' We heard him
say those broad principles and applied them in our context. It doesn't
take a lot of thinking to hear that concept and go forth and apply it.
. . . So [a part of my job] is a feet-up-and-listen-and-apply kind of

function. That is what a person should do as a director, aside from running the show."

Separation from the governor as a person pushed appointees into a position where they had to dwell on his philosophy. If they were to do a responsible job as the governor's administrator, they had to continually assess their plans in light of the principles he had laid down. But such principles as were needed to win elections, to persuade legislators, and to lead the state as a whole were usually broad and could be interpreted in numerous ways. Yet plans taken to implement those principles in departments and agencies had to be precise. Appointees had to deduce the correspondence between the governor's ideas and their own, between his principles and their plans. To do this they had to know the governor's philosophy, for if they were to be loyal, it was to the philosophy and not the person that they had to adhere.

Chapter Four

THE GOVERNOR'S ADMINISTRATORS (CONTINUED)

ALTHOUGH THE PEOPLE whom Reagan and Brown appointed to administrative posts were either top executives or prominent policy advocates, most recalled feeling delight and a bit of self-satisfaction at their invitations to high government office. Indeed, several said the feelings of self-importance became even stronger with the full realization of their enormous powers.[1]"[Being an appointee] is a very heady business," said a Brown cabinet officer. "Nobody can look you in the eye and say they don't like it, because it's powerful. I don't know how you could avoid that. I thought that I was dealing [in my previous career] with big business. But when you get up here you realize the impact that you can have. It just, you know, turns you up a little."

An appointee's authority was of a very different nature from the "borrowed" authority of the staff.[2] The authority of agency secretaries and department directors was their own, conferred by the positions they occupied and the mammoth bureaus they managed. Every day they were treated as centers of influence in their own right, made to feel important and indispensible. Although defined by legislative mandate, the authority of appointees was not a simple unitary force; it was Janus-faced. On one side, it looked toward the duties of managing a large complex bureaucracy, and on the other side, toward the tasks of assuming a role in the larger sphere of state government. The first face of appointee authority was that of command, the second that of persuasion.

AUTHORITY OVER THE BUREAUCRACY:
THE DUTY TO COMMAND

Having the prerogative to give commands, appointees had to take on the responsibilities and obligations of command. These were diverse and, for the most part, routine and time-consuming. One of Brown's department directors stated, "What you have to do as a department head, unless you're a figurehead, is to make sure that people get work done. That is a very different thing from discussing issues and overall direction and what we are trying to do with the assignment of staff, the projects, and coordinating what's going on in different parts of the organization, budget issues, project delivery, just making sure that when once we've decided to do something [it] gets carried out, and that we are appropriately checking with other parties that have to be involved in a decision, and so on—ninety percent of [the director's job], I would say, is that type of thing." Said a Reagan department director, "I don't think people understand the authority that the director of a department has. . . . The director of a department has a lot of authority. It sort of scared me at times. You have to make decisions almost every minute it seems like. And for the big decisions, you had to have staff work and all kinds of stuff to back up the decisions. What always worried me was whether the day-to-day, minute-to-minute decisions were correct. The budget of the . . . Department was in excess of $50 million, and you're trying to make decisions in the public interest. . . . What was it that the general public wants? It's tough. It's hard to get. That's why [a director] spends so much time traveling around the state meeting with groups, so [he] can get a feel for these sorts of things . . . [But] I never went to the governor on any decision that only involved the department."

The range of routine tasks performed daily by departmental directors and agency secretaries grounded these appointees in their bureaucracies;[3] they had to achieve an understanding of their units sufficient to make knowledgeable decisions. They had to listen to the civil servants under them in order to understand their problems and to field their requests. They had to learn the positive and negative aspects of the previous administration's programs in order to manage those that remained intact and to change those that needed alignment in the direction of the policies of the current administration. They had to be familiar with their personnel in order to know when and where to apply pressure. Not all appointees were equally proficient in accomplishing such tasks, but all appointees, by virtue of wanting to provide direction for their command, were drawn into the organization they headed. There, as a Reagan department director put it, "I was on my own. I knew what I wanted to do. I had to call my own shots."

The necessity to devote a large portion of their time to intradepartmental affairs usually created in appointees a respect for, if not always an appreciation of, the work done by those in their command, the civil servants. In a fashion typical of appointees in both adminstrations, one of Reagan's agency secretaries said, "I always felt that the state government workers were probably the best qualified and the best trained of those in any government I've found anywhere, in the federal or in the local. They are really top flight people. The people on the governor's staff with no prior experience had this idea that we're on this embattled island, and all those civil servants out there are against us. I'd say no. It's not like that. They're all troopers, they're all professionals. It's as if they were once in General Patton's army and now they are in General Bradley's army. They are still Americans and still trying to win the war. They are still government employees, trying to do a good job. . . . They will take orders." Not all appointees waxed so enthusiastic in their praise of civil servants, but even the most cynical ones acknowledged at the worst that civil servants were worthy opponents.

INFLUENCE IN THE ADMINISTRATION: THE DUTY TO PERSUADE

Appointees were pulled by necessity towards the bureaucracy, towards its people and its problems, and the first face of appointee power was directed there. The second face of appointee power was simultaneously directed outward, beyond their own units.[4] Based squarely on their rights to make decisions within their departments or agencies, appointees had, at various times, to cooperate and battle with the legislature, with other appointees, with constituencies of one kind or another, and with the governor and his staff. With these groups appointees did not have the right of command. They could not tell the legislature what to do any more than they could tell the governor or other departmental and agency heads what to do.

Outside their organizations, appointees had to establish a place for themselves by influencing people. They had to become influential with the governor, his staff, and the legislature to approve their programs; with the State Personnel Board for the appointments and promotions of their employees; with the governor and Finance for their budgets; and with local, federal, public, and private constituencies for support of one kind or another. Appointees phrased their initiated contacts with the governor as "solicitations" or as attempts to "persuade" him concerning issues about which they felt strongly.[5] Much the same was true in the descriptions of their meetings with the Director of Finance. And with legislators, the need for an ability to persuade was ubiquitous: "You know [as an appointee]," said a Reagan department head, "that you've got to work with the legislators. You know you've got to hold their hands and all that junk. We always made [supporting department programs] seem like it was to their benefit. [We would arrange it so that the legislators] were getting the credit [in public] for something they didn't have anything to do with."

Appointees had to be able to command the attention of all these individuals without appearing to command their actions. They had to attempt to be persuasive—to have knowledge of programs, procedures, and principles, and to have the personal bearing to convert others to their points of view. If not already convinced of their self-importance, appointees had to puff themselves up to meet these challenges.

Besides persuading others, appointees themselves became objects of persuasion. Constituency groups both inside and outside of government routinely courted agency and departmental heads. Farmers lobbied the Director of Agriculture; doctors, the Director of Health Services; businessmen, the Director of Corporations. Legislators, as the situation required, tried to influence them to undertake this or that project within their districts. These and other sources of influence created the image, if not the fact, of the appointees' role as one of power and independence.

These two faces of appointee power combined to produce on the small scale, with similar pressures and entanglements, the same type of situation that the governor himself encountered on the large. Said one Brown appointee, "[Appointees] are directors of large corporate enterprises. They're involved in doing things—personnel matters, budgets, speaking engagements. They become preemptive, like the governor himself." Recognizing this similarity in the roles of governor and appointee, Reagan wanted to name his agency secretaries "Deputy Governors." Reagan's move failed because it was feared that this title might be confused with the Lieutenant Governor, an independently elected constitutional officer, but the proposal illustrates nonetheless the near equality that Reagan saw between his role and that of his appointees.

Even appointees' exempt status accentuated their independent power. Most had good jobs before their appointment, and most had return rights to their old positions, were ready to retire, or were confident in their ability to find new and better jobs without relying on their public service. Thus, unlike members of the governor's staff who often used their positions to further their careers, *appointees found that the temporary nature of their tenure provided them with an additional source of independence from the governor*. As one Reagan appointee stated, "[The Governor and his staff] really had no power over me that meant anything to me. They could fire me if they wanted, but the day they did that [would be the day] I would be better off economically. It was a source of strength, frankly. . . . If you were dependent for your livelihood and survival on [a government job] or if [your appointment] was to be a stepping stone for you to become a judge or whatever you wanted to seek next, then it is pretty important to get along with a lot of people. My mission was not to get along with people. I was really very arrogant in my role, because I had to be to get the job done that I was hired to do." A Brown appointee explained his job as follows: "I'm very fortunate. I was successful in my other career, and I am [now], in one sense, playing around. In another sense, [I am] absolutely overwhelmed with the information and knowledge that I've picked up here. It's been like the best of all possible worlds. I've definitely got the best job in the United States in a real sense. I don't have any political ambitions; I asked nobody for the job; I'm here and

I've got it for a short period. There's nothing I can do wrong. I could be fired publicly, and probably end up being a hero in the Republican Party, or I could do this job and have somebody say, 'He brought some sanity to the government.' I've got the best damn job there is."

The appointees' power of independence, along with the other dimensions of separation from the governor, undermined the open expression of personal loyalty. In order to play a role in state government, both within and outside of their departments or agencies, they had to portray their ability to make decisions and to plan courses of actions *apart* from the governor's explicit guidance. They had to handle most of the problems within their bureaucracies on their own as best they could. They had to activate their own ideas and set into motion their own sense of mission for the direction of their units. And for their programs and budgets and personnel, they had to become their bureaucracies' advocates within the wider sphere of state government.

In all these roles, an expression of personal loyalty would have undermined an appointee's effectiveness, because it would have been seen by others as sycophancy or as a sign of personal weakness.[6] Appointees had to try to blow air into their personalities to compensate for their lack of certainty that all the decisions they had made were correct ones. A particularly good example of this drive to develop an aura of assurance was demonstrated by the trappings in appointees' offices. One of Brown's agency secretaries, for example, had lined his office walls with laminated plaques bearing exerpts from his own speeches. No staff member would have had an impulse for such self-display. Appointees had to act as if they were autonomous and self-assured, in order to direct their units toward their own goals. Not all appointees performed these roles equally well. Some were good managers, but lacked ideas. Some were very persuasive, but lacked the knowledge to transform ideas into workable programs; others lacked the firmness to give orders, or the tenacity to see that they were obeyed. But regardless of their shortcomings, appointees interpreted their job as one that required that they have strong commitments to themselves, as well as to the governor. It was the ambiguousness of the overlap of commitments to oneself and to the governor that created and maintained the standards of allegiance.

CHECKS ON APPOINTEES' INDEPENDENT POWER

Because of the separation from the governor and the considerable power of their posts, it would seem that appointees might have developed independent fiefdoms within the state government. To some extent, this certainly happened, but there were factors that kept appointees bowed to the wishes of the governor more often than not. These factors were institutionalized parts of state government and aimed directly at limiting the kinds of actions an appointee could take.

Appointees were obliged, of course, to take direction from the governor and were subject to his removal; they were there to put his policies in place. But at this level the bond between the governor and appointee was more symbolic than coercive and was based more on mutual cooperation than on any kind of ability of the governor to force an appointee to comply, short of firing him.[7] After a short time on the job appointees were drawn towards the bureaucracies they headed, and away from a comprehensive view of the administration as a whole. Appointees for the most part came to value the autonomy of their departments and worked to increase it, if possible, because it was autonomy and the freedom to make independent choices that made a department or agency important and its head powerful. They submerged themselves in their departments and became caught up in the welfare of their units, which was their own welfare, too. But the needs of the department and those of the administration as a whole were never perfectly compatible; inevitably a gap widened between their direction and the governor's, between their philosophy and the governor's philosophy. This gap was kept as narrow as possible in at least three ways: first, through technical controls on appointee power; second, through required public displays of allegiance; and third, through conflicts that taxed appointees' energy and required they justify their actions in terms of the governor's philosophy.

Technical Checks: Budgetary and Legislative

All appointees were linked to the governor and to each other by the technical aspects of organization. It was at this level that the governor most effectively limited the discretion of the appointees and stemmed the centrifugal force that pulled the departments out of his control. The governor had the ability to use sanctions in the form of organizational controls, and these sanctions increased the importance of the governor's philosophy as a normative standard by making it the nexus of appointee negotiation.

At an organizational level, the governor controlled two spheres of state government upon which every appointee depended, finance and legislation.[8] The governor, through the Director of Finance, was able to control departmental and agency budgets, and through this means approved or disapproved the direction taken by each unit.[9] Said one of Reagan's appointees, "Every department director knows that his success depends in part on convincing Finance of the need for people or money or supplies or whatnot. [So] when the Department of Finance would call me over to talk about my budget, I used to go into rehearsal. I would get in the staff room and have [my staff] feed me questions to see if I knew the answers. When I went over there, it usually turned out to be more social. . . . But you were nervous. . . . I'd be briefed on everything in the department, because you never know what Finance is going to take an interest in." "I make my decisions [about departmental programs and priorities]," said one of Brown's department directors, "and then I meet with the higher-ups in the Department of Finance. If I feel they have good reasons [for opposing my increases], I'll back down. But when it comes to assessing the priorities of the administration, I know where the Governor is, and many of the program changes that I've initiated are as a result of my working with the Governor. . . . So for priorities, if the Department of Finance starts knocking things down, we're just going to go to the Governor."

The second sphere of the governor's administrative control was that of legislation. The governor, unlike his appointees, had the power both to introduce and to veto legislation. Each bill introduced into the state legislature, whether from the governor or a legislator, was analyzed by the departments most affected by its possible passage. For this purpose departments and agencies, with the exception of Finance, maintained their own legislative sections housed within the units. Once completed, a departmental bill analysis was forwarded to the agency legislative section, where possible conflicts between departments were resolved and a separate analysis was done. Both the analyses were then sent to the legislative unit in the Governor's Office, where the governor's aides formulated the administration's position on the bill. In addition, the Department of Finance personnel analyzed every bill involving revenue, and forwarded this analysis to the legislative section in the Governor's office, where the governor's legislative aides developed an "approved" position.

Through their control on legislation, the governor and his office staff were able to approve or reject programs to which some appointees were strongly committed. A Brown department head explained the procedure as follows: "Ultimately a departmental legislative program is debated with the agency, and the agency will finally say, 'This is the agency position we want you to file.' If the department director is not satisfied, he always has the option of appealing that to the governor, meeting with him and the agency secretary. The governor will resolve the issue, and the department director will carry forth whatever the decision is, or resign." In both administrations, however, the governor seldom got involved to this extent. Typically, a legislative aide in the Governor's Office issued the administration's position in the governor's name. Said a Reagan appointee, "The legislative liaison people had a lot of power and they were physically close to the governor. And although they listened to us, they did have a lot of power. . . . They were often tangled [with Finance]. But I'd say that they did the job as they saw it and they were very powerful."

Both governors, through their Directors of Finance and close aides, controlled departmental and agency budgets and legislative programs. Therefore appointees had constantly to justify what they wanted. For such justifications, they seized the governor's philosophy—that amalgamation of press statements, campaign slogans, policy guidelines, and general political orientation—and appropriated its principles for their own use. After all, their ideas, in theory, lined up with the governor's, so what they embraced was not so much his ideas as their own. But in the conduct of state government, the governor's ideas were those that carried the most weight. Thus, the fine line between their ideas and the governor's ideas began to blur as appointees dressed their own plans in the fabric of the governor's rhetoric. So dressed, their goals

subtly and by degrees became the governor's goals and their principles, the governor's principles. Through appropriation, the governor's
philosophy became the appointees' tool of persuasion. It served as the
symbolic means to solicit cooperation from others, and the shield to
stand behind when doing battle for what one wanted.

*The necessity to rely on the governor's philosophy in order to legiti-
mate their own goals was the paradox of appointee power and independence.* If appointees were going to be independent in their action
and powerful in their role, they had to cast themselves as representatives of the governor's philosophy. They had to be seen as capable
of making decisions that the governor would agree with, at least in
principle. Although pulled in different directions, as their plans and
the needs of their departments required, appointees had to act as if
they marched in unison, with the governor as well as with other appointees. Some appointees were astute in manipulating the governor's philosophy to their own ends, and some were sincere in trying
to employ it faithfully. But regardless of their astuteness and sincerity,
appointees found themselves in a situation that forced them to maintain an obligation to the symbols of the administration. However clear
or blurred, these symbols were the strings that tied each to the governor and to his administration. To break these strings, to part openly
and publicly from the governor's philosophy, was to lose the power
of independence, rather than to gain more.

Public Displays of Allegiance

The precariousness of the balance between one's own ideas and the
governor's ideas became apparent when appointees spoke in public
forums about their departments and agencies. Did they represent the
governor and his administration, or did they present a departmental
view? Often the two points of view coincided or overlapped sufficiently so that an appointee had no difficulty. But sometimes they did
not, and on such occasions appointees had to decide whom they were
obliged to represent, themselves or the governor.

An important aspect of the job of being a departmental director or
an agency secretary was to represent their bureaucracies beyond the

sphere of the executive branch. As administrators in charge, they, more than the governor, were able to present the goals and programs of their own unit in public arenas. Appointees regularly gave speeches to interested groups of constituents. They held press conferences to discuss major or controversial issues. They were called before the legislative committees to testify on the merits of particular legislation affecting their departments or agencies. Some of the larger departments and most of the agencies even had their own public relations units, headed by their own press officers. At public occasions, appointees spoke on their own behalf. Their statements did not need to represent the governor's view. In fact, a frequent question asked of appointees at such public appearances was whether an appointee's views on an issue corresponded with those of the governor.

Despite the recognition by others that appointees speak on their own behalf, appointees in both administrations felt the obligation to act in public as representatives of the governor's administration. One of Brown's agency secretaries noted that reporters and others often ask appointees the question, "What do *you* think?" when they know that the "you" being referred to is "the collective governor and his staff. . . . I don't think there is any way to appear that you're not representing the governor; you do represent the governor." Said one of Reagan's department heads, "The position [I held] had a lot of authority. There was a lot of authority given to me by virtue of that piece of legislation. But when I was public I certainly felt I was representing the governor then. I was very conscious of that; at a press conference, which there were a lot of, and any time I was making a radio or press release, any time I was giving a speech, then I felt very conscious of who I was representing. It was more than myself." As another Reagan department head put it, "[In public appearances], I always felt that I represented not only [this] department but also the administration as a whole."

Insofar as the department policies lined up with those of the governor, appointees had no difficulty. But sometimes the two did not coincide. "In 90 percent of my public speeches, of which I gave 200 to 300 in eight years," recalled one of Reagan's agency secretaries, "I didn't feel constrained to consult the governor at all. I was speaking, and I felt I was speaking, as a cabinet secretary. If I got out of line,

[Reagan] could call me on the carpet. But I would say that I seldom felt constrained, except if a cabinet decision went against me, which happened occasionally. Then, of course, I did feel I just couldn't speak on that subject. If I felt so strongly about it, which I did once or twice, I could just resign." If they knew the governor's position on an issue, appointees felt the obligation to alter their views in public, so that an appearance of unity within the administration was maintained. Such alterations were calculated in advance, as the following example from a Brown appointee shows: "I addressed a [public group] recently. . . . A speech was written by a group [of my aides] on what I wanted to say, the things I was interested in. [The speech] came back, and I had to have inserted in it references to the governor's policies, because [the policies in the speech] were too much my own. The point I wanted to make was, 'this was the governor talking,' so the speech [had to be] directed in that fashion."

Sometimes appointees felt strongly enough about an issue that they chose, in public, to make a distinction between the governor's position and their own.[10] According to one Brown appointee, "[Department directors], if they oppose [a policy] will end-run you and your legislation. They deal directly with the legislature and say, 'The administration feels this way, but I feel the other way.' " He added, "In dealing with complaints, constituents, business people, consumers, you're the governor. There's no way to divorce yourself from that. . . . You do represent the governor in everything you do. . . . But there are too many [appointees] who do act as if they're not [the governor's representative]."

Despite occasional exceptions, however, most appointees publicly supported the governor's policies. They acted allegiant, and felt obliged to do so not only because this was an implied condition of their appointment, but also because *public silence preserved their private leverage within the executive branch*; to oppose the governor publicly was to undermine their ability to persuade the governor and his staff privately to support their programs. Nonetheless, if they saw their goals threatened, their programs subverted, and their ideas neglected, appointees came to resent their self-imposed silence, and as the following quote shows, they privately desired the impossible: complete independence from gubernatorial constraints. "Somebody who is running a department or agency," said one of Brown's agency secretaries, "has the advantage over members of the Governor's Office because they have things they can accomplish, which they are fully and legally capable of doing, whereas somebody who is on the staff doesn't have anything. They are just an extension of the Governor. I am not an extension of the Governor, except in some respects for political purposes. The Governor's policy was my policy for public purposes. I might argue with him about it in private, but I certainly wasn't going to contradict him in public. Certainly to the extent that an agency head or a department head could operate without the Governor they could do a much better job."

CONFLICT

In public, appointees were obliged to support the administration's policies. But in the privacy of the executive branch, this obligation conflicted with the standards of allegiance. Appointees were hired to manage and direct large organizations. Yet, because of the complexity of government, appointees found obstacles blocking the attainment of those goals that they had been hired to reach. The position in which they worked forced them into a role of acting powerful and independent, which in turn made them resent all the more the constraints placed upon their actions. Finance, the governor's staff, other appointees, the legislature, and even the governor—all these and more periodically became obstacles that had to be surmounted if they were to put their ideas into action. Many appointees bristled over these instrusions into what they regarded as their spheres of action, for without such intrusions they could have accomplished more. And the more they were able to accomplish the more they were able to demonstrate to others, as well as to themselves, their allegiance to the governor. But appointees had to deal with Finance, the governor's staff, the legislature, and of course the governor; appointees had to learn either to live with such obstacles or fight them. Though they might pick their battles carefully, they typically chose active conflict over passive consensus. The stronger their allegiance to the governor's philosophy and the stronger their personal commitment to perform the role of the governor's administrator, the more appointees felt obliged to enter the arena of government and do battle.[11] They fought for their programs and they battled over priorities, because *allegiance required they oppose those forces that constrained their actions, even if that meant opposing the administration's policies within the executive branch.*

According to our interviews, appointees saw potential conflict on four fronts: the staff in the Governor's Office, the Department of Finance, other appointees, and the civil service. In both administrations some conflict occurred in all four areas. But because the two administrations were structured differently, Reagan's appointees felt the primary confrontation occurred between them and the governor's personal staff, whereas Brown's appointees felt it occurred among appointees themselves.

Conflict in the Reagan Administration: Cabinet-Staff

In Reagan's administration, the cabinet was the forum for making decisions, and because of this role the cabinet concentrated the confrontation between the governor's staff and governor's agency secretaries. As one of Reagan's agency secretaries who had previously been a departmental director explained, "When I was a department director, I knew what I wanted to do. I could call my own shots. . . . As soon as I became a cabinet secretary I had to go to two cabinet meetings a week and prepare for each one by reading a lot of stuff that I had never heard of but was supposed to have an opinion on. . . . So suddenly instead of looking out at your constituency, you're looking inward at the governor and the governor's staff relationship. . . . There was a great time pressure, for one thing. You felt constrained. Second, you became much more aware of the differences between a cabinet secretary and the governor's personal staff. They always figured they were closer to the governor than you were. And that was true, because they were right there in the suite, and we might be across the street or someplace else. When we were in the [Governor's] Office, we were in somebody else's office. . . . The cabinet situation was a period of conflict and high tension and disagreement. It was also a period of accomplishment."

Open rancor between Reagan's staff and his appointees seldom occurred in cabinet sessions. Such sessions were the setting of deliberation and sometimes heated exchanges, but because of their formality, they were not the setting for hostility.[12] Most of the conflict occurred in the wings, which created a feeling of bitterness in many cabinet members. "[As an agency secretary] you always felt you were in the second tier, even though you were supposedly a deputy governor. It never quite worked that way. Supposedly you were exercising the governor's authority in your area of responsibility, but it always seemed to me that you were subject to being overruled immediately by [some of Reagan's staff members]."

The objects of the confrontation between agency secretaries and staff members typically concerned the approval and jurisdiction of programs. "[In the cabinet meetings] the staff sat behind us all the time. You kept hearing this voice over your shoulder. [One of the staff members] would be saying, 'Governor, that's not quite the way I see it,' and he would be shooting down one of your favorite programs." Said another secretary, "The legislative liaison people had a lot of power and they were physically close to the governor. . . . [They were] quite aggressive and trespassed somewhat in my field. I had to set [them] down a couple of times, or try to." Said another, "It was necessary for me to intervene with [some staff members] on a regular basis [in order] not to allow them to give away too much of the program [in compromising with the legislature] in their attempt to show what a reasonable person Ronald Reagan was. And I felt that people were taking authority over the program away from me. It was going into the hands of [staff members] primarily. [It reached the point] where I was never sure, if I said 'Do something,' whether that was going to be followed through or not, in my own organization and the departments under me."

The staff/appointee conflict was heightened by the belief among cabinet members that the Department of Finance sided with the staff more than with departments, a belief verified by Reagan's Director of Finance. "The Governor's Executive Secretary . . . was the leader of the cabinet. No question about it. I suspect it sounds a little egotistical, but I think the Director of Finance was clearly in second position, not by reason of any personal magnetism, but simply by rea-

son of the office. You have so much to say about all of the departments'
successes and failures, or about how the money was allocated that I
think [this ranking] was recognized. . . . [The Executive Secretary]
and I . . . didn't like to be on opposing sides. I sure didn't with him
and I don't think he particularly did with me. . . . Sometimes you
had an individual cabinet member who would be giving you a little
bit of trouble. . . . [The Executive Secretary] and I would talk about
how to find a way to head [an undesirable program] off, without
bringing it out in cabinet and getting into a knock-down, drag-out
fight."

The confrontation between appointees and Finance was particularly bitter largely because Finance, much more than staff members,
intruded into departments and into programs.[13] "Finance has too strong
a role," explained one of Reagan's agency secretaries. "None of my
department heads were happy with Finance. They *had* to work with
them. [But the people from Finance] were kind of necessary evils,
and they were just into everything. . . . The budget process was eter-
nal. They no sooner would finish one budget in March, and have
this great punching crisis—it's like baseball and basketball and foot-
ball—they would no sooner finish one season than they're starting to
talk about the next. . . . They were powerful. . . . There was really
no protection [from Finance]. That's why there was a lot of antagonistic feelings. They usually had the Governor's ear, and everything
was so complex that there was no really good protection. They pretty
well called the shots." Another of Reagan's cabinet members explained the threat posed by Finance to the departments: "[As soon as
I became an agency secretary] I started my classical conflict with the
Department of Finance. I wouldn't put up with their jazz of holding
hearings among the governor's appointees. As far as I was concerned,
the departments were coequals; they were all part of the team, and
we were not going to have a cop sitting around telling us what our
programs are going to be. I'm willing to make the financial deal and
negotiate the budget, but it will be on the basis that we are all trying
to arrive at the same reasonable goal."

Many of Reagan's top appointees felt that the governor's staff members were not aiming at the "same reasonable goals" as the appointees
were. "[A staff member's] concept of what the governor ought to be

doing and my concept very often did not coincide. I think I respond to the governor's basic [philosophical] urges. Now a lot of [staff members] think that is foolish, that is radical, that is impolitic. [They say] 'We're going to hurt somebody, or we're not going to be able to get our bill through, or the governor's veto is going to be overridden,' which was a big deal for those [staff members]. I always felt, what the hell, *stand up to principle*. If the Democrats and the wayward Republicans in the legislature want to override a veto, so be it. [Reagan] can go around and make an issue of it. But if there was a fundamental principle [involved] he could go without having his veto overridden. [Staff members] conceded a great deal. . . . So I indicated to everyone in the cabinet that I was going to be strongly supportive of the governor's positions, *what I interpreted them to be*, regardless of all their arguments that we ought to be doing something else" (our emphasis).

Allegiance to the governor's philosophy and by implication to those programs inspired by that philosophy required that appointees defend their programs and their jurisdictions from those less committed to the philosophy than they were. From the viewpoint of Reagan's appointees, the governor's personal staff members, while committed to the governor, were not committed to his basic philosophy.[14] They were "so inexperienced," recalled a number of appointees. They were ready to sacrifice philosophy, by "negotiating with the legislature," in order "to prove what a reasonable person Ronald Reagan was."

Worst of all, the staff members blocked their access to the governor. Reagan appointees felt that they did not have an adequate opportunity to try to persuade the governor privately that their programs were good ones, and should be funded or framed into legislation. One of Reagan's staff who had been an appointee explained the conflict over access as follows: "[Appointees] are responsible for certain areas, such as [the Resources Secretary]. He is responsible for the whole of the resources area which includes fish and game, the parks and recreation, water and so forth. So he is separated [from the governor]. Well, he thinks, naturally, that his agency is the most important thing around. He feels over a time that this [importance] has to happen all the time. He feels that he is not getting access to the governor because of the governor's personal staff. Well the personal staff has another problem. No matter who the governor is, the demands on his time are unbelievable. So they have to manage his time, so that in their opinion he's getting his job done, rather than puttering his time away on a lot of other things. So this is where the conflict is. . . . That's a natural conflict; there is no way in the world you can avoid it." From his perspective a cabinet member made this point more bluntly. "[We] had to go through some young guy who didn't know a damned thing about the agency to get to the governor. It made it difficult."

Conflict in the Brown Administration: Among Appointees

Because Reagan delegated to his cabinet the task of making decisions, agency secretaries had strong leverage over departmental matters. This organizational strategy forced the major conflicts in the Reagan administration to rise to the cabinet level, where the appointees saw that their main obstacles were the office staff and Finance. Brown, however, did not use his cabinet as a decision-making body, and reserved the right to make the decisions on major issues himself. Said one cabinet member, "[Brown] doesn't delegate a great deal to anybody of those things that he feels are his decisions to make. He tends to move slowly. It isn't [that he has trouble] making up his mind, rather it's making sure that he gets all the input he wants before he makes up his mind." Because his appointees knew Brown's style of decision making, the conflict within the administration was less focused than it was in Reagan's administration, but no less present.

Some Brown appointees felt that a few members of the Governor's Office had too much influence with the governor; but the typical comment made about staff members was that the governor needed their "calming influence" or that they were "necessary" for him to accomplish his work. An extreme version of this view of Brown's staff was the following: "[The governor] is like a person who has a mansion—twelve rooms, four thousand square feet—and has two servants, a cook, a guard, a chauffeur, a private secretary, a handyperson, plus a legal advisor. All live there and all have no other jobs.

They are all available seven days a week and twenty-four hours a day, as a requirement of the job. I don't know if you can say they work hard; there may almost be nothing to do most of the time. They may go days without having anything to do. That's how the staff operates." Staff members were less seen as obstacles than as resources, as conduits to the governor. Said one agency secretary, "I don't find myself fighting them, I find myself using them."

In the Brown administration, the principal disputes occurred between appointees themselves rather than beween appointees and the governor's personal staff. Like those in Reagan's administration, these conflicts most often concerned approval of and jurisdiction over programs. Department heads vied among themselves for control of this program or that one, and with agency secretaries, who tried to coordinate and often to control the departments, sometimes to no avail.[15] A Brown department director described this conflict as follows: "The department director is in charge of that department's programs and policies, and he wants to do that job and be as successful as possible in his programs. Sometimes a department director will be so focused on that department, that it's hard to see the overall picture from the standpoint of the agency or even the administration. Maybe what's good for the department in the larger context really isn't the best thing for the agency or the administration. And sometimes it's hard for a department director to accept that. You get into a conflict there."

The conflict among appointees was exacerbated by Brown's approach to decision making and management. In interviews appointees repeatedly characterized Brown as "very independent in his judgment," as a person who solicited everyone's opinion but took no one's advice, as a person upon whom a schedule could not be imposed and who avoided routine of any type. They perceived that his philosophy was his own and that he did not impose it directly upon them or upon the conduct of state government. This pattern caused anxiety among some Brown appointees. Of Brown's procedures for making decisions, said one cabinet member, "It's entirely unorganized, and that is part of the problem, because at the moment of truth, that eleventh hour, I often wonder who he's talked to. Have I said everything I should? If I feel that I have something more to say, I just call and listen to whatever he has to say."

Brown did not impose his thinking upon his administration. Instead he desired that his appointees develop their own ideas. "I don't mean this negatively," said one of Brown's top administrators, "but [appointees] have their own agendas, and [Brown] encourages that; that's the key point. He encourages independent thinking, which sometimes he doesn't like, but he encourages it, and he encourages it through the lack of a clear, firm policy. . . . It's his style; he encourages it, because then he can walk away from it." Another cabinet member described Brown's approach as one that "tests the waters." "[If there is] an issue where he really hasn't thought about it that much, [Brown will tell an appointee] 'Whatever you think is right, why don't you try it out and we'll see how it looks. If there is opposition that comes out of the woodwork, then at least we'll know what we're dealing with.' "

Recognizing that Brown made his own decisions in his own time, Brown's administrators often felt they had to make their own decisions on pressing issues, even though those decisions might affect the jurisdiction of another department or might impinge upon the plans of the agency secretary. One of Brown's agency secretaries described this problem: "There's not enough early decision making. If you know where you're going, you can tell everybody, 'Here's where we're going, boys,' so everyone is consistent. When you don't really know what the final judgment is, [policy] lags, and people will talk, 'Here's where we're going,' and based on what they see, they're wrong. It's their idea, not the governor's. . . . It's a problem, because after a while you conclude that it's up to you." Therefore, because most decisions concerning departmental programs were not made by agency secretaries in a cabinet meeting, many departmental directors thought themselves justified in making the decisions or in consulting the governor or one of his staff directly rather than have the agency secretary perform this role. Said one departmental director, "I usually make the decisions [concerning major policy issues]. *I know where the Governor is.* The Governor gives an awful lot of latitude. Sometimes I take the issue to the Governor directly or to [Brown's chief of staff], but come to think about it, most of the initial action is taken by myself. *I know where I want to go*" (our emphasis).

Brown's encouragement of independent thinking allowed department directors to expand upon what they knew of his philosophy. They became newspaper readers and television watchers in an effort to construct for themselves an image of what the Governor favored. They attempted to meet with the Governor whenever possible, in order to learn of his plans. Taking the impressions that they gained, they meshed these with their own vision of what they should have been doing in their own departments and agencies, and took action upon them, sometimes independent of coordination with the agency or the Governor's Office.

Department directors and agency secretaries each had their own ideas and drew their own conclusions about the proper direction for their organization. This process of appropriation inevitably led to jurisdictional conflicts. Many of the disputes were between agency secretaries and department heads, and stemmed from the fact that the secretaries retained many of the responsibilities for coordination of the departments that Reagan's secretaries possessed, but did not have their leverage to enforce coordination, because they did not have the authority to make final legislative and budgetary decisions in cabinet meetings. Thus, in contrast to Reagan's, Brown's agency secretaries had much less command power over department heads, and had to try instead to solicit their cooperation, sometimes without success. This point was made by one of Brown's agency secretaries: "[Department directors] impose policies because of their ability to do so. They institute policies that are antagonistic to what [the agency] is trying to do. . . . Impotent is the only word I can think of that really describes the feeling [of an agency secretary] when an appointee, a department head, can tell you 'Shove it.' It makes you feel very impotent."

In fact, the most intense conflicts reached the California newspapers on a regular basis. One of the longest running stories concerned whether the Secretary of Health and Welfare or the Director of Health Services had the final authority to appoint career executives within a department.[16] Other articles were over similar jurisdictional disputes. One department director phrased it this way: "There is just an awful lot of subtlety to California's government that didn't exist in [my other jobs]. This is much closer to the federal [system]. Suspicion, people wondering about hidden agendas, that's the only way I know how to describe it. There is more time wasted in Sacramento on wondering what the other guy is going to do two or three steps down the road and there are more political agendas here than [in any other place] that I've worked, and in some cases even more than in the federal government. Wondering why someone is going to do something—it is a tremendous waste of time."

In transforming agendas into programs, department directors had to often take on Finance, in addition to their agency secretary. Rather than final budget decisions being reached in cabinet sessions, as occurred in Reagan's administration, Brown's department heads, usually in the company of their agency secretary, met with Finance one at a time. If an appointee disagreed with Finance, he likely met with the Governor for a final decision. This approach, unlike that in Reagan's administration, diffused some of the conflict between appointees and Finance. One department director explained his problems with Finance as follows: "It's only natural that the Governor, in working with his directors, would focus on programs and priorities. There's a lot of signals to go ahead in those areas. At the same time [the Governor] is giving signals to the Department of Finance in talking about budgets generally. [Finance] hears more conservative hold-the-line figures. So there's a tendency to clash. These things have to be resolved, and the Governor's the person who ought to do it when it comes to priorities and program direction." To a large extent, Brown used the Department of Finance, with which he maintained a close and continuous relationship, as a means to keep tabs on his administrators, in whom he encouraged independent thinking.[17]

Despite the difference in the concentration of conflict between the two administrations, there was an overriding similarity: In order to be loyal to the governor in power, appointees were forced to battle for their programs, for their ideas, and ultimately for themselves. They saw these battles as part of their job, as a requirement of being the governor's administrator. Accordingly, appointees did not conceptualize the conflict they experienced in the same manner as staff members saw competition within the Governor's Office. *Whereas staff members personalized intra-office competition, seeing it as unnecessary and as a manifestation of obstreperous egos, appointees saw their conflict as a confrontation of roles.* Said a Reagan cabinet member who was one of the most critical of the Governor's Office: "[The Executive Secretary] did a good job. The staff did a good job. Good staff. But there was constant friction between the secretaries' offices and the Governor's Office." Much the same was true for the conflict among Brown's administrators. Perhaps it was the case that appointees understood that the necessity for conflict was built into their jobs, rather than in their persons, and recognizing that in themselves, they projected it into others.

Nonetheless, appointees did acknowledge the difficulty and personal tolls in constantly having to struggle to attain their goals. Turnover among appointees was as high as it was among the staff. They tired of the hassles of government, and despaired of the lack of support for their ideas. They returned to their old jobs or went on to something new or retired. But while they were the governor's administrators, they embraced and in part embodied ideas, regardless of whether those ideas were the governor's or their own. Said one appointee, "When you are in a position like this, you have to hold onto something and believe in it."

DEPARTURE AND PROTEST: BREACH BETWEEN ACTION AND ROLE

As compared with personal loyalty, allegiance was a less emotional and less binding form of commitment. Accordingly, resignations in the middle of the administration were more common, public reasons for leaving more varied, and departure in protest more frequent than was true for the Governor's Office.[18] Like personal loyalty, however, allegiance shaped both the normative and nonnormative ways to resign. For the normative exit an appointee maintained the appearance that the governor and he continued to agree on the symbols, goals, and methods of the administration, that at the level of ideas they were still going in the same direction, even if the appointee was no longer able or willing to perform his role. For the nonnormative exit, which breached the standards of allegiance, an appointee acknowledged in protest that there was a divergence in ideas between him and the governor that precluded his continuing in the job.

The standards of allegiance obligated an appointee to harmonize his ideas, plans, and programs with those of the governor. This obligation required that an appointee overlap his commitments, in effect, synchronize them with what he perceived the governor's commitments to be. Although both commitments remained distinct and separate, they were joined by means of the symbolic bridge provided by the governor's philosophy. This was a flexible bridge, because the circumstances of appointee work, as well as that of the governor, tended to widen the gap between the two and to stretch the substance of the symbols. Appointees and governor alike found that policy formation, program implementation, and plain politics were molded as much by happenstance and sheer pragmatism as by political philosophy, however clear and forceful its tenets. And appointee work itself, as one Brown appointee put it, was frustrating and exhausting: "[Public bureaucracies] are large corporate entities unlike any others. . . . [It is] a very rigorous environment—understanding government. It is not as easy as it appears on the outside and accomplishment only comes with such careful preparation that it almost exhausts the individual. To accomplish major things in government, to get everyone agreeing that this is the right course of action, is perhaps one of the most difficult and most demanding orchestrations around in terms of seeing that something happens. Frustration, not understanding government, not having management background, not understanding the role of the legislature, not understanding how to work with people—[these] cause a lot of fatalities."

Because the work was exhausting and frustrating and because the symbolic bridge joining the appointee with the governor was so flexible, appointees resigned their posts with regularity. For whatever reasons they resigned, appointees typically gave a politically acceptable reason for leaving.[19] The essential aspect of allegiance was the appearance of a continuing close correspondence of the appointee's ideas with those of the governor. Any reason that did not violate that appearance was an appropriate reason for resignation. Thus publicly stated reasons varied greatly and ranged from health, family, and business commitments to the simple statement that the appointee had originally agreed to serve a specified length of time and, now that the time had expired, he or she was returning to private life. In addition, the appointee and governor typically exchanged "regrets" that he or she was leaving the "governor's team." The parting amiable, the standards upheld, the resigned appointee left government with no further obligations of allegiance, except for an absence of protest in public. As if he were reciting the expected standards of allegiance, one Brown appointee said, "I'm very loyal to [Brown]. I take pride in being loyal, because to me loyalty is a very, very important factor in government. And I'd say I'm loyal not in the sense of failing to disclose something illegal, not that kind of loyalty. [Instead I'm] loyal in the sense that when a decision is made by an administration either you abide by the decision or, if it is a matter of principle, you quietly leave, [and] you leave not to write a book or to make the circuit, but you leave grateful for having had the experience of being able to be of service to people."

Philosophical Disputes

Occasionally, however, appointees left in protest. Such departures were seldom the occasion for writing an article or a book. A statement to the press usually sufficed. Typically this statement rose to the level of the loyalty being breached, and with appointees it was usually expressed as either a disagreement between the governor and the departing appointee over the appropriate principles and goals of government or an accusation that, because of the lack of fair play or undue restrictions, the appointee was unable to accomplish his intended goals.[20]

There were several examples of appointees leaving California State Government in protest, the most notable of which was that by James D. Lorenz, who was Brown's Director of the Department of Employment. He recorded his tenure in the Brown administration, his departure, and his protest in a book, *Jerry Brown, The Man on the White Horse*.[21]

In the first weeks of his administration Brown appointed Lorenz to be the Director of the Employment Development Department, a post he was to hold for about a year and a half. According to Lorenz's account, even before he was appointed to this position, Brown had asked him to draft an employment program. After becoming the director, Lorenz began to lobby Brown, as well as other appointees, staff, and legislators for support for some legislative programs for which he had received a tentative approval from his agency secretary. Brown, however, decided not to support the legislation, and Lorenz proceeded to formulate a new, more comprehensive program, by squaring it in part with what he knew of Brown's philosophy: "I began working on describing the jobs program in . . . terms that Jerry would like. . . . Every observation Jerry had made over the previous six months I regurgitated back to him, packaged and symbolized in his own likeness. It seemed a little unnecessary to me and slightly hokey, but if those were the cosmetics he wanted . . . I was willing to stand on my head to get a jobs program."[22] Approval of the program, however, stalled in the Governor's Office and became tangled in the programs of other departments. Lorenz continued to push his ideas and to confront agency appointees over the autonomy of his department in relation to the agency.

The growing confrontation came to a head when Lorenz's program proposal was leaked to the press and was labeled "revolutionary" and "wild-eyed." After having had the agency secretary request his resignation, and his refusing to comply, Lorenz met with Brown, who also asked him to resign: "You and I," Brown reputedly told Lorenz, "just aren't on the same wavelength." Lorenz again refused, and Brown fired him, giving the following as his public reason: "Jim is a man of high ideals with a commitment to serving people. But despite his considerable talents, I don't think he can adequately manage such a large department of state government and effectively help meet the state's responsibilities to the one million unemployed people in California." In his final press conference, Lorenz, despite his frustration with the administration's approach to decision making and his realization that he and Brown differed greatly in their philosophies, Lorenz selected the mildest possible protest, the same as that selected by most protesting appointees. " 'Jerry was a fine person,' I told the assembled reporters. 'We had a disagreement about how hard and fast to push a jobs program. I wanted to go further than he wanted to.' And so on and so on."[23]

Several of the appointees interviewed disagreed with many of the details of Lorenz's book. But they did agree that the confrontation between Brown and Lorenz basically concerned philosophic differences and misunderstandings. "[Brown and Lorenz] just thought differently. I think Jim took a lot of things for granted. I think he took for granted some things about where Jerry was coming from philosophically that just weren't true. And because he was assuming those things, he didn't understand why Jerry wasn't reacting the way Jim thought he should be."

As Lorenz's example of an appointee's departure and protest illustrates, in a breach of allegiance, even one as public as his, both participants cast it as a fundamental disagreement between them over the philosophy, goals, and methods of government. *Because allegiance rests on the mutual assumption of overlapping commitments, the bonds break when appointees must publicly acknowledge a divergence of sufficient magnitude to prevent them from working behind the facade of allegiance and still maintain their commitments.*

THE DILEMMA OF ALLEGIANCE: BREACH BETWEEN SELF AND ROLE

Our interviews with administrative appointees differed greatly from those with members of the governor's staff. Unlike staff members and career bureaucrats, appointees spoke of their own commitments, accomplishments, problems, and frustrations. Whereas the others talked about their roles, appointees talked about themselves. Staff members and CEAs, who had in part to submerge their own commitments in order to serve their bosses, only reluctantly and under questioning revealed their personal reflections about their jobs. But appointees were full of themselves, and talked as if they served the governor by putting these "selves" on the line for him. And, in fact, the roles appointees played forced them to do just that. *In a sociological sense, an individual's self was given full vent in his role as appointee.* Appointees had to put on a show. They had to act forceful, persuasive, understanding, and demanding—even if they did not actually feel any of these. They had to call upon their inner understandings of how one acts these parts and in so doing they became exaggerations of themselves.[24] In this sense, they did put their "selves" on the line for the governor. This was the substance as well as the source of the dilemma that arose out of this form of loyalty, for the dilemma of allegiance concerned how much of those "selves" they were willing to give up for the governor.

The organization of state government structured the web of interaction in which appointees found themselves, molded the roles that they had to play in order to be effective administrators, and defined a set of obligations for which allegiance was the most viable form of loyalty for them to feel. Ideally, the recruitment process selected individuals primed to fit into this organization. Judged according to the excellence of their skills and the worthiness of their ideas and commitments, appointees felt handpicked. They envisioned at the outset of their appointment their overlap with the governor; they were suited to share the "aura" of the governor and to be "a part of a big team." Regardless of whether they inwardly regarded themselves worthy of this honor, they had to build upon themselves in order to fulfill that initial obligation of being the governor's administrators. And once in position they had an even greater need to build upon themselves; they found themselves separated from the governor and in charge of large complex organizations that demanded a great deal of them. In this position they were obligated to assume the role of independent, autonomous decision makers, regardless of whether they saw themselves able effectively to play that role or not. Yet, because of their own and others' expectations, they had to fill that role as best they could with themselves, with their skills and commitments and mannerisms.

But this role had a complementary side to it. Even as they affirmed or redefined their own commitments to the organization they headed, they were called into the wider sphere of state government. There they were forced to defend and to align those commitments with the commitments of other appointees and the governor. This dual obligation of maintaining one's own commitments and of making them overlap with the commitments of others created the condition that gave substance to the standards of allegiance. To bridge the gap between diverse commitments, loyalty was elevated beyond people and specific ideas to the level of those principles that could incorporate them all. For the state government, this was the level of and the role played by the governor's philosophy.

Allegiance capitalized upon the ambiguity and generality of such principles. Both were apparent in our interviews. Repeatedly we heard such comments as these from a Brown appointee: "Brown was responsive to my ideas. We were sympatico. I am in total agreement with Brown's ideas." By agreeing with the governor's philosophy, whose ideas did this appointee support, his own or the governor's? This ambiguity allowed all appointees to expand their own ideas, as well as to redirect them to fit in specific ways the conditions they found in their organizations. And the generality of principles allowed them to haggle about concrete plans without jeopardizing their commitment to the philosophy as a whole. On this a Reagan appointee said, "There were differences [between appointees] constantly. . . . Yet we never became enemies." A Brown appointee reached much the same conclusions: "If there are different points of view, they have to be resolved. . . . We all work for the government, so . . . [we] can reach other ideas and question them. I don't see any problem, [with resolving different points of view], but we have to decide where we're going. If everyone knows the plan, we go ahead." Allegiance was, therefore, a flexible form of loyalty, which allowed one to do what one wanted to do, while simultaneously justifying those actions in terms of the good of the whole.

But for some this very flexibility created a dilemma. Being able to justify their goals in terms of the whole, they focused on and sometimes became obsessed with those obstacles that blocked the attainment of their goals. Other appointees, Finance, the governor's personal staff, the legislators, the civil servants—all of these and the governor himself came in for their share of resentment, and each decision against appointees shook their resolve to continue pursuing what they felt they had been hired to do. They were constantly put in a position where they had to compromise their commitments, or resign. They had to choose to adjust their goals, or quit. Most decided to give a little here or there, so that a loss here meant a gain there. But they resented the necessity to haggle, because in the end they were negotiating their commitments; they were negotiating themselves. Being loyal to principles, they at some point wanted to "stand up to principle." Said a Reagan appointee, "There was an awful lot of negotiating going on. Lobbyists [from an interest group or the legislature or the Governor's Office] try to convince the other side that they're being unreasonable and that they really ought to compromise and if they compromised then everybody would be happy and would get a vote on this, that, and the other thing; and everything would be fine. That's pure negotiating technique. I [the appointee] was on the sidelines of [this negotiating] and I always felt we were giving them too much. We were not being tough."

Each stand they took in opposition to others exacted its toll. But because the line between their commitments and the governor's was so ambiguous, they could never be sure when the two diverged. For this reason most appointees resigned their post not in breach of allegiance, but from the sheer frustration of having so little to show for their effort and from a sense of having given up so much of themselves in the process.[25] As one Reagan appointee who resigned in midterm said, "Unless you have some ambition like [running for public office], it is probably not a good idea to get into public service, because if you try to be a public servant, you will end up faceless and subservient, and wouldn't be too effective either." Or as another Reagan appointee put it, "Everytime you have a battle, you lose a little here or there, and you can only have so many battles till you're all used up."

The dilemma of allegiance was how much appointees were willing to compromise their commitments in order to gain their commitments. The only solution to the dilemma was to be a gamesman, someone more devoted to the strategies of power than to the attainment of goals. But for those dedicated to their ideals, there was no solution, for the stronger their commitments came to be, the more they had to compromise them and the less willing they were to do so.

CONCLUSION: MANIPULATIONS OF THE APPOINTEE ROLE

In this and in the previous chapter, we have shown that the governor's administrators must strike a balance between independent action and political conformity. All architects of state executive organization, at least since Barrows in 1915, anticipated this balance and built into state government the structure and routines necessary to maintain its continuity. However, these builders of administrative organization did not realize the practical precariousness of their creation. Nor did they recognize the continuous need to repair the structure of state government so that this executive role would retain the necessary tension and would draw out of administrators the requisite reliance upon the governor's principles.

As these chapters demonstrate, Reagan and Brown used their appointed administrators in strikingly different ways. Their divergence in this regard altered the structural factors maintaining the role, resulting in the formation of two distinct variations of the role itself.

Reagan and his aides specified the role. They spelled out the duties and responsibilities of appointees and distinguished sharply between agency and department officials. As in the Governor's Office, in the executive branch this stereotyping strategy centralized the administration. Because it took up Reagan's well-known political views, the strategy helped define what were important issues and it moved these issues to the top, to the cabinet and to the governor, where they could be dealt with in some way. But this same strategy also centralized the conflict inherent in state government. Cabinet members stood against cabinet members, against staff aides, against the Director of Finance, and against the Executive Secretary. But Reagan insisted that the cabinet meeting be formal, and he always came in telling jokes. This facade of good form shaped the conflict, converting it, at least in the open, to being merely disagreements among gentlemen. The set procedures and centralized forum for making decisions, the constant need to articulate the rationale for programs, and the clear-cut character of Reagan's philosophy—these tipped the balance between freedom and conformity, and made Reagan's appointees advocates of political conformity. They became loyalists, exaggerated proponents of Reagan's philosophy, and hence willing, in the name of team play, to relinquish some of their own freedom of command. In this fashion, Reagan, a man of great personal charm and without open rancor for any person, emerged as the friendly arbiter of ubiquitous conflicts and as the pacifier of his own philosophy. This stance increased Reagan's flexibility and centralized his rule.

During Jerry Brown's administration, the role of appointee tipped in the opposite direction, towards the freedom of command. Brown did not set down clear philosophic guidelines for his appointees, did not establish procedures for making decisions, and did not distinguish sharply between levels of appointees. Brown opted for the substance of the executive, rather than its procedures. He studied the complexity of issues, instead of the methods by which they should be solved. As a consequence of Brown's emphasis, appointees developed their own guidelines, their own procedures, and their own networks to support their goals. They tried to increase their independence of action so that they could better obtain what they wanted. Such autonomy within state government soon reached its limits, as turf battles among appointees became a constant feature of the Brown administration, and responsible in large part for the proliferation of departments during his administration, as well as the ambiguity of their placement. Having allowed and even favored the development of his appointees' autonomy early in his administration, Brown became increasingly hampered by their freedom, so much so that he turned repeatedly to ad hoc means to get his programs developed and implemented. His approach to government isolated his own ideas, and his solutions to the important problems of late-twentieth-century mankind became eccentric projects for his staff, instead of a general program for state government. Brown's management style undercut the very goals he sought, the very principles for which he stood. It is, therefore, ironic that Brown, who remained wedded to the morality of substance, ended his administration with the stigma that he had been, all along, a mere politician, a person without principles and without scruples.

Chapter Five
THE GOVERNOR'S EXPERTS: HIGHER CIVIL SERVANTS

I N THE REAGAN AND BROWN administrations staff members assumed the role of the governors' surrogates, and administrative appointees assumed a collegial role. The group we consider in this chapter, California Executive Assignees (CEAs), performed yet another function in the exercise of gubernatorial power: the role of the expert.[1] CEAs were the highest level members of the permanent bureaucracy and had proven skills and knowledge. They were used by the appointees precisely because of their expertise and ability to understand the often complex and confusing world of government programs and procedures. CEAs were analysts, expeditors, mediators, and planners. Their job was to divine and interpret those conditions most suited for achieving the governors' political ends, without necessarily approving their content.[2]

All experts, whether they are doctors, accountants, or CEAs, play a role that demands two attributes, specialized knowledge and objectivity. Because important decisions rest on their advice, experts must display competence (and often a certifying credential), and they must always give their advice without regard to personal preference. Experts do not have the right to make decisions, only to help the client decide the best route to the goals he defines. CEAs had to be apolitical even though they worked closely with politically charged issues, and as we shall demonstrate, the conditions of their place in government reinforced their neutrality. Because competence and impartiality are the two bases of an expert's position in a social system, the expert's role relations rest on a code of ethics that incorporates these tenets, often referred to as "professionalism" today.[3]

CREATING A NEW CIVIL SERVANT

Most organizational roles emerge gradually as new management needs arise. Typically, some person takes on additional duties or gives an existing job a new character in response to changing situations. Over time these small changes may coalesce to constitute a new position or classification of positions; this is how the personal staff role came into being.

In contrast, the CEA role, although the product of years of government change, did not evolve.[4] Rather, it was created by legislative fiat in September 1963 after some considerable thought and lobbying on the part of the Brown, Sr. administration, the State Personnel Board, the state employees' work organizations, and interested legislators. All of these groups recognized that some transformation was needed at the top levels of the career service but each had its own designs and fears of a new service of high-level officials.[5]

The pressure for change came from the maturation of the civil service system itself. At the turn of the century there were 800 state employees and they could be easily rearranged or dismissed when a new administration came into power. Over the next decades, however, a succession of civil service laws strengthened the independence of public workers and made them largely immune from political manipulation.[6] This immunity allowed people to make state government a career and to develop specializations in the different program areas. Indeed, modern California government has had a reputation for its competence and relative absence of patronage. But this stability, coupled with growing numbers of state workers, led also to a relatively immovable executive branch, from the governor's viewpoint. By 1959 there were 112,500 state workers protected by tenure, and those who held the top positions had sometimes been in place for twenty or more years.[7]

This stable career service, while it had obvious attributes, could not meet the quickening pace of government that began in the Warren administration. Three top California personnel managers cited "the vociferous demands" of a population that was increasingly diverse, politically active, and insistent on government's protection of high living standards. "The key to meeting these demands is the responsiveness

of top-level civil service administrators to the need for program innovation. Entire programs succeed or fail as a result of the commitment, expertise, and responsiveness of individuals in key management positions."[8]

Pat Brown and his appointees had been frustrated by entrenched
senior officials who could successfully thwart political programs that
threatened existing bureaucratic arrangements and interests. Brown's
response, which met with opposition, was to try to add to the number
of political appointees in the departments available to his discretion.
A compromise was proposed based on the recommendations of the
1950s Hoover Commission study of the federal civil service. The
Hoover Commission, seeing in Washington much the same conditions as California faced, had recommended a senior executive corps
that bridged the gap between the permanent bureaucracy and the political administration.[9] Although that idea did not take hold in the
federal government until President Carter formed the Senior Executive Service in 1978,[10] the Hoover study became the basis of the CEA
system in California in 1963.[11]

Although drawn from the ranks of state workers, CEAs were to be
a flexible group and to differ in important respects from regular civil
servants. Certain top-level government jobs of a policy-influencing
nature were designated as CEA-only positions and required that the
employee filling the job qualify for and accept CEA status. This meant
he had to be selected by an appointee from the corps of CEAs and
that he had to accept a condition of all CEA posts—no guarantee of
tenure. If an appointee did not like a CEA, he or she could send the
CEA back to a position in the regular civil service at his or her last
rank with a warning of only 20 days. Removal from a CEA position
was not considered removal for cause and was not normally appeal-
able. Accepting a CEA position was a decision that involved a degree
of risk for the employee.

While having some features of the regular civil service and some
of the political appointee system, the CEA plan developed its own
distinctive character during the Reagan and Brown, Jr. administrations.[12] Like the civil service, selection for CEA status was based on
merit and one had to have moved up the regular government ladder;
no one could enter state government as a CEA. This prevented the

governors from politicizing the system by bringing in their own people as CEAs. Like regular civil servants, CEAs had a guarantee of employment. But CEAs were like exempt employees in that they had no tenure in their posts, making them a far more flexible instrument for political appointees who could remove and reassign career executives at their discretion. If CEAs did not carry out the political will of the governor or his appointees, they were back in the bureaucracy in a few days with a significant loss of status, responsibility, and pay. They were also more like appointees in that they were engaged in politically sensitive, policy-related work. They did not just implement programs; they helped formulate legislation and provided data for political decisions. Because CEAs were in top, often visible jobs, and because there were so few of them, they became a distinct cadre in their own eyes, and in the eyes of those above and below them. They tended to be young for their job levels, usually achieving CEA status in their mid-to-late thirties, and claimed to be less tied to the state for employment and security than other senior civil servants.

Although important, CEAs were never numerous. In 1980 there were over 130,000 state civil service employees (not including another 90,000 that work for the judiciary, legislature, and state university and college systems). That same year there were about 500 employees that held Career Executive Assignments, less than one-half of one percent of all executive branch employees. CEAs occupied positions just below those of the governor's appointees and filled both line and staff positions throughout the upper levels of state government. Typically, they were well educated, many with advanced degrees, and all had sufficient tenure in state government to have proven exceptional managerial skills or technical expertise. They were considered the elite of government employees and held highly sought-after positions.[13]

THE CEA-GOVERNOR RELATIONSHIP: PROFESSIONALISM

CEAs, as much as staff people and appointees, expressed a strong sense of loyalty to the governor. And as with these other groups loyalty infused their actions with justification and meaning. But the meaning CEAs gave to their work and their relationship to the governor differed dramatically from that given by staff and administrative appointees. Like appointees, CEAs said their loyalty lay ultimately with the governor, *but CEAs identified their loyalty as being strictly to the governor's position, and not to his person or to his philosophy.* In articulating this type of loyalty, they described a bond similar to that connoted by the feudal term "fealty." As distinguished from other aspects of European feudalism, the oath of fealty was quite simply a subordinate's pledge to obey a superior's command and was "a unilateral undertaking to which there was seldom a corresponding oath on the part of the lord," according to historian Marc Bloch.[14] Because pledging fealty without also pledging homage (deference) did not signify a reciprocal or even a personal relation, a subordinate's pledge was more a promise than a contract of obedience. The act of homage, not fealty, established vassalage, the obligation of the lord to protect the subordinate; this gradually changed from a personal relationship to a contractual one. Fealty, however, was frequently exacted from a wide range of individuals for whom vassalage would be inappropriate. Says Bloch,

> Royal or seignorial officials of every rank took it on assuming their duties; prelates often demanded it from their clergy; and manorial lords, occasionally, from their peasants. Unlike homage, which bound the whole man at a single stroke and was generally held to be incapable of renewal, this promise—almost a commonplace affair—could be repeated several times to the same person. There were therefore many acts of fealty without homage.[15]

And as a promise, the oath of fealty, as well as the acts of obedience it required, became a point of honor, an anchor in the medieval code of behavior. Weber recognized this in his discussion of bureaucratic loyalty:

> Entrance into an office . . . is considered an acceptance of a specific duty of fealty to the purpose of the office in return for the grant of a secure existence. It is decisive for the modern loyalty to an office that, in the pure type, it does not establish a relationship to a person, like the vassal's or disciple's faith under feudal or patrimonial authority, but rather is devoted to *impersonal* and *functional* purposes.[16]

It is in this sense—promised obedience incorporated within an impersonal code of behavior—that fealty describes the loyalty felt by
CEAs, what is usually referred to as "professionalism" today.[17]

Loyalty to Position

As CEAs repeatedly stated, it was their professional responsibility
to respond faithfully to the demands of the governor and his appointees. Loyalty, however, was not defined by the CEA as mere
obedience; as it was put to us many times, professionalism prescribed
the *appropriate mode* of obedience. Said one CEA, "We work for any
governor, and we can change hats in sixty seconds. . . . We're going
to do whatever the governor directs us to do. He's the boss. But we're
going to do it in a professional manner." So defined, their relationship to the governor or to his appointees was professional, and not
political, loyalty. It consisted foremost of performing one's managerial, policy-making, fiscal, or legislative functions with a high degree
of technical competence and objectivity, but without regard to the
political implications of those functions. "Policy analysis," remarked
a high-ranking CEA in the Department of Finance, "is best done if
you, the politician, say, 'Here's my objective and I want to get there.'
Then you can put the professional to do the analysis. And while we,
the professionals, may not agree that you should be doing that objective, we can usually give you your best course of action and identify
all other courses of action to a governor for his consideration." Or as
another CEA stated, "Somebody else's job is to make political decisions. We don't make them. The governor is the guy who has the
monkey on his back. We provide the best input we can on a strictly
professional basis." Although, through their collection of facts and
analyses, CEAs may have tried to shape policies and procedures for
implementing programs, once the governor or an administrative appointee made a decision, it became the CEA's duty to follow that
decision.

CEAs were not merely functionaries, however. Their professionalism was employed in the service of the governor, or more often one
of his appointees, and CEAs felt a strong sense of obligation to serve

their superiors not just mechanically, but with the intention of helping the appointees further the political goals they defined. For example, one of the chores CEAs were frequently called on to perform
was testing political waters and warning appointees when they were
likely to encounter controversy. One CEA spoke of how he saw his
responsibility in this area to the department director for whom he
worked. "If I'm aware of something that he is going off on, and it's
going to amount to walking the plank, I'm going to make sure he
knows why. And if he has reasons better than that, that he should in
fact still go, fine. But I want to make sure that every act he commits
is an informed one." This desire to protect is not personal, as in the
case of staffs, but rather an expression of duty to the superior.

The loyalty that CEAs described was a promise of *skilled* obedience
to the positions rather than the people of government. The commitment was enacted within a code of behavior which CEAs called
"professionalism" and involved an obligation to work impersonally and
apolitically in the service of partisan administration. Although they
acted out their loyalty to the appointees of the governor, with whom
they worked closely and often enjoyed, CEAs would do the same for
any governor and any appointee to whom they might be assigned.[18]

ORGANIZATION OF THE CEA ROLE

As was the case with appointees, the conditions favoring CEA loyalty represented a combination of selective recruitment and organizational supports. Where appointees anchored their role relations in
the person or philosophy of the governor, however, CEAs defined their
positions in terms of a structurally determined code of professionalism.

Selective Recruitment

All CEAs came from within the ranks of the state civil service, and
therefore, unlike appointees, they had common origins with other state
employees. Individuals desiring a Career Executive Assignment had

to go through a series of examinations conducted by the State Personnel Board to determine their qualifications. Typically, a civil servant had considerable experience in the civil service before qualifying for promotion into the CEA ranks. This experience gave a prospective CEA sufficient time to observe the role and functioning of state government, as well as of the CEA system. Because of this, a certain amount of self-selection was inherent in the CEA recruitment process. Unlike appointees, or even people entering the state civil service, prospective CEAs had an opportunity to preview their new status and were very aware of its requirements and benefits. Not all eligible civil servants chose to take this step, for it required them to transfer their commitment from a department, its programs, and fellow workers to a professional cadre not based, necessarily, in any organizational unit. For example, a civil engineer who had risen through the Department of Transportation by successfully developing and managing highway programs would have to accept the possibility of directing water projects, conservation programs, energy research, or parks and recreation projects. And frequently, CEAs were sent as teams into problem departments as consultants and management analysts; they had to be willing to float about government as needed, doing a variety of high-level and often problem-ridden assignments as required by the administration in power. Many CEAs were not assigned out of their departments; others were moved about frequently.

The CEAs we interviewed saw the step into their status as more than simply a promotion; it was a qualitative leap given much forethought, a leap that required obedience to an appointee as a condition of holding the position, a requirement to which regular civil servants are immune. As one CEA put it, "A CEA official understands pretty clearly who he or she identifies with. It is the director who has the appointing authority. So there is no question you won't be there if you don't identify; you are subject to twenty days' notice."

Not only must CEAs feel comfortable working with a variety of policy-related issues and at the behest of political appointees, they must feel professionally and personally secure because of the tenure they relinquish with CEA jobs. Typically, CEAs minimized the importance of guaranteed job security. According to a former CEA now working in private industry, "The protectionism of civil service status isn't that big a thing. It wasn't to me in my career. I'm probably not unique, because those that reach the level of CEA have typically come up the chain of command, have been very successful in administration and management positions, and have reaped the rewards of the system. So you have, generally speaking, a cadre of experienced, professional people who have something to market inside or outside government. They could care less [about security]."

This indifference to tenure, the willingness to take on risks and relinquish ties to the department that was the source of their previous successes, and the acceptance of a code of professionalism in lieu of program commitments distinquished CEAs from other high-level government employees. But more than self-nomination was required for CEA recruitment; a prospective CEA had to prove himself to an appointee. Appointees had the statutory right to hire and fire CEAs within their departments, and although new appointees tended to keep the same CEAs in the positions they occupied under the previous appointee, this was by no means always the case. There were numerous examples of CEAs being rearranged in different positions or terminated soon after the arrival of a new director. According to one CEA who had seen removals of CEAs after the elections of both Reagan and Brown, "These major shifts can get very ruthless. It is a troublesome time to live through."

Because CEAs were drawn from the ranks of the civil service and had years of experience, and because there were only a limited number of them at any time, CEAs obtained a reputation beyond their own department. Therefore, when a CEA was terminated, when a new CEA position opened, or when a troublesome problem arose, CEAs in one department were often recruited or loaned to a director in another department to fill a vacancy. Over time CEAs came to resemble a pool of specialists and consultants, some of whom appointees repeatedly asked to handle particular types of problems. Appointees often attempted to recruit CEAs who had a good reputation for competence, that is, for their skill in performing tasks, as well as for their professionalism, their neutrality, or absence of previous politicization. A CEA's reputation, therefore, became his most important commodity.

Organizational Supports

Just as individuals were recruited for their professionalism and their competence, the structural situations in which CEAs found themselves tended to support these attributes. Several structural factors were particularly important: incentives, uncertainty, and most importantly, the requirement to act as a middleman.

Incentives: The incentives for being a CEA were well-defined: more money, more prestige, and more responsibility than is ordinarily the case with a classified civil servant. CEAs were well paid, earning as much as appointees in some cases. Promotion into CEA posts always involved an increase in pay of at least 10 percent and some CEAs made considerably more money in their executive assignments than they did at their classified rank in the regular civil service. As much as CEAs enjoyed the additional income and found it a powerful incentive for retaining their CEA posts, they were aware of the dangers the additional income possessed. Said one CEA, "If [the appointee] doesn't like what I'm doing, [he] can, without cause, tell me that within 20 days I will not be in this position, and I won't be. I won't be out on the street, but my income will be cut about in half." Said another, "You must live so that you are not dependent on money. . . . I've got to be free. I feel sorry for colleagues of mine who wrapped themselves up in $120,000 houses on the salary they were making, which they could barely afford at that salary and who were then looking at a demotion of $1000 a month. Now that is rough. I never want to be in that spot, because I want to be able to walk out that door if I need to." The added income a CEA earned was a powerful incentive to be compliant with the political demands of an appointee, but, as we will show, it was an even more powerful incentive for building a reputation for professionalism.

CEA positions carried with them considerable prestige and responsibility. According to Government Code 18547, which outlined the CEA Plan in 1963, a CEA position was

> a high administrative and policy influencing position within the state civil service in which the incumbent's primary responsibility is the managing of a major function or the rendering of management advice to top-level administrative authority. Such a position can be established only in the top

managerial levels of state service and is typified by broad responsibility for policy implementation and extensive participation in policy involvement. . . .

Typically, this meant directing a small department, being deputy director of a sizable department, managing programs with considerable legislative interest, or being an appointee's top aide. CEAs also filled key policy-making, fiscal, legislative, and liaison positions in departments and agencies. Everyone in government recognized that these were important jobs that required considerable expertise; to occupy such a post was both rewarding and prestigious. According to a former Department of Transportation CEA, ambitious civil servants wanted to become CEAs because "that's where the jobs are," and because of "ego." For those who found high levels of responsibility necessary to an interesting career, CEA jobs were a powerful incentive in and of themselves. Said one CEA in the Department of Finance, the type of work they do "adds to the professional feeling of professionals. We're important. We do important work. Our judgments are used. And we have to do above average. We always look upon ourselves as being a very highly talented, highly trained, and highly trusted group of public servants." According to CEAs, the prestige and responsibility of holding CEA positions had to be matched by the competence to perform the job well. Competence, in turn, had to be coupled with professionalism, with the willingness to do what was asked. CEAs worked hard at establishing reputations for these qualities.

Uncertainty: Although the incentives for being a CEA were well-known, so too was the uncertainty of their tenure. As one CEA put it, "this has a very extensive impact on the way people work." Without showing cause, an administrative appointee could dismiss a CEA at any time, and in the first year of Brown's administration about 14 percent of the CEAs were nonvoluntarily terminated.[19] According to a CEA who was in the health area, "When a new fellow comes in, usually there is a grace period of about 45 days on the average that they keep the old staff to get themselves established. Then comes the day of reckoning when they say, 'Well, I'd like you to stay'; or 'The truth is your identity within this party is more than I can accommodate,' which is very common. You cannot be offended by [their] saying 'Thank you, but no thank you.' You realize that's the circumstance when you get involved in this." At first glance, uncertainty of tenure matched with the inducements of money and prestige would seem to favor the development of a personalized loyalty, such as to an appointee, or of an open allegiance to the current governor's philosophy and goals. Even though these types of loyalty developed in some CEAs, as we will discuss, in most the combination of incentives and uncertainty favored the development of professionalism—an impersonal, apolitical responsibility. The reason was quite simple: A CEA wanted to be able to survive the next transition to a new governor. *To adopt any type of loyalty other than professionalism was to jeopardize one's longevity as a CEA.*

CEAs recognized the danger of being identified with a particular administration, and stressed the need "to build a good reputation" and to keep a "low public profile." The Brown administration made this professional discretion difficult for CEAs to maintain: "[The Brown administration] is more personalized than the previous ones, and therefore many more people think [some of us in this department] are in his hip pocket. More of our names appear in the paper under this administration than ever appeared under any other administration. I'm concerned about it. It's all right for me. I'm at the top slot in civil service. They can't do a hell of a lot to me other than drop me back. But I don't want those people that are comers getting their names in the paper too much, because the next administration will have the list and will say, 'Your name is on the paper with Brown's administration. You must have been a Brown man.' " These fears were not unjustified. One CEA, who was placed in charge of reorganizing the Department of Health at the beginning of the Brown administration, recounted the following incident: "There was one individual who was [closely associated] with a Reagan appointee. In my opinion he was one of the stronger managers in the department. The department desperately needed stronger managers, and my recommendation was to leave him in his place. That was shot down. [Brown's appointee] said, 'No, he's tainted. We can't have tainted people.' He was too close to [the Reagan appointee], so [Brown's appointee] dumped him."

Middleman Dilemma: The third, and probably the most important factor, was the structural conditions in which CEAs found themselves, conditions that produced what we call the middleman dilemma. By virtue of their location in the organization, they were wedged, like noncommissioned officers in the army, between those who commanded and those who carried out commands, between the governor and his appointees on the one hand, and the civil servants on the other. Not only was their position in-between in terms of hierarchy, their job was structured in some ways like those above them and in other ways like those below. They were like appointees and like civil servants, but they were neither.

On the one side, appointees expected compliance to their demands to adopt a certain program or managerial philosophy or mode of implementation, rather than some other ones. The CEA's job was to be flexible and responsive to those above them, and as we have discussed, there were important incentives that pushed CEAs in that direction. They expected to be good soldiers to the superiors above them and were often called on to do battle in the name of the appointees. For example, one CEA was sent into the Department of Health early in Brown's administration; the department was having major problems and the CEA was sent in as a trouble-shooter. One of the first things he did was organize a high-level team of operations analysts from outside the health organization to investigate the delays in the implementation of some of Brown's new programs. "So I sent this group down in and they literally got locked out. I mean the people who were running the program just ran and held their stuff like this (tightly against their chests). They actually grabbed their papers off their desks and said, 'You can't see this stuff, you can't come in here. Who said you can come in here?' And they came up and screamed at me for sending those 'outsiders' in."

On the other side, the civil servants expected CEAs to represent their interests as well, although their interests and loyalties differed from those of staff, appointees, and even CEAs. One Department of Transportation employee defined civil servant interests as program loyalty: "Program loyalty causes a lot of problems. The people in the organization, I subconsciously do it myself, search for supporters of that program. And we may tend to appear, and sometimes are, more loyal to a commission, like a highway commission or a legislative committee, that sees things the same way as we do than we might be to the administration, even though we are part of the executive branch.

That's a difficult problem to wrestle with—that question of program loyalty or product loyalty versus loyalty to an administration that may change every four years. And God knows we go through enough agency secretaries and directors. We have to find our own way."

In finding their own way, civil servants, we suggest, built commitments to a department, a program, and to occupational specialties. Their vested interest was to maintain the continuity of such commitments, for these defined the organizational roles they played, as well as their network of interpersonal relations. These commitments were, in fact, codified. Job descriptions, position evaluations, promotional hierarchies, and merit reviews were all formal means to instill commitments and role expectations into employees. When civil servants complained or even tried to sabotage an administration's effort to reorganize or to change program direction, it was more accurately seen as an attempt to maintain commitments, rather than as an act of disloyalty per se.

CEAs understood the commitments of civil servants to their departments and programs because they were former civil servants themselves. CEAs tried to provide what civil servants wanted and needed to do their jobs: clear instructions, attainable goals, and the material means for carrying out their programs. CEAs also knew that their CEA status might be terminated and they could find themselves back in the bureaucracy among hostile civil servants if they had ignored their demands. Also, CEAs were usually managers of state employees and as managers tried to respond to the legitimate demands of their subordinates, even when they were in conflict with the demands of appointees; this was an obligation CEAs often felt quite strongly. One CEA, the deputy director of a large department, put it this way: "You know, the main dilemma is trying to carry on and satisfy the people under you who are much more committed with doing the job. Most of us, at least from my level down, their commitment is on the program side and they need certain things to do a job. My job is to try and get it for them." One of the items that appeared on a budget request in his department was a popcorn machine for a disabled children's program. "Okay, I can understand that a popcorn machine can be very important. [But] I will never let it appear on the [budget] list. I will get it some other way, because I know what would happen when [the budget request] goes upstairs. Jesus Christ, so find me another name [for the popcorn machine]."

CEAs also recognized the dangers of what they, and civil servants generally, defined as "politics." The administrative paralysis caused by conflicts between appointees, by programs that were designed to build political images but were impossible to implement, by confusing assignments and conflicting goals, and by appointees' disrespect for personnel procedure and civil service rights—all these and more came under the definition of politics, and as managers, CEAs had to resist their intrustion into the department. As one CEA put it, "the way to [keep the department running smoothly] is to keep the politics out of the department. Let the politics be here in [my] office. My job is to try to keep *me* from being sucked in, and that is an art."

Caught between two opposing forces—the politics of the appointees and the departmentalism of the bureaucrats—CEAs had to deal with both, without identifying too closely with either. To be too political was to lose one's credibility with the civil servants, as well as to jeopardize one's job in future administrations. To be too committed to civil service goals, such as strongly supporting established programs, was seen as recalcitrance by appointees, and as deserving termination. By supporting either side consistently and strongly, CEAs ran the risk of losing their jobs.

THE AUTHORITY OF EXPERTISE: THE DUTY TO ADVISE

From this discussion of the CEA role it might appear that CEAs had relatively little room for action. They were squeezed between two groups, one powerful by virtue of position, the other by virtue of size. The structural factors we have described might appear to have stifled CEA activity and to have neutralized them to such a degree as to have made them high-level functionaries.

This was not at all the case. *CEAs had power that was based on expertise, on professional skills that were rendered impersonally.* This was the sort of power that doctors and lawyers wield in relation to patients and clients. People allow professionals to have power over them as long as they believe that the professional has superior knowledge and is dispensing it impartially, without consideration for whom the client might be. Professional codes of ethics demand, for example, that a physician use his skills equally in the service of a rich man as a poor man, or that a lawyer work as hard to defend an evil person as a good one.

California government has structured the CEA position like that of a professional and, indeed, CEAs often used "professional" to describe their role. Many were professionals by virtue of their education as well; there were CEA doctors, lawyers, accountants, and engineers. CEAs had to prove superior expertise to achieve their positions, they had to use their knowledge to serve whomever was in office, and they had to do the best job they could without regard to personal inclinations or judgments. This commitment to professionalism was publicly recognized and organizationally buttressed. It led to the CEAs' preoccupation with "reputation." This was not an egoistic concern; *reputation was one's right to wield power*. Without a professional reputation a CEA could not act.

But with a reputation for objective expertise the CEAs became available both to those above them and to those below. For example, CEAs typically saw themselves as intermediaries between appointees and state workers, and sometimes as departmental representatives to the legislature.[20] One former CEA explained that he was used as a sounding board by appointees contemplating controversial programs. "It was interesting to me, because when I went through the Reagan welfare reform, I was not part of the welfare reform team, but [appointees] used to ask me to come in to talk over their ideas with them, because they wanted to get a feeling for how reasonable the other side (the department employees) would react. And you come around to [the Brown appointee], who viewed [me] in the same way. He viewed me as the reasonable other side."

As middlemen, CEAs were used to mediate disputes, but unlike labor-management negotiators they never achieved a lasting settlement. Negotiation tended to become a permanent posture and had to be anticipated by CEAs. One career executive in a position just below the appointed department director described one of the small ways in which he tried to maintain an aura of access to civil servants intimidated by his high level. "I never wear a tie unless I have to go to a meeting outside of the department because the director [always wears a tie] even on the hottest day. The [directors] have an obligation to, in fact, look the part, because there is a lot of role playing in terms of power. If *I* mirror that in the department, it seems that it is actually putting up a barrier. I like access to every clerk in this department. When we have a real crisis, when I call someone, they already know me. They are comfortable with me. Anybody who occupies this [CEA] role, if they think about it, can make use of that confidence."

Conflict between appointees and state employees was a recurring phenomenon and stemmed in part from their very different commitments. A CEA brought into the Department of Transportation to manage a dramatic program shift described a typical form of this conflict, as well as the CEA view of it. "[Bureaucrats] tend to respect the limits of hierarchy, but they tell me to tell the boss he's full of shit. But once the boss says, 'Okay, I want to do it anyway,' they say, 'Okay, goddammit, we will do it.' Now I would say that the average director would not accept my view. They far more believe that the organization is out to get them, and that [the bureaucrats] aren't being loyal. But I sit kind of halfway between, and my observation is that they really are trying to be loyal and progressive and do what is right. They just want to argue a lot about it because their hearts and their souls and their whole lives are in what they are doing." CEAs were constantly torn to support one side or another in the natural antagonism between politics and administration, but the conditions of their position assured that there was danger in either course. They had to carve a precarious perch of neutrality and skillfully place themselves where they could be seen as belonging to neither side in order to sustain their power with both. One CEA described this dilemma. Although officially the director's chief assistant, he called himself "the department's assistant." "I'd be very foolish to think that I am only here to help the director, and any requests from anyone else I can ignore."

By clinging to professionalism CEAs became power brokers, not only between groups in the executive branch but in legislative matters as well. Legislators respected their objectivity and gave their analyses and recommendation real weight. For this reason, CEAs were frequently invited to testify before legislative committee hearings.

Skillful objectivity also assured that their opinions would be taken seriously by appointees. They had a knowledge of the system few appointees could ever achieve, and because they were known not to favor any particular interests, at least publicly, their advice was heeded. Department directors often spoke of how they would have been lost without CEAs. CEAs, by acting objectively, could affect proposals, influence courses of action, and turn opinions one way or another. In short, they could be very powerful.

THE LIMITS OF THE ROLE

Departure and Protest: Breach Between Role and Action

Resignation in protest was an act of betrayal on the part of personal staff members, and to administrative appointees resignation in protest was typically the result of a philosophical dispute. In both cases, resignation broke the bonds of commitment, be they personal loyalty or allegiance. For a CEA to have resigned in protest, however, had a fundamentally different meaning. It could have been an act in *affirmation* of loyalty, an expression of commitment to one's professional code. To understand how this could be so, one need only look at the meaning of professional responsibility. Professionalism demanded that loyalty to political figures be stylized and that interaction with appointees and the governor be impersonal and apolitical. Role expectations for a CEA were not shaped by the person or philosophy of a governor, but rather by a code of behavior that placed real bounds on the appropriateness of action. An attempt on the part of appointees to force a CEA to violate his professional code by behavior that he defined as improper and, therefore, threatening to his reputation, had to be met with resistance. The ultimate form of resistance was resignation. When a CEA resigned in protest he was in fact saying, "I will not be politicized."

Of the CEAs we interviewed, a number had resigned, more had threatened to resign, and all said they would use resignation as a last resort, in order to prevent their professionalism from being compromised by an appointee. CEAs recognized the ease with which politics could compromise their job performance, and stated that an important facet of their positions was their ability to resign: "You can resign as a CEA appointment just as you can be terminated by your employer. [This] puts me in a better position [than that of a regular civil servant], because I can tell [an appointee or a governor] to screw it. 'I don't agree with what you're doing, I am going back [to my civil service classification].' " Said another, as a CEA, "one of the things I have always had is a reputation of a loyal rebel. I'm loyal until I walk out the door. I won't backbite. I won't go behind his back. I'll fight [appointees] like hell, if I think they are wrong. This is the reputation I have gained. I've earned it and it is a useful one." This same CEA, one of the only survivors in a massive termination of CEAs in the Department of Health at the beginning of the Brown administration, credited his survival to his forthrightness with the new director. "I said to him, 'You either trust me to run this division or move me. . . . I've seen you guys come and go. Now you either use me and let me do my job or move me.' "

CEAs did not like to resign under such circumstances, of course, and more frequently resisted politicization if at all possible. Resisting one's superior and the attractiveness of power politics was not an easy task for people as ambitious and involved as CEAs. CEAs avoided making decisions that they viewed as having political content and were uneasy when forced into that position. According to a CEA in Finance, "The thing that we believe is that we are not elected to office. It's the other turkey that is, and it's his game, right or wrong. The only thing we want is some direction. Don't put us in the position of telling what to do [politically] because after a period of time, what happens, if you have an [appointee] who is part of the administration for a long period of time, you work out kind of a rapport with him and then that person really begins to lean on you for a whole lot of things. And you can't do that. You have always to guard against that. If you don't, then [CEAs become like appointees and] the bureaucracy will run the goddamn government, and it shouldn't."

Resignation from CEA status was therefore an act in conformance with the norms of professionalism; resigning removed the CEA from the possibility of besmirching the code of professionalism. There were three normative forms of departure that a CEA could choose. First, a CEA who found himself pulled to the governor or his philosophy could accept an exempt appointment, most often as a deputy director of a department or agency. In accepting such an appointment, a CEA became, for all to see, the governor's person, and no longer needed to maintain an impersonal bearing. Second, a CEA who did not feel comfortable with politics and who identified strongly with program commitments could return to regular civil service status. He avoided violation of his professional code and saved his reputation for apolitical behavior. He became available to the next governor as someone who was not tainted by rival politics. And third, a CEA could leave government service, usually to accept a job in private industry with a firm that served the same constituency as the CEA's former government department. All three actions were seen as "understandable" and honorable.

Resignation with honor was an important option because of the tensions inherent in a CEA position. Career executives were caught between the conflicting demands of appointees and bureaucrats and should the pressure from either side be too much a CEA had to be able to leave. Resignation was the CEA's pressure valve, it was the acceptable "out." As professionalism defined a normative posture that allowed a CEA to create an apolitical and impersonal haven, resignation created an exit if the haven was violated by either side. But for the pressure valve to work a CEA had to accept the possibility that he or she would resign or be fired rather than be unprofessional. It was a danger to love one's CEA position too much, as one CEA told us. "I want to feel free to quit and I have to be free to be fired. And I don't want to worry about it. Enjoy it, have fun, it's nice, and I like the power. But I am expendable. When I took the job, I took it with that attitude."

A CEA could, like staff members and appointees, breach the norms of the role as well. The professional code was both rigid in principle and ambiguous in application, but there came a point when a CEA's behavior was unmistakably unprofessional. CEAs who departed from the standards of professionalism while remaining on the job were seen by others as having become corrupted, either by being lap dogs of some appointee or by being inhouse spokesmen for some special interest group. One former CEA, who was hung in effigy by state workers during a conflict over a massive layoff in the Department of

Transportation, described his reason for resignation. "I was becoming a symbol of an irresponsible and unfair political action. . . . That [position] was most uncomfortable for me because I spent a lot of time building a reputation. Although I had a reputation of being tough, I didn't have a reputation of being unfair. What bothered me the most were situations where I'd explain the options and make my recommendation and explain what the reaction was going to be. I'd be told [by appointees] to go ahead and implement it and I'd implement it. The reaction [of department employees] would occur and then [the appointees] would back down and modify it. I knew what was happening to my own reputation; that was the thing that really bugged me." It was a CEA's obligation to use his abilities in the interest of appointees, but there was a point beyond which he or she was seen to be working with them, and not for them.

The Dilemma of Professionalism: Breach Between Person and Role

The role of a CEA was that of a finely tuned instrument that could be employed in a variety of ways and with a high degree of reliability. The professional code required that CEAs do the will of appointees and do it with competence, but without becoming so involved that they became "political." They had to serve many masters well but without control over whom they served or how they were used. Sometimes this led to what some could see as duplicity. For example, in California the outgoing governor typically prepares the budget for the year after he is gone from office. Usually the governor-elect has neither the time nor expertise to do this in the months between election day in November and inauguration in January when the budget is sent to the legislature for approval. Jerry Brown, however, attempted to create his own budget in these three months with the help of the Finance Department CEAs and civil servants. The Finance Department was, at the same time, preparing a budget at the direction of outgoing Governor Reagan. One Finance CEA recalled the experience of working for two masters at once. "We immediately, and I mean that afternoon [the day after the election], we were meeting with [Brown] saying, 'We stand aboard at your command, whatever pleases you, we will try to give you what you need.' At the same time we conducted the affairs [of the Reagan administration] and kept the two separate. If we picked up something that we knew but were not told of a confidential, political nature in the morning over here [in Reagan's office], and we worked with Brown in the afternoon and night, we'd go over there and he wouldn't know about it. And this is a shitty thing to do, what the hell, we never said a word. We think we can keep a confidence."

They had to be willing to work not only for one master after another, but had to be willing in one administration to build up a department and in the next administration to tear it down, if that was required of them. They had to be willing to provide a governor with their best analysis of policy alternatives, and watch him select only the most politically expedient. Finance CEAs who did policy analysis were frequently put in this position and according to one, they had to be willing to listen to the governor say, " 'That's my decision, that's what I want done.' And you [the CEA] have done a good job, and you've had your day in court. Your job is to appear in front of a [legislative] committee on Monday morning at 10 o'clock and argue for his selected alternative, rather than the one you know is right and that the statistics support and [has] the weight of evidence. But can you do it, without feeling you've sold your soul?"[21]

CEAs were not by "nature" self-effacing technicians, people without souls. They became CEAs by being ambitious, active civil servants who performed their duties in the bureaucracy with skill and even zeal. They were the "go-getters," the "fast-track" stars of state government. Becoming CEAs allowed them to use their considerable talents in even more important ways and with greater potential impact, but it stripped them of something else: the luxury of commitments. Departmental employees worked in furtherance of programs they felt were important and in the interest of their department's constituency; they were building better highways or delivering quality health care services. The people above, the governor's staff and appointees, had commitments as well, to a political philosophy or to the governor himself. Exempt employees often came to office having been campaign workers or advocates of a policy position. But CEAs could not attach themselves to programs or to politics; they had to be neutral if they were to keep their jobs. They had to become people without content.

Their only home was their professionalism, their code of ethics. They had to attach themselves to that and use it as a guide for their behavior in an environment that always tried to pull them in one direction or another. Surrounded by the seductiveness of political power on the one side, and the departments that were the source of their earlier successes and commitments on the other, they had to opt for the aloofness and detachment of professionalism if they were to survive the tension and remain a CEA. But this too was problematic. If they attached themselves too firmly to the CEA code and learned to accept and enjoy that status, they risked becoming attached to it too much. Dismissal was always a possibility; their "home" was not a secure one.

The structural situation in which CEAs found themselves required them to develop a loyalty to apolitical and impersonal action;[22] this was the role of the CEA. But the people who filled those roles were not mannequins. Nor were they unaware of the sacrifice of their own commitments and opinions that they were required to make. The person and the role did not always match and therein lay the dilemma. The dilemma of professionalism was described in the following way by a CEA that had been in state government for 15 years. "While we may disagree with the administration's programs we'll make a decision to be able to get out, or we carry them out. As long as we have the opportunity to have some input before that decision is made we feel that we've tried. We've had our chance to try and influence it; if we were unsuccessful, then we say, 'Well, can I do this? Is it against my professional ethics or my moral responsibilities?' Or do I swallow my pride and say, 'Well, okay, that's the decision, he's the boss, so I'll do it'?" Being a CEA required that one often swallow one's pride, and, in a sense, swallow one's self.

A tension was produced when the CEA was continually asked to do things that were in accordance with the code of professionalism, but against his own inclinations. Sometimes a CEA would try to talk an appointee out of a course of action that he did not approve. "If they can't talk the director out of it," said a Health Department CEA, "then in their implementation of it, they try and do what they see as respectable a job as possible. They have a very sensitive thing to do because they're walking a tightrope. They can't look like they're trying to obfuscate what the director has commanded. They have to, as sensitively as they can, do the best by both worlds. Sometimes by trying to do the best of both worlds there is still no way you can do what you think is right. You are in a situation where you must transmit completely unrefined exactly what a director has submitted. It's sad because it makes working a miserable thing."

Professionalism showed CEAs the way to submerge themselves in the role by providing a rationale for neutrality; concern for responsibility and reputation took the place of political and program commitment. But most CEAs drew limits to how they would allow themselves to be used or to how far they would bend in a direction they disapproved. When the stress became too great, when the gap between the role and the person was too wide, then quitting was the way out: resignation resolved the dilemma. A CEA who managed several controversial programs and finally left state government because he could no longer stand being pulled apart said of being a CEA, "Everybody has to have their piece of you, and you have to realize that."

CONCLUSION: MANIPULATIONS OF THE CEA ROLE

Although the formulators of the CEA plan could not foresee how their social invention would work out in the decades ahead, it is clear that they had some fear of creating an administrative monster, a monster who might grow to embarrass or turn on its inventors. Political scientist Lloyd Musolf, a close observer of the birth of the CEA program, said at the time that the State Personnel Board "neither intends to establish an elite, at one extreme, nor to open the door to partisan plunder, at the other. Yet, only time can tell for certain whether the Plan will surmount these dangers, or even if it can survive impending court tests of its constitutionality." [23]

Although the CEA program was formed with trepidation under Pat Brown, it was only under Reagan's administration, after some of the initial classification, testing, and compensation problems had been resolved, that its functioning became stabilized. The Reagan administration's concern with procedure and the hierarchical definition of tasks was conducive to the early routinization of the CEA plan, and the problems anticipated earlier never materialized. CEAs, under Reagan, were simply a new, more flexible classification of bureaucrats. They were used for their technical abilities and understanding of the systems of government; several department directors suggested that they never would have gotten through the first months in office without the orientation and aid of CEAs. But as the Reagan appointees grew familiar with their jobs, the CEAs, for the most part, assumed the role of skilled career officials and did not become junior politicians, as had been feared. This observation is, of course, a generalization, but our interviews indicated that the CEAs' functioning in the Reagan years was definitely skewed toward the administrative and analytic components of the expert role. Few members of Reagan's personal staff, for example, knew much about CEAs as a group and almost never met them during the routine course of business. CEAs were departmental subordinates and were rarely brought into the center of political activity.

Although most of the CEA positions were filled by the same pool of people in the Reagan and Brown administrations, the CEA role bent in another direction during Brown's years as governor. Brown used all of the people around him—his staff, his cabinet, CEAs, career officials, people outside of government—as resources in formulating and debating ideas. Anyone, no matter what their formal position, could be useful in divining a political route or a moral stance. Indeed, one of Brown's appointees said that an idea could as easily come from Brown's waiter at lunch as from a cabinet officer. Where Reagan was obsessed with correct procedure and businesslike management, Brown was obsessed with ideas that inspired correct action.

In this setting CEAs were not limited to duties as impersonal experts and analysts. Jerry Brown used CEAs as he used the others nearby, as aides in his highly personalized search for the best forms of political action. While his individualized personal and political use of staff members and appointees was something of a managerial innovation, it was certainly accommodated within the role expectations of Brown's political officials and aides. For CEAs, though, being caught up in a personalized maelstrom was simultaneously exciting and forbidding, and sometimes clearly beyond their commitment to neutrality.

This personalized use of CEAs began with the Finance CEAs' guidance of Brown through the budget process in the months before the inauguration, which we mentioned earlier. In spending long hours and many days cloistered with the Governor-elect, they became, in fact, his political tutors and first aides. Brown used the budget process not just to learn the financial procedures of the state, but to probe the history and substance of existing programs. These CEAs were pulled into political decision making because Brown refused to let them remain aloof; according to them, he demanded their opinions and advice. This bending of the CEA role toward a posture more akin to that of a personal aide was a source of consternation for some. Brown appointed Roy Bell, a top Finance CEA, to his cabinet as Director of Finance, and over the next few years a few other CEAs accepted political appointments. But most stayed on as CEAs and to varying extents felt the tension between their apolitical role commitments and their sometimes politicized usage under Brown. What this latest working out of the CEA role will mean for the CEA corps as a whole, and for individual CEAs, will only be told as the Deukmejian administration unfolds its own management style. It is interesting to note, however, that during Jerry Brown's second term the State Personnel Board made it easier for CEAs to reject politicization and return to the ranks of the civil service; return rights were strengthened and the cut in pay for giving up a CEA post reduced.

Chapter Six
POWER AND
ROLE PERFORMANCES

THE FUNDAMENTAL PROBLEM of sociology is understanding the fact of social order—why everyday life is more or less organized, rather than a Hobbesian chaos of individuals. Sociologists have attempted to analyze this problem in a number of ways, but two approaches have been dominant. The first approach, structuralism, assumes a top-down perspective on social order. Structuralists focus on such larger patterns of social life as institutions, social classes, and roles. In this macrological tradition people are assumed to act in terms of these structures, thereby explaining why people behave in similar ways in any given society. The other sociological approach, phenomenology, looks at social life from the bottom up, examining how individuals *create* society through their interaction with each other. People assign meanings to their interaction and orient themselves in terms of shared interpretations. Order, according to phenomenologists, arises from mutually understood patterns of meaning.

In this study we assume that both of these perspectives are important to a complete explanation of social order, in this case the order exhibited by California government. We believe that the organizational activities of contemporary government can be understood only by identifying how structural properties of government, especially social roles, influence the activities of individual actors. At the same time, the social life of government is not determined by structure; it is far more complex. Our informants acted within a web of meanings that they created and reproduced through their daily activities. But these meanings differed systematically according to actors' places in the social structure and were related to the possibilities and obligations of their social roles.

If individuals in government are in fact guided in their behavior by the shape of government organization, then understanding the structure of government and the patterns of action it prompts is critical to understanding the possibilities for government activity today. Government structure supports some types of political action, we suggest, and constrains others. Regardless of the formal powers granted to governors by the constitution and by legislative fiat, governors cannot arrive in office and make government operate in any way they choose. They must initiate programs that accord with the organization's structural inclinations. They must command subordinates in ways that do not do violence to established patterns of meaning. Executive power, as Weber described, must be exercised through a structure of domination, and every structure supports a range of meaningful social action and excludes, as deviant, acts outside that range. *Governors, no less than the subordinates we have discussed so far, must orient themselves to the possibilities the organization makes available.* We elaborate this point with regard to the very different strategies of wielding power of Ronald Reagan and Jerry Brown in the next chapter. In this chapter we explore the relationship between government structure and social action by examining three closely related points.

The first point, which we discuss in the following historical analysis of structural change, shows that *the growth of management roles accompanied changing ideas about the proper shape and place of government.* Early state government was an assemblage, not a systematically organized whole. The movement toward a formal and centralized organization led to the differentiation of executive authority into distinct management roles.

Secondly, we argue that *power in government depends upon role performances*, that is, acting in terms of the publicly understood patterns of meaning appropriate to different roles. Executive authority in state government is institutionalized into three qualitatively distinct subordinate positions—staff, administrative appointee, and CEA. In order for individuals in these roles to use their particular types of executive authority effectively, they must demonstrate to others that they are legitimate bearers of the governor's trust—that they are competent and that they are loyal. The process of gaining personal legitimacy requires the performance of competence and loyalty, and this involves routinely practicing the ethical as well as the task obligations embodied in the different roles. This is seen particularly in power relations and decision-making processes. We develop a sociological theory of decision making based on substantive rather than economic rationality.

Third, we suggest that *widespread adherence to role obligations is the basis of continuous, predictable administration.* The complexity of government is only possible because actors conform to the demands of social roles. Even during a normal period in executive government goals, procedures, and personnel change constantly. And then, once every four or eight years, even more changes. New people come with new procedures with which to accomplish their new ideas. The lack of stability in the organization of government is often a problem because planning, decision making, and all the routines necessary to put political goals into action require a measure of organizational continuity. Adherence to role obligations expressed as loyalty is the basis for this continuity in public administration.

STRUCTURAL CHANGE IN THE EXECUTIVE: THE GROWTH OF ORGANIZATION

The top management positions in today's executive branch are the outcomes of a developmental sequence based upon two fundamental ideas. The first idea is the view that the executive branch ought to be an organization, and the second idea is the belief that the chief executive, the governor, ought to be the person in charge of the organization. Both ideas, which date from the last decades of the nineteenth century, set in motion a developmental process that continues today.[1]

Preventing Organization

The framers of executive government in the United States had neither organization nor unity of command in mind when they shaped the first models of government.[2] For California, even as late as 1879 when voters ratified the present constitution, lawmakers and delegates to the constitutional convention did not view the Executive Department as something that required organization.[3] Even the term *organization*, meaning "the arranging and coordinating of parts into a systematic whole," was a fairly new concept in 1879, coinciding in part with the intellectual movement of Darwinism and with the recent formation of the first large-scale business enterprises in America, the railway companies.[4] The writers of the 1879 constitution used the term organization several times, however, first to refer to the system of superior courts in California, then to the arrangement of a state militia into a systematic body, and later to the system of county governments.[5] But in describing the executive branch, they made no suggestion that it should be organized, that it should be a unified, systematically arranged unit of government. In fact, the writers of the constitution clearly had in mind something quite different.

In keeping with the ideas of the time, those who wrote the 1879 constitution wanted to prevent a unity of command, which was an idea Americans had for some time associated with kinglike powers, sovereign capriciousness, and citizen oppression.[6] Accordingly, they divided the exectuive into separate elective offices. Besides a governor, there were eleven other positions having executive responsibilities that were filled with individuals elected by popular ballot.[7] Each position had separate duties, with the governor being assigned the most important. Moreover, the framers of the 1879 constitution overlapped many duties by requiring several independently elected officials to serve jointly as members of some important boards and commissions, such as the Board of Examiners.[8] Even the governor's specific duties had nothing organizational about them, either in conception or in practice. The duties formed a list: "The Governor shall be commander-in-chief of the militia. . . . He shall transact all executive business. . . . He shall see that the laws are faithfully executed. . . . The Governor shall have power to fill . . . vacancies by granting a commission. . . ."[9] In the state constitution the governor was not styled as a manager of an organized unit but rather as a mediator of vested interests. The constitution appropriately called him "Chief Magistrate."[10]

Organizing for Efficiency

Beginning in the 1890s governors began to lobby for a more unified conception of executive power. Martin Schiesl's study, *The Politics of Efficiency*, clearly shows that the move towards political centralization under a single executive was a widespread movement in public administration throughout the United States from the 1880s on,[11] including California. California governors argued strenuously that unification would lead to the elimination of wasted revenues and wasted time. The first step, said Governor Henry Markham in his 1893 and 1895 biennial messages to the legislature, was to establish a uniform system of accounts throughout state government. Besides calling for fiscal reforms Markham also wanted some of the elected officers made appointees instead.[12] As boards and commissions multiplied in the 1890s and 1900s, the connection between centralization and cost-cutting appeared more obvious and the demand for both grew louder. "Immoderate decentralization," reasoned Governor Henry Gage in 1903, "leads to disintegration."[13] Expanding this theme, Governor George Pardee wrote in his 1907 Biennial Message to the legislature:

> Division of responsibilities never makes for efficiency in the conduct of either public or private affairs, and I am strongly of the opinion that if most of our state boards and commissions were abolished and departments substituted, each being under a responsible head, holding office at the pleasure of the chief executive, with the executive strictly responsible to the people, a marked improvement in efficiency and economy in the dispatch of public business would result.[14]

The centralization of executive authority does not lead, even in theory, to a unified and wholistically conceived administration.[15] But in America in the first two decades of the twentieth century the idea of unity of command went hand-in-hand with an explicit conception of organized wholes.[16] In fact, Americans, so reluctant to acknowledge chains of command and a sense of political domination, made centralization seem an unfortunate but necessary consequence of the need to be organized.[17] As a result, the most often stated goal of reorganizations that swept America during this period in both public and private sectors was, quite simply, to establish an organization; the desire was simply to be in a state of organization and to accrue the benefits that supposedly flowed from this condition, benefits identified, often with a Protestant fervor, as being those of economy and efficiency.

In California, the first comprehensive effort to make the executive branch an explicit, unified organization occurred in 1919, and the committee charged with making the recommendations was named, appropriately, The Committee on Efficiency and Economy.[18] Appointed by Governor William D. Stephens in 1918, the committee was directed to assess the costs of overlapping governmental services and to suggest ways to eliminate waste without reducing public welfare. In line with then current theories of scientific management, the committee concluded, "There are no factors which are greater causes of inefficiency than decentralized control and inadequate supervision and review."[19] In pursuit of "efficient governmental management," the committee recommended, the *"important features . . . of reorganization are the establishment of certain principles."* These principles are "(1) centralization of responsibility; (2) cooperation of the larger organization units; (3) coordination of agencies which perform similar or allied functions."[20] The purpose of reorganization was to establish organization itself. With the implementation of these principles, which occurred piecemeal over the following two decades, the executive branch of California gradually became a consciously constructed, deliberately manipulated organization, in fact as well as in conception.[21]

Reorganization and the Differentiation of Executive Roles

Once people in positions of importance had defined the executive branch as something that ought to be an organized whole with the governor in charge, then that definition formed a justification, as well as an abstract model, for subsequent reorganizations. In fact, the pleas for a strong governor did not lessen but rather gained in intensity after executive unification had occurred. Once governors had been placed in the role of managers, they began to argue for more resources in order to live up to the responsibilities of that role and for more political clout in order to make the state government run smoothly. In outline, the developmental sequence ran as follows.

The first round of reorganizations in 1919 and 1927 aimed at *unifying the executive branch*, at making it an organizational whole, by identifying the necessary state functions and giving the governor the authority to use appointees to manage and coordinate those functions in the public interest.[22] Out of these reorganizations came a definition of the governor/appointee relationship, as we indicated in chapter 3. Appointees ran departments, departments formed around state "functions," and functions reflected groupings of bureaus, boards, and commissions that had originally been established to deal with areas of citizen dissatisfaction. Later reorganizations would build on this conception of executive organization, and would continue, as the 1959 reorganization report put it, "to pull together the many units of government into a cohesive, unified, and internally sound structure."[23]

Defining the executive branch as a unified structure set the stage for the emergence of a second organizational theme. Beginning in the 1940s and continuing to the present day, the second round of reorganizations attempted to *strengthen the governor's unity of command*. As we described in chapter 2, the governor's personal staff was one result of these reorganizations. Warren justified the expansion of the Governor's Office on the grounds that the executive organization had become so complex that the functions of the governor were not being filled. Later attempts to expand the Governor's Office used the same justification: "Give the Governor the management tools to get the job done: budget, program development, management analysis, and personnel."[24] The responsibilities of the Governor, argued the reorganization report, "must be balanced and coordinated either by the Governor personally, or by an office organized to extend his personality into all these activities."[25] The continuing role of the personal staff was to help the governor achieve centralized authority over an executive branch that had been previously defined as an organizational whole composed of functional divisions.

With the executive defined as an organization and the governor defined as manager in charge, a third round of reorganizations aimed at *loosening the organizational rigidity of the executive branch*. Once a goal in its own right, organizational unity is now identified pejoratively by the term "bureaucracy," and is itself the object of attack. Out of these attacks emerged the role of CEAs. As we discussed in chapter 4, CEAs are professional civil servants whose jobs are to use their technical expertise to make the bureaucracy respond to the wishes of political appointees.

A related development aimed at making executive organization more flexible and move under the governor's control. A constitutional amendment, passed by voters in 1966, permitted the State Legislature to delegate to the Governor the prerogative of executive reorganization.[26] The constitutional revision, noted a legislative report, recognized that the governor had "primary responsibility for determining the structure of the executive branch," needed "increased flexibility" to make organizational changes, and required the "freedom to make far-reaching modifications in government in order to keep pace efficiently and economically with changing social and economic conditions."[27] Its status as a unified organization no longer in question, the executive branch is now subject to the logic of fine tuning.

The developmental sequence we describe led to the formation of new organizational roles designed to accomplish distinctive kinds of duties with respect to the overall organization of state government. This role differentiation is not simply a division of labor, but goes beyond that to distinguish, in a qualitative fashion, types of executive authority.[28] Each role—staff, administrative appointee, and CEA—draws upon a distinctive relational bond with the governor that identifies in broad terms both the *duties* embedded in that role and the *authority* required to accomplish those duties. Therefore, authority is not simply a matter of degree, with some roles having more authority than others. Instead, authority is also a matter of kind, a matter of distinctive styles of action.

THE POWER OF OBEDIENCE

The unification of government and the centralization of executive power in the governor were in large part carried out by developing the three positions we analyzed. Appointees responsible to the governor organized government, personal staff centralized control, and

the CEAs made bureaucratic organization more responsive to executive manipulation. Each of these roles shares some aspect of the
governor's own authority; each confers on occupants the right to exercise executive power in certain ways.

But there is a dilemma here: in order for a person to be powerful,
he or she must *only* exercise the power legitimate to his or her role.
For a staff person to become powerful, for example, he or she must
couch all action as being in the name of the governor. Acting in any
other way, such as in self interest, which might be appropriate to a
Cabinet officer, is outside the norms of the staff position. It is an abuse
of power as defined by government's system of meaning. In this section we examine this dilemma of power, that is, how *individual power
in organizations is a matter of conformity to roles.* In the next section
we discuss the place of role performances in policy formation and decision making.

Power vs. *Authority*

At this point we need to make an analytic distinction between power
and authority. Power and authority are terms more precisely distinguished in academic than in government circles.[29] But even in politics the two terms have slightly different, though often overlapping,
meanings. On the one hand, government workers use authority to
mean *a sphere within which power may be rightfully exercised.* This
sphere is defined by the position a person holds. But authority also
means more than a jurisdiction; it also suggests a manner or *style of
action* that is defined and required by the role.[30] For example, a person in the Governor's Office may hold the position of legislative liaison; this position identifies a sphere within which the person may
rightfully act, but also identifies the appropriate manner of action. In
this case the person should act as the governor's surrogate. Both sphere
and style of action adhere to the role and are implicit in the term
authority, as it is commonly used. "Authority," said one Brown appointee, "comes from the job; nobody has authority personally. . . .
I exercise the authority of the job. . . . The state statutes describe
my authority." But appointees know that beyond the statutes their au-

thority is also based upon acting in a certain way: "The ground rules
are you have to stay in sync with the general philosophy of the administration." In academic as in governmental language, authority
means "legitimate power,"[31] that is, power defined apart from individuals and in reference to a role in an organized structure.[32]

Among government workers, there is a usage of "power" which is
more specific than the meaning of authority. In this usage, power is
applied to specific individuals with reference to their *effectiveness* in
exercising the authority of their position. Unlike authority, which applies to a role, power in this usage applies to an individual and refers
to a person's *role performance*, to whether that person conducts himself or herself in a manner befitting the role.[33]

One Reagan aide talked about this more personalized notion of power
as follows: "The influence [one has] depends upon performance and
integrity, you know, your performance over a period of time. If you
burned [someone] on something, your influence with him is going to
be limited, and you're going to have to run through somebody else
[in order to accomplish what you want]." Most people we interviewed
referred to this same theme. Many talked about their "credibility" or
that others must have "confidence" in them or said simply, "You've
got to be honest." As another Reagan aide said, "You better make
sure when you're [in this job] that what you're saying is right, because
you may not have your job very long if you're not. If you don't know,
don't try to fake it. That was my byword: Don't fake it." *In this usage
power implies the personal legitimacy needed to exercise the authority
of one's position.*[34]

Whether or not this common sense distinction between authority
and power is the best or even an adequate way to define the two terms,
the distinction still serves to emphasize an important component of
action in state government. An individual's power to control the actions of others does not flow simply from the fact that one has a position of authority. Although having such a position is certainly a requirement for exercising power, one's power is also based upon others
seeing one's commands or requests as appropriate given his or her role
in government; a person's power depends, in part, on how he performs his role.[35] Therefore, whereas authority is continuous, is
embedded in the role, and is available in theory to any person who

performs the role, power—the ability to control others—varies from person to person, from situation to situation.

We have already given a number of examples for both administrations that show the characteristic ways that the power of individuals in the three roles waxes and wanes. Therefore we will briefly summarize some of the vicissitudes of power in order to illustrate the importance of personal legitimacy in the exercise of authority.

Authority in Roles

The authority of staff aides rests on the presumption that they are acting on the governor's behalf, strictly as his surrogate. This type of authority is defined by the staff role and is common to all staff members. Nonetheless, individuals on the governor's staff have varied a great deal in their power, in their ability to exercise the authority of their role, largely because of two factors that legitimize an individual's right to be the governor's surrogate. First, legitimacy depends upon access or presumed access to the governor, and second, legitimacy depends upon the presumption that the aide is personally loyal to the governor, that he is faithfully doing his job. If a staff member was seen to be close to the governor in some capacity, his personal ability to influence specific events was often great. This point was brought out by one Brown aide, who recalled an incident that revealed to him the potential power of his role. "I didn't know a soul when I came up here, except [one other aide]. [Shortly after joining the Office staff], I set up a meeting with a legislator and [a CEA] from the Department of Finance, and I said, 'Do you want me to sit in on the meeting?' The guy from Finance said, 'Well, you're like an 800-pound gorilla; you can sit anywhere you want.' " But if the access of staff members is known to be limited, their power—their ability to do their jobs— diminishes accordingly. Said one Reagan appointee, "When I would get directions from members of the staff of the Governor's Office, I would ask if the Governor said that. I'd pin them down and if they finally said, 'No', I would say, 'Well, I don't intend to do that.' I ended up really just taking all of my direction of consequence from the Governor, or from someone like [his Chief-of-Staff] who I thought was tied in so close [to the Governor] that [what he] said would be correct." In both administrations, but particularly in Brown's, access did not always depend upon one's staff assignment, but rather upon more personal factors.

Although a reputation for closeness to the governor contributed to an aide's power, his reputation for personal loyalty was even more important. A Reagan aide made this point as follows: "One of the greatest abuses of power that takes place in a Governor's Office is those people who play a role of representing the governor when they really aren't sure they are, and they really aren't sure where the governor is. . . . You only get yourself in trouble if you try and play the role that you really don't have or try to represent something you really don't know, even if you have the right to represent [that sphere]. You're going to get exposed sooner or later. You may represent the governor to a person down there, and then what you told them doesn't seem true. First you're embarrassed but then the word goes through the community: I lied to them and tried to snow them, [telling them] where I was or where the governor was. They will have caught me in my own lack of integrity. People will say, 'You had better watch out when you deal with [this aide] because he's not quite leveling with you.' Now you are ineffective. And I enjoy being effective. The way to be effective is to be straightforward." The way to exercise power as a staff aide was to be "straightforwardly" the governor's surrogate.

An appointee's authority was of a different order from that of a staff member and required him to make decisions affecting his departmental or agency jurisdiction that were aligned with the governor's philosophy. As one CEA said, "The statutes set up that legitimacy. The role of appointees is absolutely legitimate. They are responsible for the programs they're running. . . . But they're also responsible up to [the governor], to be part of the team." In regard to a department or agency, an appointee's authority was great; he had a capability to exercise many different options and to influence many different people. But an appointee's actual power, like that of staff members, varied greatly. If an appointee was generally viewed as an ineffective administrator or as being disloyal, his range of options was at times reduced to the point that he became merely a figurehead.

Appointee power could be undercut from all sides. The governor's staff easily assumed some of the policy-making responsibilities that were legislative or budgetary in nature. The Department of Finance, as one Reagan appointee pointed out, relied on their own specialists, rather than on the appointee, for making budgetary decisions. "If we found a weak department director, we would bring in a strong budget analyst and we would, at times, look to the budget analyst as the guy who really knows what's going on in the department and is really running the department, even though he had no line responsibility. That was the methodology sometimes used. The Department of Finance, because of the fact that our analysts were in every department, would probably have a better knowledge in terms of the specifics of the problem [than would a weak director]."

Likewise the top level of civil servants within the department or agency, usually CEAs, were able to usurp line authority, an appointee's decision-making capabilities that affected the operation of the department. Said one CEA, "[Civil servants] grant the director a great deal of legitimacy and all of them understand that this is the fellow whose policies and ideas in fact affect [their area]. Most of these people are oriented towards a sense of responsibility to [this area], and he's accorded a great deal of respect by virtue of his office. He confirms that, or dispels it, by the sagacity of his decisions. If he makes decisions that don't correspond with what appears to be a wise decision-making process, the people in the ranks will tolerate the director, but they certainly will have no allegiance . . . with his decision making." If an appointee proved incompetent or disloyal, the CEA continued, then a staff of loyal CEAs provided the director with an "enormous screen, to screen out anyone who would think that he is, in fact, dumb or unfit. . . . Now let's say the director has hired a skilled, well-informed, good decision-making staff, who in fact starts out loyal. Let's say, the director, after he's made those wise commitments for hiring, absolutely blows it; he starts making obviously poor decisions or is contemplating some or is saying, 'Here are the things I'd like to do.' Before they're implemented, this staff is going to do everything that they know how to do that will block him, if they're wise, which includes saying to him, 'That's the stupidest thing I've heard, and here are the reasons why'. . . . When this sort of thing happens, then it is the role of the staff to try and compensate."

The authority of CEAs rested on yet a different foundation, that of expertise. Perhaps the best example of the power of expertise was the authority of the Budget Analyst, a CEA position in the Department of Finance. "The Director of Finance, in his organization, had specialists," said one of Reagan's agency secretaries. "They camped out in our departments as they were formulating budgets. . . . I had five departments and five or six other boards, and Finance would have typically three or four specialists who kind of camped out while they were formulating the budget. They would camp out over a two or three month period while they were formulating these budgets. They would come to our meetings but then they'd go back to Finance the rest of the year, when they were presumably studying all this stuff. Their job, of course, was to submit sound and balanced budgets, but they just got into everything. . . . Their input was very, very strong, and very, very frequently a cabinet secretary would have a proposal that seemed pretty good and they would shoot it right down." Although their influence did not spread out over the whole of state government, CEAs in departments other than Finance possessed equal abilities to influence the course of events by virtue of their technical skills, which included knowledge of how to work the government to a department's or an appointee's advantage. Recalled one Reagan department head, "We had a fellow in the department (a CEA) who worked on the legislative problems. He was really great at that. We never lost a bill." As we show in chapter 5, the power of CEAs was also regularly undermined or ignored, for example when an appointee or the governor made a political decision contrary to the technical advice of a CEA or when a CEA seemed too political or too bureaucratic to be trusted.

Role Performance and Power in Organizations

Each management role represents a type of executive authority. Ingrained in governmental routines, the authority of these roles, according to the perception of state workers, is a constant. An incumbent's use of authority is not constant, however, but varies according to person and to circumstance. *State workers see their influence over*

*others as being directly tied to their role performance, to their ability
to show others that they are upholding the standards of their roles.* They
understand that they must act in a way that others can recognize their
role-defined loyalty, and that such performances contain *interaction
rituals.*[36]

For example, one Reagan aide described the care with which he
would deal with others so that his loyalty would be apparent to all.
"The staff really is the extension of the Governor, so we would have
to be very careful that we are not usurping the Governor's power, using his power other than in his name. . . . If I were talking to a
legislator, I would never say, 'Here's what I want to do' or 'Here's
what you should do.' I would be very careful to say, 'I *think* the Governor would take this position.' While I would say 'I think,' I knew
darned well what position the Governor would take, and they understood that. But I would never set myself up as an intermediate power,
or power broker, between the Governor and a legislator. And I think
that was an important part of that role. . . . These were things you
don't think about every time, but you have kind of a background philosophy of how you were doing it." In this example the notion of
personal loyalty provided the background philosophy—the model by
which he could frame his actions, in the form of an interaction ritual, so that his actions became legitimate in the eyes of others. Or as
one CEA put it, "The need to get legitimacy for your actions . . . is
a very important skill that bureaucrats, as well as exempt [people],
learn with any administration. And those that don't develop that skill
and go off and do dramatic things without good sense are the ones
that are going to end up getting fired or called to task."

Role performances and interaction rituals aimed at having *others
define one's act of power as an act of obedience.*[37] Any other definition
might result in a decreasing ability to exercise the authority of one's
position. For instance, if an act was seen as stemming from one's disloyalty, it was viewed not as *an act of power, but rather as an act of
abusing power.* Therefore, in order for staff members to have been
influential in state government, others had to see them as being obedient to the governor's predilections. For appointees to have been a
potent force, others had to view them as being able to make independent decisions that were in line with and, hence, obedient to the gov-

ernor's philosophy. Similarly, for the CEAs' technical expertise to have been important in shaping the course of state government, others had to recognize their obedience to professionalism, which made their advice appear to be unbiased assessments of political situations. In each case, being seen as loyal—as honest, as possessing integrity—provided the means by which they were able to be *repetitively influential*; when they were seen as "just doing their job," state workers could do what they were doing again and again.[38] But just doing one's job involved considerable personal costs; there were tensions within each set of obligations that made loyalty a difficult impression to manage, and a more difficult emotion to feel. And it was always tempting to make an impact beyond that defined by one's own sphere and relationship. This was a temptation to which more than a few succumbed.

If they survived long, people in the top management positions learned that their own power was fragile; its only solidity rested on performing their roles. But even the motives of someone who remained faithful to his role and to his authority in that role were always open to question. Those people who showed a moment's open disregard for their obligations found others willing to see in their subsequent actions the impression of disloyalty. To act without regard for one's role, to play someone else's game even for a short time, was potentially discrediting. Acting in a single instance as a politically tainted CEA, a philosophically idiosyncratic appointee, or a self-serving staff member was enough to erode one's power in the long run. Not everyone acted loyally in this sense. Nor did everyone understand what loyalty meant in regard to their own actions. But in judging others and in acting on that judgment, they assessed loyalty by looking at how others used their role authority—obediently and disobediently.

A DECISION-MAKING THEORY OF
SUBSTANTIVE RATIONALITY

Nowhere in state government was the connection between role performance and power more apparent than in the course of planning and making decisions.[39] In most complex organizations, including the California executive branch, these activities are ostensibly the job of top-ranking managers. But in comparison with many private organizations the executive branch employed more people, incorporated more loosely coupled units, and was subject to greater and more continuous changes in goals, procedures, and personnel.[40] The State Legislature added another dimension of complexity by being an extraorganizational source of approval for most key policy and budgetary matters.[41]

Despite the size, complexity, and changeableness of state government, programs were planned and decisions were made. Each year both governors delivered a budget to the legislature that outlined and provided revenues for executive programs, appointed hundreds of people to public posts, and decided whether or not to sign the thousand and more bills that passed the legislature. The governors and their top-ranking managers found themselves in a position where they had to plan and decide without adequate time and without adequate knowledge. Yet planning and making decisions became routine tasks, despite the difficulties in doing both.[42]

How were planning and decision making accomplished routinely in a complex and uncertain environment? Our analysis reveals that role performances were the key component of these routines.[43] *Roles and role performances supplied a measure of organizational continuity, not because they gave people's behavior a formal, script-like character, but rather because they provided flexible models of personal conduct that encompassed ethical and practical dimensions of action in state government.* These models of conduct contained definitions of authority in roles and supplied interaction rituals, vocabularies, ethical standards, and emotional bearings. Using these models of conduct, individuals were able to compare the behavior of others with the roles they occupied; this allowed them to plan and to predict the outcome of negotiations. It was through understanding the nuances of roles that people in government interpreted and controlled each others' actions; roles are at the foundation of government's system of meaning.

To analyze in greater detail the place of role performances in the processes of governmental planning and decision making, we divide these processes, in an analytic but artificial fashion, into three common components: goals, strategies, and negotiation and compromise. Each component was inseparable from roles and role performances.

Goal Setting

As in all public governments, goals in Reagan's and Brown's administrations were seldom distinct and unambiguous.[44] Both groups arrived in Sacramento with a general sense of what they hoped to accomplish. But faced with the task of putting ideas into practice, people of both administrations found that even the most clear-cut campaign goals lacked the specificity needed for being run through the legislative and executive branches. And when legislators and executives added practical details and interpretive slants to goals to make them attainable in some sense, the goals themselves changed. They became intertwined in organizational routines, entangled in roles and role performances.

People in most positions, especially those serving as agency secretaries and departmental directors, had to have lists of goals. For instance, because an obligation of the administrative appointees' role was to implement the governor's philosophy, they tried to translate into specific terms abstract principles. The appointees' power in both administrations rested on their ability to specify the governor's goals and to implement them in their respective departments. As managers of large bureaucracies, appointees also had to respond to the needs of civil servants and to the requests of organizational constituents; they had to monitor or at least have an opinion on continuing programs from previous administrations. Appointees had to form goals or more or less consistent accounts to justify actions taken, or actions that might be taken.[45]

The projection of oneself into the role of another and the presumption of goals appropriate for that role were the standard means in both administrations to evaluate the role performance of people in executive positions.[46] The circumstances of one of Reagan's Secretaries of Health and Welfare, the largest agency in state government, illustrates the multi-sided quality of such evaluations. Reagan came to office promising to run government as a business and to cut the cost and influence of government. This secretary knew that in his area this was translated to mean cutting the welfare rolls and reducing the cost of the welfare program. According to the secretary, "I knew that [Reagan] wanted efficiency, knew he wanted to reduce the size of government. I always felt that every time the welfare rolls went up, they'd look at me and say, 'That goddamn [secretary], he's got to reduce welfare.' " This cabinet officer was in fact seen as a poor administrator because he did not seem to be embracing the goal of cutting back welfare payments, a large budget item in California. But from where he sat, things looked somewhat different than to the critical aides in the Governor's Office. According to him "We could not get the [state] legislature to modify some of their programs. They had some very strict formulas for welfare grants. So our hands were tied in that respect. And we soon realized, and I told the Governor, that two-thirds of the people on welfare were kids under 15 years of age. Or they were aged and disabled. The average taxpayer's concept of the welfare recipient is a 28-year-old able-bodied guy sitting in front of a color television set, drinking a beer while he could be out working. But that wasn't the profile." Federal regulations also controlled the disbursement of welfare payments because much of the money came from Washington.

The governor's staff tried to undercut the secretary because they questioned his competence to reduce the welfare budget. According to a top Reagan aide, "He was basically a nice guy, and what we needed in there was a son-of-a-bitch, to be very honest. A terrible department, it was so big. You really needed somebody in there that could just go back and do a lot of things that [the secretary] wasn't equipped to do." A CEA who worked for the secretary in the agency during the disputes with the governor's staff reflected on how the situation appeared to him. "I don't think [the secretary] was that weak in my opinion. But my perception was that Reagan and/or some of his key advisors had this more traditional or stereotyped Republican feeling about these programs, and as [the secretary] got more and more exposed to the programs and saw some of the people [they were] helping, and then he got orders to cut back, blast away regardless, he couldn't stomach it too well, and he got the reputation of being the weak sister of the administration. And, also, you couple that with the fact that our hands are tied by federal rules and regulations and laws on the books, he was hamstrung by these, and perhaps by a feeling that the programs weren't as horrible as some of Reagan's people [would] think."

Because this cabinet officer defined his goals differently from what the governor's aides, and perhaps the governor, wanted them to be, he experienced constant difficulty in having his opinions taken seriously. He was slowly squeezed out of the administration. Had he been able to redefine his goals to align with their perceptions, or change their thinking to appreciate his interpretation of his role obligations, his tenure might have been more fruitful.

But the important point is that goals and interpretations of goals were implicit in and relative to specific roles, that others evaluated incumbents in light of their role performances, and that goals implied by one role were seldom in harmony with the goals implied by another role.

These points were summarized by another Reagan appointee as follows: "You've got a natural conflict built into the two types of roles. . . . The governor's staff, in representing the governor say, 'Those damn agency secretaries. All they want is to give everything away to those damn department directors out there, who have become the captives of the bureaucracy.' And the agency secretaries say, 'Those damn kids over there [in the governor's office], who aren't even dry behind the ears—all they worry about is politics. We have to do what's good for the people of California.' The two roles have to meld in some manner . . . but [the conflict] is one that's absolutely essential. [For example, in one] conflict, the Governor's Office had a singular role, and made a singular political decision.[47] In that case we had a weak agency secretary, who people [in the Governor's Office] thought had become captive of the bureaucracy. He was not good in terms of verbalizing his positions and not well thought out in terms of being able to develop a good plan. There was a tremendous distrust of the agency. So the Governor's Office took over [this particular] decision, and the decision was chaos in terms of the whole political impact in California. It was something that it took us five years to recover from. But you can find it going the other way [with the agency secretary bypassing the Governor's Office to the detriment of all]. You can find the agency secretary that is so strong, he'll go off and do his own thing and the Governor's Office getting very upset because he's now become the hero. [They say] 'Hey, wait a second; he works for the Governor. He shouldn't have his picture on the front page of the *L.A. Times.* That's supposed to be the Governor's picture. Why is he announcing this great new program? Does he have his own political ambitions? . . . [So there is] the necessity to try to meld those two roles."

As this appointee implies, bias was built into any person's evaluation of goals and of role performances more generally.[48] Evaluation occurred in a hall of mirrors. All people in government occupied some role. Each role implied different commitments and gave different meaning to the actions of the incumbent. There were no outside observers in this system, because there was no place to stand and no relationship that gave an unbiased view of government. Whether a goal was good or bad depended in part on the role one had. Hence, there was no single, let alone correct, assessment of a goal. In commenting on the Brown reorganization of the Department of Health, one CEA made this point as follows: "The administration supported [the reorganization]. They pushed it. They proposed it. The agency proposed it. [The director] disagreed with it. There was some conflict there, but whether it was significant or not—everything's relative. I mean, I don't know. There were some who said that it didn't have to be broken up, that it could have been managed better. I guess I really don't know how to answer your question. *It depends on whose eyes you're seeing it through.* It's a dilemma."

Strategies

Goals and strategies, defined here as plans designed to produce an outcome, were not discrete steps in the process of decision making.[49] Rather, they were concurrent and often indistinguishable aspects of the same act. For example, a CEA who was sent into the Department of Health described the process that he, and everyone else in government, had gone through in setting goals and in calculating the means to achieve them. "Now when I went in, the first thing I did was try to figure out what it means. I didn't know [my program] from a hacksaw. And in effect what I did was just sit and talk to people, both inside and outside, talk to the industry, took a look at what the specific issues were, dealt with all of the actors in the issue, and then came up with what I thought, in my own opinion, was the course the state should take." In determining what course the state should take, this CEA was seeking the appropriate goals for the department, but implied in his seeking was knowledge of the limits of the possible means to achieve the goal. When he made his recommendation it involved not only a suggested end but implied parameters to a set of means. He would not recommend anything that was too costly, that required more manpower than was available, that was against the known philosophies of the governor or important industrial constituents, and a host of other factors. His proposal of a particular goal for the department was also a simultaneous calculation of the possible ways to achieve the goal, and some assessment of their probable success.

Although goals and strategies are usually aspects of the same set of practices and calculations, it is useful analytically to consider the calculation of means to an end apart from the end itself because such calculations emphasize a slightly different dimension of role performances. Unlike the formulation of goals, which result from reflection upon one's own role in light of how others perceive it, *the calculation of strategies results from reflections upon other peoples' roles and role performances, and upon how one's own role is related to theirs.*

A key component of building a strategy was being able to envision alternative courses of action that might lead to the same outcome.[50] The ability to put together several scenarios and to pick the most likely to succeed was a skill that was learned only through much interaction with others or by probing the knowledge that others had gained through their interactive experience. In trying to figure out the possible ways to fulfill his commitments, an individual conjured up an image of all the players in government that might have an impact on his goal. He projected himself into the roles of others, tried to see his goals as they saw it, and deduced what actions they could take in light of their obligations. The knowledgeable actor calculated whether they would be friend or foe.

A manager in the Department of Health discussed how this process took place. "Smart directors will understand who the players are in an issue, and will try to deal with those players. Suppose there's a proposal you want to make. Suppose you want to change [a program]. I know if it's got money [written into the legislation], I'm going to have to deal with Finance. I know if I want the administration to support it, I've got to deal with the Governor's Office. I know that I've got to deal with the agency. What I do is I try to laundry-list my cast of characters, and then I try to make damn sure that I know what *their* needs are. My ultimate goal is to get some legislation through. And if I am missing any parties, it's more often than not they'll stop it, roadblock it, or change it significantly where I don't like it and I have to can the whole thing. So I try to make sure that the staff, the employees working for me, are conscious of those interactions. What they see is a director who can make decisions in an environment of teamwork, and the environment of outside influences. But if he or she does not consider those or figure those out, ain't nothing going to happen."

Knowing "who the players are" was absolutely critical in planning successful strategies, but learning the players and government's structure of meaning takes time. Not understanding the environment of forces was frustrating for people entering government or changing jobs. One Reagan cabinet officer recalled his entree into government. "You start from scratch. You don't know anybody, you don't know who down in the bureaucracy is reliable or not reliable, and you make a lot of judgments on whether they are retained or not retained on just hunch." One of Brown's legislative aides felt powerless at first because of the overwhelming task of learning about the 120 legislators upstairs in the Capitol and their numerous committees and staff members. According to this aide, learning the job "takes at least six months, even if you work hard at it." Learning the public commitments of legislators, the environment of influences in which each of them worked, and their personal abilities and willingness to meet those requirements was necessary if the staff aide was to be able to select a way through the pitfalls of the legislative process. The aide recounted the kinds of information that were necessary for doing the job well. "The key, from my perspective, is really knowing what makes everybody tick. You know, you have to study their district a little bit. That's why I get so involved in watching their [election] races to know what kinds of battles they went through. Who was active in their campaign, what groups brought pressure to bear on them, all of that's going to be important when you go to them and ask them to support or oppose something, if you can know what their frame of reference is. And then, too, learning the procedures, learning where a bill is referenced, what the process is, how a bill is introduced, who is a good author, who's on what committee, what the committee structures are, what the strong committees are, what the less strong committees are. How to get a bill off the floor if it's on the floor and you want it to go back to the committee. So from that standpoint there's quite a bit to learn in just finding out where the players are and how they want to do it."[51]

Planning strategies called for knowing people well enough that one was able to predict what they would likely do given their role in state government. For most individuals, this sort of knowledge about people in government existed prior to the specification of goals and the formulation of strategies, but was clearly gained in anticipation of doing both. Gaining such knowledge about people is called, in the language of politicians and government officials, "networking," "building a power base," and becoming "well connected," and its acquisition means that one "knows his way around town." It was an understood part of many positions, especially those involved in liaison work, such as the governor's press, legislative, legal, and appointment aides, whose incumbents had a recurring need to work with and through other people in order to do their job.[52]

The assessment of strategies rested upon the evaluation of what interested individuals might be predicted to do in light of what their roles obligated them to do. In thinking through a plan of action, state executives looked, therefore, at the *predictability* of the individuals upon whom they might base their strategies. Predictability, or credibility as it was more often called, was a measure of role performance. And, according to state workers, one's ability to exercise the authority of his role—his power—was directly tied to the predictability of his role performance.

It might seem that to be predictable in regard to certain issues or policies would weaken an individual's strategic ability to move unexpectedly. To some extent, this was the case. But to build a network of support an individual had to be predictable; others had to know that they were able to count on him or her to push, for example, health care bills or to oppose liberal economic policies. Only by standing firmly on a publicly known set of commitments did others call a person into their strategies as someone "who can be counted on." People did not want to miscalculate about each other; the cost was often too high. One of Brown's aides spoke of this in the relationship between the legislators and the governor's legislative staff. "For the most part I think it's based on an ongoing relationship. It takes a while to develop that relationship with those people who you know you can go back to, who you're going to be able to see, because you helped them, or you've been courteous to them, or you've done something for their constituents."

Being predictable, having credibility, was the only way in which a person was able to build a power base, a network of supporters that could be called on to take a role in the strategies of the individual. And being predictable in one's own actions and expecting others to be predictable in turn meant that an element of trust among the ranks of executives had to be established. Another Brown aide made the point this way: "You get information by giving information, and the only way which you can do that is by trusting, by knowing that the person is what we call a 'good person' as opposed to a 'bad person.' A 'bad person' is a person who lies or won't live up to what they say or promises more than they can deliver, or one who misleads you. That's a bad person. A good person is someone who deals with you honestly. So before I can be honest with you, I have to know you're an honest person, too. So that's why if you look at state government, you'll find that most of the CEA positions are filled by people who are [in the good person] network. They know each other, they came up through the ranks together, and they have winnowed out the good boys from the bad boys and the good girls from the bad girls. So you've got to be able to establish that sense of trust."

Like goals, strategies were embedded in trust, in sets of interaction rituals that informed all parties involved that people were faithfully fulfilling the obligations of their respective roles. And like goals, strategies and the evaluation of those strategies carried the bias of different roles; they varied among roles and among people acting in those roles. Importantly, strategies and goals were not the discrete, one-time-only calculations assumed by some decision-making models. Nor were they, in a formal sense, means-ends calculations. Although subject to considerable calculation, embracing goals and forming strategies only worked in an atmosphere of continuous role involvement. State executives wanted to be repeaters, wanted to be effective time after time and not just on a one-shot deal. Repeated effectiveness required long-term role involvement, which meant that one's goals and strategies had to be shaped in calculation as well as in practice by the requirements of roles.

Negotiation

A central component of forming goals and planning strategies was the knowledge that reaching final decisions usually necessitated negotiation and compromise.[53] State executives were aware of the "natural" conflicts in government—between the executive and the legislative branches, between appointees and bureaucrats, between staff and line positions—and recognized the importance of cooperating with people whose jobs required opposition.[54] Negotiation and compromise arose from the knowledge that others' commitments were role-based and were in conflict with one's own, and that individuals in those roles potentially had long-term relations with each other.

At one level, negotiations were acts of mutual persuasion over items of common concern. But at another, equally important level, *negotiation was bargaining over the limits of one's role obligations.* Negotiation tested the limits of role performances by locating the points at which people were willing to relinquish some role commitments in order to uphold others. Compromise was the point of resolution at which both parties were able to maintain their commitments sufficiently well so as not to feel, or appear, disloyal. A person who was seen to have negotiated poorly, to have not sustained the minimum standards demanded by his role obligations, was said to have "given away the show." Successful compromise, that which did a minimum of violence to the loyalties at stake, allowed all parties to say, "I can live with that," meaning that commitments had been upheld.

The logic and routine nature of bargaining in terms of roles is clear in the following statement by one of Brown's department directors: "I say, 'Look, I really think I have to do it this way because I have to have a consistent policy, and what you're doing is contrary to that.' Generally speaking, it will work out the way I want it 100 percent or some compromise we all can live with. When I'm dealing with the head of [another department] on a mutual matter, I don't feel I'm the Governor's representative. I think we are both the Governor's representatives; we both have different institutional viewpoints that we're projecting there and our job is to come to some mutual understanding, and we usually do. If we don't, I guess it has to get resolved above us."

Negotiation involved trying to convince the other party that a given act or policy did not threaten their commitments or did so to an "acceptable" degree. Usually, this meant changing some point in a piece of legislation or modifying a budget. But sometimes negotiators tried to get the other party to *redefine* their commitments so that they were in line with the negotiator's. A director in the Department of Motor Vehicles tried to get the Department of Finance to redefine their commitment to cut costs, to a commitment that embraced a notion of service, as well as cost. "[I told them] I really insist you do something about the [hiring] freeze in those field offices. When I go out there myself and stand at the back of the line for an hour and a half, this is not reasonable service, and what you people [in Finance] don't understand is that if you give me a driver's license examiner tomorrow, it takes me six weeks to teach him. There is a game that is played—if you want to save money, you don't fill the position. But this destroys my department out in the field office. I can live with that [here in the department headquarters]; I don't need another manager some place; some supervisor can take over his function, but who is going to give the driver's test? We actually took the Department of Finance people, when we felt that they just didn't understand our system out there, and made them stand in line. We got a blanket exemption [from the freeze] to the division of field offices."

Redefining commitments made negotiation seem less problematic, and support for the other seem less of a loss. Concessions were easier to give when both parties were able to envision their commitments as coinciding or overlapping, so that they were able to see "eye to eye." People negotiate to achieve at least some of their commitments in the face of opposition, but there are limits to how much one can nego- tiate away and still be seen as loyal to one's position. If a person ne- gotiates too much, he doesn't uphold his loyalties and loses credibil- ity—also a sign of weakness. One of Brown's legislative aides put it this way, "See, I could make all the deals in the world, and I would. I'm the biggest whore in the world. I mean, I'm a pragmatic expert at it. Alright? But it wouldn't do any good. I would give it away in two days. I mean, there'd be nothing left to trade." People must tread a careful line between negotiating too little and fighting with the pos- sibility of total defeat, and negotiating too much, which suggests not standing up to principle and having no credibility. The bases of de- termining when to negotiate and when not to is always at the level of loyalty. What is most efficacious for meeting the obligations inherent in one's role commitments? Loyalty and commitments must always be the foundation of one's negotiating stance.

The stance is well demonstrated by a scene between Governor Brown and the head of a department, as recounted by an aide. Brown made all of his department heads personally justify their budgets during his first year in office, especially if they wanted more money. He was a notoriously tough negotiator whose argumentative challenges many found intimidating. "It was very interesting to watch people's reac- tions to that process. Some people hung very tough. I remember [one director] who was the head of the Youth Authority, really hung tough. I can't even remember what the issue was. He was really very pas- sionate about his responsibilities, that is, to the people who are in the Youth Authority. He felt very strongly that they were not being ade- quately supported. He wanted more money. He was very eloquent, [and] I think the Governor was very impressed."

Negotiating is a routine activity of government, and because of this people looked not only to fulfilling their immediate commitments but considered their future negotiations. Some might try to negotiate un- fairly if they thought that they could get away with it, but in practice most tempered their desire to win with the knowledge that they had to go back to the same people again and again. Therefore, like goals and strategies, negotiation occurred under conditions of trust generated by people adhering to the requirements of their roles and to the parameters of their authority.

During both administrations, the *consequences* of planning and decision making—the plans and decisions—were, of course, shaped by the issues of the day, issues that had little to do with the actual organization of government. But the *process* of planning and decision making within government also exerted a great influence on the final form of ideas and their implementation. Insofar as it required goals, strategies, and negotiation, decision making in government departed from the abstract evaluation of ends and means and became entangled in the organization of government, in the connection between role performances and individual power.

PUBLIC ROLES AND PRIVATE LIVES

Executive authority is differentiated and institutionalized in the top roles in state government. But the ability to exercise executive authority does not rest on mere incumbency. Rather, authority rests as well upon performances, upon demonstrations showing others one's willingness to uphold the obligations of one's role. Such performances are based upon tacit understandings and interaction rituals that insiders to state government regard as common sense. Those who knowingly ignore the understandings and violate the rituals place their power, their own ability to control the behavior of others, in jeopardy.

But disregarding mutual rules of conduct jeopardizes more than one's own power. It also disrupts the continuity of administration by decreasing overall the calculability of strategies. It heightens the degree of uncertainty, making the career of a policy depend more upon chance. This is a point that Reagan's top aide, Edwin Meese, understood well: "My personal philosophy of power is that the more power you have potentially, the more you have an obligation to utilize restraint when you exercise the power. . . . If positional power was not restrained and not used to a degree consistent with other members of the cabinet, then that would shatter the teamwork concept. It would make my job, in the long run, a lot more difficult, because I would have lost the confidence that existed among all the members of the cabinet. Because they knew that I was not going to sandbag them, they would make it a point to come and kick things around with me before they went to talk to the Governor."

Seasoned executives in state government, especially the CEAs, recognize that personal qualities, as perceived by others, have a direct bearing not only on one's ability to exercise power, but also on the success of an administration. Although they use many different words to identify these personal qualities—integrity, honesty, dedication, credibility, but primarily loyalty—all these words pertain to another's perceptions of one's personal trustworthiness, and make these a precondition of exercising power. Just as they recognize the importance of this quality in others, people also recognize the importance of being seen this way themselves. Hence, by a subtle process, accomplished political players come to see loyalty as one of their principal assets. Or as one of the most influential and respected members of state government said in reflecting on his thirty years of service: "Loyalty is absolutely the most important thing in government; I've been telling [Brown] since the day he became governor that the most important person he can appoint is the person who will be loyal to him."

Notions of loyalty and commitment permeate government, in large part because the people of government are in the business of exercising power. These notions provide the standards of obedience by which people both legitimate their right to exercise power and assess the right of others. *As such, loyalty, as a construct, provides a system of meaning and a reflexive framework for understanding the complexity and changeableness of government, and how one operates in the face of both.*[55]

But the framework of action and interpretation provided by roles and loyalty is not to be likened to a machine or to a method without content. At least at the top, executive organization is not a bureaucratic tool, impersonally solving the problems of a society. It is not something to be sheared off from politics and put down as mere administration. Instead, the framework of action in government is founded upon *emotional beliefs and ethical standards* that are themselves rooted in the performance of roles.[56]

In performing roles, most people deferred their private interests and personal goals. As one Brown aide put it, most "have just thrown themselves" into their jobs. The same point was made by one Reagan aide in reflecting on Nixon's presidential staff during Watergate, "I just felt it was quite an experience to be around someone with a level of ethics that Ronald Reagan had, especially when my classmates were up in the White House and I was in Sacramento. They were going to jail and I wasn't, because I had never been asked to do any of the things that they were asked to do. That's a very fortunate thing. It would have been pretty tough to say no. . . . It is very easy to lose your perspective."

Often people lost sight of their original goals and abstract notions of morality. They adopted the standards of their positions, and treated these standards as if they were objects of their own creation. Such individuals manufactured the emotions to match the standards expected of them. They saw that others constantly interacted with them as if they expected the inner commitment to correspond to the outer behavior. If they did not enter government with a sincere commitment, they were drawn into feeling genuine loyalty—a sincere love for the governor, or a deep devotion to his philosophy, or a real dedication to the code of professionalism. Their future goals became more distant as they were caught in present activity. One Brown aide said: "Everything I do is to benefit [Brown], which ultimately benefits me."

But the distinction between people and the roles they occupy was often ambiguous. Some felt a constant temptation to enlarge their roles in government beyond what their job and relationship committed them to. With sincerity, they wanted to do all they could to help and they wanted to be appreciated for what they did and felt; so to do a little more and to feel more deeply what they already felt seemed a logical way to gain that appreciation. They overplayed the game, ignored the constraints, and acted as if their loyalty gave them the right to go beyond their job. Some succeeded at this, but most did not. Said one Brown aide, "[Working in the Governor's Office], you become convinced you're important, but you are not. You're only important if your project succeeds, and then you have to find another project. . . .

The lecture I gave to [newcomers] is 'Don't become arrogant. Don't become inflated. It's not that you're nothing. It's just that you're just a little cog. Don't let it go to your head because if you let it go to your head, there will be a dozen people to bring you back to reality very quickly'. . . . There's a joke that goes around here. The only real power you have in working for the Governor's Office is knowing that your phone calls will be returned. We toss that around to keep ourselves in touch with what we're doing."

Not everyone was able to throw themselves into obedience with equal ease. Many felt frustrated by having to conform to other people's expectations, to yield to other agenda, to exercise constraint to satisfy someone else's patterns. Some felt they had higher commitments than those defined strictly by their role relationships. Said one Brown aide, "I have a very strong sense of public service, of a commitment to serving the public. That's one piece of naivete that I still carry around with me. It makes me feel good, so I cling to it. . . . Sitting where I sit now, I'm in a position to move [others] closer toward my own personal agenda. But I have almost no control over the calls, or the assignments that come from [the Governor]. . . . [I would like to tell others], 'I want to go back and do [my job]. Why don't you just leave me alone and let me do [it]. I've got my own agenda.' That's really the question, to what extent do you control your agenda? If you control your own agenda [in the Governor's Office], it probably means you're being ignored. On the other hand if you are working on [the Governor's] agenda or [someome else's] agenda you don't get a chance to do some things that common sense tells you needs to be done or that your own agenda says you want to do." To such people, genuine role performances were hard to pull off. Sincere loyalty was a difficult emotion to create, because such loyalty negated other commitments. They acted loyal, without feeling it. They swallowed their pride, without showing it. They felt resentment, without revealing it. Gradually misery or guilt set in; they found themselves in the dilemma of loyalty. Their private motives did not match their public presentation, so they had to choose to continue as they were or to declare themselves publicly so that all could see where their loyalties lay, or to exit. Such choices were difficult.

State workers knew there was a gap between public roles and private lives, between public justifications and private motives. But they seldom knew the extent and content of the gap. Was a person sincerely loyal, or was he or she just acting that way? The question couldn't be answered with certainty by observing another's actions; so in the absence of clues to the contrary, people acted towards another on the assumption that his commitments were real and expressions of loyalty genuine. They treated another as a legitimate holder of his or her position, and endowed one's actions with motives appropriate to such a person. They had to do so, for at stake was their own personal legitimacy, and, with that legitimacy, their own ability to exercise power.

Chapter Seven
EXECUTIVE STRATEGIES AND THE STRUCTURE OF GOVERNMENT

IT IS DIFFICULT to imagine two more different politicians or managers than Ronald Reagan and Jerry Brown. Reagan was a traditional Republican who delegated extraordinary powers to his staff and appointees. Jerry Brown was an eclectic thinker and a Democrat who delegated reluctantly, and often not at all. One sought to minimize the role of government in society, while the other sought to improve social arrangements. In previous chapters we have mainly emphasized the considerable similarities of their administrations, such as their organization and use of subordinates. These similarities, of course, had little to do with Reagan and Brown as individuals, and were the result of the like structures they worked within.

Despite the considerable organizational pressures that limited their administrative choices and activities, Reagan and Brown did manipulate in different ways the roles of their staffs, appointees, and CEAs, as we described. Although constrained, each managed to push their subordinates in this direction or that, emphasizing one aspect of a role rather than another. These manipulations—management strategies, if you will—were not at all idiosyncratic in either instance. Rather, they were logical consequences of the governors' larger visions of the function of government in society and, more importantly here, the role of the governor in securing those visions. Reagan and Brown each had explicit, and very different, views of how government should run and the role of the governor in running it.

In this chapter we shall describe how two governors with markedly dissimilar orientations, but faced with the same organizational structure, tried to take hold of the government. This is not a political analysis, rather an analysis of the difference that management style makes given a particular organizational arrangement. Because their management styles derived in large part from their philosophical stances, we shall describe briefly the ideas that each held about the proper function of government in society. We shall show how each operationalized those ideas as management practices, and, finally, describe the consequences of those practices for the outcome of political activity in this country today.

THE ROLE OF THE GOVERNOR

Reagan and Brown, no less than any of their subordinates, had both the powers and limitations of their own roles as governor to work within, and like other government positions, the role of the governor had changed over time. For example, the years between the Progressive era and World War II marked what Larry Sabato described as the "modern decline of the governorship" in this country.[1] During that period, the establishment of the federal income tax and New Deal programs ballooned federal influence relative to that of the states: Governors, including California's, were not terribly important and contented themselves largely with partisan political functions and routine administration.

In Governor Earl Warren's administration (1943–53) state government became active again. Warren had a wartime surplus to spend, and the federal government began delegating programs and monies to the states. According to J. Oliver Williams, during the postwar period governors became the "federal systems officers" at the state level, because of huge amounts of money funneled through revenue-sharing programs.[2] In the 1950s and early 1960s state expenditures went to large-scale economic development and public works projects, and later, Great Society social programs. In eight years, Governor Pat Brown presided over the construction of 1,000 of California's then 1,650 miles of freeway, three new University of California campuses, six state colleges, and a $1.75 billion flood control project.[3]

The growth of state government, in both size and importance, continued during the Reagan and Brown, Jr. administrations. By the time Reagan assumed office in 1967 the executive organization had 115,000 employees and a budget in excess of $13.3 billion. It was a massive enterprise that demanded considerable management attention. In addition, by the fact of its large size and financial resources, state government had acquired the potential to greatly influence California as a society—to attract industries, to fund research, to educate, to clean up pollution. The governor's position during the Reagan and Brown, Jr. years combined both great executive powers and the capability of directing the state's influence toward public concerns. On assuming office, Reagan clearly emphasized the management functions of the governorship, and Brown, with equal fervor, the substantive issue-oriented aspects of gubernatorial power. In emphasizing one aspect of the gubernatorial role so decidedly, each was clearly hampered, in part by intent, from effectively performing the other.

GOVERNOR REAGAN

Philosophy

Pat Brown, Reagan's gubernatorial predecessor, was a proponent of President Lyndon B. Johnson's Great Society.[4] Brown was mindful of the power of government to intervene in the lives of citizens and believed strongly that that power should be used compassionately to resolve social inequities and to be a force for the good. Personally, Brown was an old-fashioned politician. He shook hands, kissed babies, and was in the center of a well-established party network.

In contrast, Reagan was a new-style media politician more aloof from voters and with a clearly different view of government. First, he believed that the large government California had developed was neither healthy nor efficient. In his view, social programs undermine individual initiative to frightening effect; he felt that a sound society depends on the cumulative acts of individuals pursuing self-interest. Reagan thought it arrogant that bureaucratic officials ("planners") claimed to know better than citizens how to manage society. He told a campaign audience that "the people themselves have the strength and the ability to solve the problems that confront us," and did not need government officials meddling in their affairs or pocketbooks.[5]

More specifically, Reagan believed that the free enterprise system and business concerns should provide services and jobs in the state, whenever possible. He saw large government organization as inefficient, "bloated," and unable to perform as well or as cheaply as the private sector. His intention as governor was to encourage business to take over as many social functions as possible, by curtailing government encroachments and by providing a healthy climate for private enterprise in California.

Finally, he believed that what government the state did require should be run efficiently and in a businesslike manner. He saw no reason that government agencies could not apply the techniques of corporations to their activities and he wanted to infuse private sector thinking into government operations. For example, he spoke of inviting a group of California hotel managers to inspect the state's hospitals and mental institutions, whose housekeeping functions he thought to have much in common with hotel operations.

Reagan's philosophy stressed individualism, free enterprise, and a limited and businesslike government. It was a simple, straightforward set of ideas, and in fact, was reducible to one page. Early in his administration Reagan aides circulated a single sheet to his appointees expressing the Governor's philosophy, a credo he followed closely during both of his terms. This was not a list of platitudes for public circulation, rather a document distributed to members of the administration for their guidance in daily decision making.

Governor's Philosophy[6]
—Keep the size and cost of government as small as possible.
—Solve problems and perform governmental functions at the lowest possible level.
—Avoid the creation of additional layers of government.
—Government should not perform a function which can be effectively performed by the private sector.
—Promote innovative and creative approaches to governmental programs.

—Utilize the skills and experience of the private sector in carrying out governmental programs.

—Federal government should communicate and administer its programs though the state government to local governments.

—Government exists to protect us from each other. No government on earth can possibly afford to protect us from ourselves.

More than anything, this philosophy expressed a belief in the importance and possibilities of good management. It contained not a single substantive idea or program intention; the only reference to ideas ("Promote innovative and creative approaches to government programs") spoke to the process, not the substance, of innovation. Reagan, despite what has often been portrayed as his conservative ideology, was wedded to a belief in good management, not to a belief in a set of specific ideas. Good management practice and the analytic techniques it represented constituted his response to the issues of the day, not party doctrine.[7] A *Christian Science Monitor* reporter wrote that "It is never hard to see his philosophy. He speaks of it daily. He measures everything against his bent toward economy in government, cutting costs, getting government out of people's social and economic lives wherever possible. He is not, therefore, a pusher of new programs."[8]

This is not to suggest, of course, that Reagan's concern with management did not have political consequences. Reagan routinely subjected political interests and social concerns to the "neutral" processes of policy evaluation and cost-benefit analysis to come up with the "best" courses of action. That some interests are irreconcilable, that some risks are never worth potential benefits, and that some persons will benefit while some suffer, are consequences often obscured by a management approach to government.

Management Practices[9]

Despite Reagan's philosophical support of businesslike government during his first gubernatorial campaign, in fact, he had almost no experience as a manager. He was a talented spokesman and a persuasive campaigner, but he had never run a substantial organization, including his own campaign. One of the managers of his campaign thought at the time that Reagan was running for office because he thought it important to express his philosophy, "But I really think he didn't have the slightest idea what the governor did."

Reagan's response to his election and the awesome management task ahead was to structure an executive organization and management style that did not depend on his active management of daily affairs. After a difficult beginning, he established management practices that enabled an inexperienced executive to run a large organization effectively and to run it in a way consonant with his philosophy. Three sets of practices were the most distinctive attributes of Reagan management: an administratively powerful chief of staff, a strong cabinet, and a routinized decision-making system. Reagan, although never active in the day-to-day management of staff or program activities, played an important role in maintaining his administration's adherence to his fundamental principles of government, and in gaining support for the activities of his appointees.

Staff Organization: Reagan's role during his campaign was to be the candidate and not run the campaign, according to one of his aides. Reagan, a political neophyte, relied totally on his campaign staff and paid political advisors to plan strategy, to schedule appearances, to write speeches, and to organize publicity. "[Reagan] was doing what he does best, which was going out and convincing the masses he ought to be governor," his campaign press secretary recalled.

After the election, Reagan continued to delegate most functions to aides, including the staffing of his administration. Those members of the campaign who were interested in going to Sacramento lobbied among themselves for positions in the Governor's Office. The first appointments secretary said that, with the exception of two appointments to the State Barber's Board, Reagan had no personal choices for administrative or staff positions. Although Reagan was consulted and eventually approved the choices, for the most part the top campaign staff filled the positions in the Governor's Office in ways that they decided. Phillip Battaglia, chairman of Reagan's Southern California campaign organization, the most powerful campaign position, became chief of staff and continued to control many of Reagan's activities as he had during the campaign. Battaglia insisted that only he or the press secretary speak to reporters, and that all staff people wanting to see the Governor see Battaglia first. In addition, he incapacitated members of the staff by not sharing information with them. "[He had] a style of secrecy and lack of openness. We would sometimes read about things for the first time in the *Sacramento Bee*," said one staff member. In addition, Battaglia made many decisions that others felt only the Governor should make. "[The chief of staff and his supporters] were concluding that they were the governor and they were beginning to use the powers of the governor far more than I thought they ought to," said one person who was on the staff at the time. In fact, according to another aide, some documents that had the chief of staff's signature had to be returned for the governor's signature in order to make them legally binding.

During the first few months the staff organization was characterized by factionalism—Battaglia and his supporters from the Southern campaign organization, versus the larger staff—and by highly politicized decision making. Battaglia, who everyone agreed was a brilliant political strategist, made decisions according to their political and not managerial impact. The result was administrative chaos, an atmosphere of tension, and the isolation of Reagan.

Only a few months into the administration, however, Battaglia allegedly became involved in scandalous personal activity. Other members of the staff notified Reagan, who immediately decided that Battalia had to leave his administration. In retrospect, several people said that the fear of scandal merely provided an excuse for ending a poor organizational situation. "The whole issue of the 'Scandal of the Summer of 67' was just the lever to get a bunch of bad guys out of there."

Reagan immediately appointed William P. Clark to succeed Battaglia. Clark, at that time, was Cabinet Secretary, a position that included preparing the agenda for the cabinet and organizing the information on decisions pending before the cabinet officers. Battaglia had frequently boycotted the cabinet meetings, thereby undermining their effectiveness early in the administration, but with Clark's appointment as chief of staff, the cabinet became an important part of the Reagan administration, which we discuss in the next section. In addition, Clark changed the role of the chief of staff and the character of the staff organization. Although Clark had participated in the campaign, he was more interested in administration than politics. One staff member described Clark as the "perfect" choice for chief of staff, "He has a judicial temperament; he's disinterested. He didn't like the legislative-political goings on." Indeed, Clark and his successor as chief of staff, Edwin Meese, III,[10] delegated the partisan political functions of the Governor's Office to the man who was the assistant to both of them, Michael Deaver. Political activity thereby became subordinate to administrative activity, and remained that way for the rest of the administration. According to Clark, he even assumed the role of devil's advocate when it came to discussing the Governor's political life. "Nancy Reagan and I were the only two opposed to the '68 run for the presidency," Clark said.

After Clark's appointment as chief of staff, politics gave way to administration in the Governor's Office, the cabinet became more important, and the staff organization became less tense and more routine.[11] Clark formalized some of the staff assignments that had been evolving, changed some others to reflect what he saw as more logical functional divisions, and created a more hierarchically arranged staff. Some persons became senior staff and reported to him; the rest reported through the senior staff members. The Governor's Office acquired a business-as-usual atmosphere and, as one person put it, "Clark settled the staff down."

Clark and Meese guided the staff toward performing what several persons called "housekeeping" functions. The staff did many of the tasks performed by Pat Brown's staff, such as legislative analysis and monitoring of the administration's bills, appointments to political offices and boards, press relations, liaison with local governments, as well as handling the governor's correspondence and schedule. However, unlike Pat Brown's staff, or the famous Nixon staff of advisors, Reagan's personal aides did not have a routine role in governmental policy making or in making program decisions. The cabinet (of whom the chief of staff was a member) was the locus of decision making, not the personal staff.

When Meese took over from Clark after about two years, the staff was generally agreed to be a smoothly operating group. Meese made a few changes, mostly to formalize and systematize further the Governor's Office. [12] For example, he reduced the senior staff to four persons, and prepared careful descriptions of each person's responsibilities to avoid overlapping assignments. Concerned with keeping everyone well-informed, he instituted more meetings for both the staff and cabinet, "So everybody knew what everybody was doing. There weren't these mysteries and rumors that usually give rise to power struggles. We had a lot of open decision making to avoid having people see who could buttonhole the Governor last," said Meese. When meetings became too routine or stale, Meese changed their frequency or place or time. During the six years he was Executive Secretary, the staff became increasingly formalized and routinized as arrangements and processes were tested for their efficacy.

Meese was fascinated by organization and admitted that he enjoyed fine-tuning the administration. One of the staff, who shared Meese's interest in management theory, recalled that they would spend hours debating such things as whether the Army's general staff system was superior to the Navy's chain of command system. "He's a management buff; it's his hobby. The size and shape of organizations, and who has what mission . . . he talked about it so much that he turned people off. Deaver would walk in and listen and he'd walk right out because it bored him stiff." Meese used this knowledge of organizations to define the staff's role in such way that it made a distinctive contribution to the Governor's command, and so that it avoided overlap with the cabinet. It had a clear and separate place in the administration, and individual staff members had clear and separate assignments within the staff organization.

The quiet hum of the staff organization was interrupted after Reagan's election to a second term. During the campaign Meese and most of the staff stayed in Sacramento to run what they called the "governmental" activities, while Reagan's political advisors ran the campaign. By then, most of the staff were attuned to the emphasis on management process. Those who were ideologically oriented, who saw ideas as the governor's most important mission and not management, had either left government or were grouped in the Office of Program Development (OPD). OPD was a think-tank that tried to figure ways to put conservative principles into practice. Although nominally part of the Governor's Office, OPD was not in the Capitol and was not part of daily staff affairs.[13]

When the campaign was over the political advisors confronted Reagan with what they saw as necessary changes in the staff. They felt that they had worked hard to put Reagan into office and Republican principles into practice, only to see them watered down and subject to management considerations in the Governor's office. One of these political aides said, "There were those who really were concerned with how you operate the store day-to-day, and there were those [of us] who thought 'Now, why was it we fought this election, and what is it we wanted to change?' "

The ensuing confrontation was a clear victory for Meese. Reagan opted for a statesmanlike position and careful management practice, rather than a strong ideological position. The Office of Program Development was disbanded and the staff became even more systematic and concerned with management procedure in the second term.

All of Reagan's chiefs of staff were strong figures. Battaglia was powerful because he closed off access to the Governor and usurped decision making. Clark, and especially Meese, were powerful because they controlled the organization, not because they controlled Reagan. Although Reagan's time was carefully scheduled by them, staff members and appointees who wanted to see Reagan could do so, if necessary. Cabinet officers had access to Reagan twice a week at cabinet meetings and were always encouraged to express their opinions there. But Reagan liked the structured interaction that was fostered by Clark's and Meese's arrangements and always deferred to it. He encouraged people to use the formal communication channels that were established and maintained by his chiefs of staff, and he almost never went outside them himself. He gently turned people toward procedures when they tried to gain advantage with him outside the routine. One staff person said that if he tried to get a decision directly from the Governor, Reagan would say, "Have you talked to Meese?"

Cabinet Government: Reagan had campaigned on his intention to bring businesslike practices to government and he established two groups in order to make good on that promise. One was the Businessmen's Task Force, and the other was the Weinberger Commission.

During the transition period after the election, Reagan gave speeches to members of the business community soliciting their support. He told them to put their checkbooks away but to offer their time, or the time of their employees. In this manner Reagan had the efforts of about 200 largely young executives donated to the state for six months. They were organized into teams coordinated by an accounting firm executive, and sent into the major units of government. "They were told not to go in and make recommendations on issues, or on what should be abolished or retained," said Meese. Rather, they were to look at procedural matters, "how you could do better with what government was already doing." The Businessmen's Task Force made some 1,700 recommendations, more than half of which were actually adopted by the Reagan administration.

The second group, called the Weinberger Commission, was a committee chaired by Casper Weinberger during the weeks after the election to look into the alternative forms of executive organization. Weinberger was a former state legislator and party official, and was familiar with California government. The other important member of the commission was William P. Clark, later to become the first Cabinet Secretary and second chief of staff. At the time, however, he was a Southern California lawyer and a Republican county chairman who was not interested in government service. He saw this commission as a limited commitment.

The formal structure of the Executive Branch had changed considerably under Pat Brown. When Brown took office in 1959 there were 24 departments and 50 independent agencies.[14] In an attempt to assert control over all of these units Brown reorganized them into eight functionally related groups called Agencies and appointed agency secretaries to manage them. These secretaries formed the cabinet and reported to the governor.

The Weinberger Commission concluded that the Agency Plan had never worked as well as intended, largely because the roles of the agency secretaries were not sufficiently well defined relative to the department directors that reported to them. In the free-wheeling Brown, Sr. administration agency heads had become involved in the daily administration of departments and from the Reagan administration's structured view, "it was really kind of a mess." Weinberger's recommendation was to reduce the number of agency secretaries to four and to carve out a distinct role for them in government. Halving the number of agency secretaries made it impossible for any of them to become involved in the affairs of the as many as fifteen departments they coordinated. The theory was that "If you had fewer of them they would necessarily become generals," limited to overseeing and policy making, according to one Reagan aide. Reagan accepted these recommendations and appointed four agency heads, Secretaries for Agriculture and Services, Business and Transportation, Resources, and Human Relations. These officials were to serve much like group vice-presidents in industry. In addition, Reagan's cabinet included the Director of Finance, analogous to a chief financial officer, and the Executive Secretary (chief of staff), who was to be much like an executive vice-president.

Those present at the beginning of the administration recalled that the cabinet system took several months to start working well. It took a while for everyone concerned to learn their roles and the way in which government operated, and in the first months the politicized and powerful chief of staff threatened the cabinet's strength. But with Clark's ascendancy to the chief of staff position he was able to move the cabinet into the role envisioned by he and Weinberger. In addition, in less than a year Reagan replaced his first director of Finance, who, although he had financial consulting experience, proved to be incapable of managing the huge Department of Finance. Reagan appointed Weinberger to the position, helping to assure that the cabinet would operate as the envisioned deliberative body.

Mini-memo Decision Making: Although Pat Brown had created the agency system, he did not use the cabinet of agency secretaries as a formal decision-making unit. Instead, he tended to rely on trusted aides to help him decide issues. In the Reagan administration, however, the cabinet was the focal point of decision making. This, like almost every other aspect of Reagan's management, was a consciously constructed and nurtured arrangement. While some members of the Weinberger Commission were assigned to look at formal structures for the state government, Clark's mission had been to consider alternative management styles. He looked to recent presidencies for examples. "I was impressed by the LBJ style of 'total cabinet,' in contrast to the Eisenhower, Nixon, Kennedy style of dealing with advisors. Johnson liked filling up a room with people," said Clark. Reagan endorsed the idea of making decisions with a cabinet because it was similar to a corporate board of directors, an arrangement in line with his philosophy. It allowed him to get routinely the advice of the prominent businessmen he had appointed, and it minimized his own lack of management experience. He was part of the deliberations, without having to have them depend on him.

Important issues that originated in any corner of the government were brought to the attention of the cabinet in the form of "mini-memos." Mini-memos were single-page briefs that summarized the issue under discussion, described the alternative possible actions and their probable consequences, and made a recommendation. They were rigorously limited to one page, but frequently all sorts of material was added as addenda. One department director recalled how the mini-memo system worked. "You read up on the subject, and you write up the thing. You recommend to the governor that he do this, this, and this, and you sign it. Then you send it to the agency secretary. He puts his signature next to yours either to disapprove, or approve, or neutral. If he disapproves or is neutral, you better talk to him because he's not going to support you in the cabinet. After the cabinet meeting, it comes back to you signed 'Ronald Reagan or Ed Meese—approved by the cabinet, such and such a date.' Or it will come back, 'More study needed in this area.' "

Mini-memos to be considered at one of the twice-weekly cabinet meetings had to be in the Governor's Office at least two days in advance so that they could be duplicated and circulated to cabinet officers and to top staff members, who typically attended the meetings as observers and commentators. The Cabinet Secretary scheduled the issues for the agenda, and at the meeting the interested cabinet officer presented his issues. Reagan invariably attended cabinet meetings when he was in town, but the chief of staff conducted the sessions. They were formal, "businesslike" sessions that began and ended on schedule, but questions and debate were encouraged. All cabinet officers were expected to study the issues and to participate in discussions even if the issue was not in their area of expertise. One cabinet officer said, "I spent a huge amount of time walking back and forth to these cabinet meetings and of course sometimes I'd have two or three issues, sometimes none. Then you'd sit there for a couple of hours listening to stuff that you really weren't interested in." The advantage to this time-consuming system, according to this and the other cabinet officers, was that "our opinion was asked. It gave us a very good team feeling."

Although there was extensive debate on issues in the cabinet meeting, those meetings were the only forum for debate. If there was consensus on an issue the chief of staff would summarize the discussion for the minutes, and Reagan typically would concur. If there was no clear agreement the chief of staff would summarize the positions and Reagan would either express his opinion then, or, occasionally, announce the decision at some later time. But no matter how vigorous or heated the issue, the cabinet meeting was the only place that Reagan would hear arguments. He expected his cabinet officers to bring the issues to the meetings, debate them there in public, and then support the group's decision once made. According to one cabinet officer, Reagan "ratified" their decisions. He avoided making decisions behind closed doors and expected his cabinet not to supplicate him in private. Reagan believed in teamwork and expected it of his appointees and himself.

Mini-memos were more than a way of informing the cabinet. They were a vehicle for systematizing information flows up and down the bureaucracy, for defining issues as decision choices, and for assuring that research had been carefully and thoroughly performed before an issue reached the cabinet. The mini-memo system, although a procedural device, was also a way of establishing the norms of participation. It "neutrally" allowed some people to enter into decision making and not others, and it limited the forms of participation.[15] But it was a public system whose rules were known to all, and it was adhered to almost without exception.[16]

Advantages of Reagan's Management Practices

This formal, highly systematic use of subordinates had several important consequences for the outcome of Reagan's administration. For the most part, but not entirely, this system worked well and to Reagan's advantage.

Reagan came to office with considerable personal skills that were useful to him in government. He was comfortable with the media and was a highly effective speaker. He was personally warm and appreciative of the people who worked for him. For example, he always gave presents to the clerical aides in the governor's office at Christmas. He encouraged and usually attended the frequent birthday parties staff members had in the office, even though Meese found them disruptive. Reagan was witty and known for his apt use of jokes in awkward situations, particularly in press briefings. "He had more jokes than any human being I've ever known," said one aide. Reagan also acted like a governor. Although friendly, Reagan was never intimate with his aides and maintained a statesmanlike bearing. He used the pomp of his office effectively—his limousine, the Governor's mansion, formal receptions—all contributed to the feeling among subordinates that he had assumed the office well and was a legitimate bearer of power.[17] He looked, he sounded, and he acted like a leader.

Some of his traits were liabilities, however. For example, Reagan disliked and avoided performing some necessary management functions, notable firing and disciplining personnel, and dealing with conflict. One person said that if the gardener was to be fired, Nancy Reagan had to do it, because Reagan could not. The establishment of a strong chief of staff and cabinet government enabled him to avoid these tasks, though. The chiefs of staff did most of the distasteful personnel work. Clark said he became "the bad guy," because Reagan "was not a shaker." Reagan also disliked managing disputes among subordinates. "He didn't like any aspect of politics—either in the purest sense, or internal politics—and he wanted that handled by somebody else," according to one of his staff. "It was handled universally in the Reagan administration by Battaglia, Clark, and Meese."

The strong chief of staff and the well-organized staff system also allowed an inexperienced manager to function without impairing bureaucratic routines. One of his top staff said, "His experience in management techniques just doesn't exist. And it didn't have to."[18] The structure kept everything orderly and Reagan relied heavily on it. Likewise, he always obeyed the routines he established. Even as the administration moved into its second term, and Reagan did gain experience, he chose to remain a delegator who relied on formal organizational processes rather than his person, to control activity. It should be emphasized, however, that the staff structure was primarily administrative, and not political, in the ways that Nixon's or Kennedy's staffs were political. Reagan was never isolated by his staff, but he used and hid behind its formalities whenever he found it useful or to his liking.

The cabinet structure also had several important advantages for Reagan. By making the cabinet a true decision-making forum, and the *only* forum, Reagan pushed his administrators toward consensus management. Cabinet officers had to come to agreement in cabinet meetings because they had no alternative; Reagan refused to decide issues alone or to adjudicate disputes. Because personal pleas were useless, cabinet officers tried, though not always with success, to minimize their differences in order to get things done. The public nature of the cabinet meetings and the use of mini-memos tended to keep what conflict arose at the level of issues, rather than personalities. Not incidentally, consensus management had political advantages. The Reagan administration maintained a unified front before the public and before legislators.

Second, by delegating decision making to the cabinet, Reagan's inexperience became less of a liability. In cabinet meetings his role was to establish philosophical standards and to ask questions, but his experienced cabinet officers for the most part came up with answers to the state's problems. One Reagan aide said, "Reagan developed a very firm philosophical framework. . . . He doesn't care so much about the nuts and bolts. So the cabinet was a very good vehicle for his style."

Third, because cabinet officers were indeed decision makers and were widely known as such within government, they were powerful managers of the departments below them. The agencies, which were relatively weak in the preceding administration, became a powerful management level. Department directors could not hope to end-run cabinet officers with any success; the system forced them to abide by the decisions of the agency secretaries. In this way, Reagan's delegation of power became centralized in the cabinet where he could oversee it.

The Liabilities of a Routine

This formal, rigid system was not without its shortcomings, however. The reliance on routine, while it was remarkably efficient in disposing of issues, limited Reagan's personal capacity to exercise power, posed a threat to innovation and ideas, and actually contributed to government's capacity to deal with social problems, something Reagan opposed.

The decision-making process reduced often complex issues to a brief written form. Although substantial research was done on issues as they moved up the hierarchy, Reagan only became involved in issues at the last moment when a decision was about to be made. "He knew what was written down," a staff member said, but the material he diligently read was a highly refined product that had already cast recommendations and problems in a particular way.

Also, because Reagan so faithfully followed the routines and norms of teamwork that he established, he limited his own ability to act unilaterally and to wield fully the powers of his role. One of his top Finance Department aides described how Reagan's regular acceptance of staffwork limited Reagan's ability to do what he wanted personally. "When the bills were finished [being discussed] in cabinet they were bundled in boxes. This box said 'Vetoes,' and this box said 'Sign' [and] the Governor would sign. Occasionally he didn't like them because he was not an unintelligent man—he was a very intelligent person. He was trying to respect the organizational structure and the responsibility and authority he had given to to his agency secretaries to run their shows the way they thought proper. He stuck by his own delegation unless he thought it was extremely bad. I don't know, I think occasionally he may have reversed things just to keep reminding them that he was Governor." Reagan sacrificed his unilateral use of power for the good of the team, and he expected his subordinates to do the same.

As individuals, there is no doubt that cabinet officers had little choice but to submit to the cabinet important programs and legislative decisions. Failure to do so would have been seen as disloyal and would have undermined one's power. However, there is evidence that *as a group* Reagan's cabinet members strengthened their powers relative to the governor. Reagan's insistence on teamwork and consensus led them to deliberate, as a group, outside of the formal meetings where the governor was present. The cabinet routinely met for breakfast before cabinet meetings to exchange views and to work out what they saw as differences among them. One chief of staff recalled, "I remember one day that we got together intially at six o'clock (in the morning) because we had to have a pre-meeting before the meeting at seven o'clock, in order to be ready for the cabinet meeting at eight o'clock, and by nine o'clock we had the thing solved."

Although Reagan knew about the breakfast meetings he did not attend them and could not hear the cabinet officers' debates. The cabinet members worked out their differences alone and, whenever possible, presented him with a *fait accompli* to be ratified. This suited his desire for consensus and preserved him from conflict, which he found distasteful. But it strengthened the position of the cabinet who knew that Reagan rarely turned down a decision they all supported.

Top staff also met regularly without the Governor, usually after Reagan left in the evening. One person characterized this meeting as a chance to compare notes and to resolve issues. "Each of us would discuss whatever particular problems we had had that day. And whatever that problem was would be discussed by all these senior advisors and then if there was anything important enough to go to the Governor, then the Executive Secretary would meet with the Governor following that meeting. The Governor rarely ever came into that meeting."

Because Reagan had so straightforward and consistent a philosophy, and the decision-making procedures became so routinized, staff aides began to make decisions themselves, confident of their approval by Reagan. One staff aide gave an example of a decision that the staff made without the Governor's knowledge. "We instituted, for the first time in the history of California, regulation of insurance agents' fee commissions under Ronald Reagan and he never knew a thing about it. The guy who had been responsible for it said, 'I know his philosophy; that's against Ronald Reagan's philosophy, but there are times where you have to overcome philosophy.' In that case Ronald Reagan never knew what had happened. And had he heard about it, he would have come unglued. But at the end [of the administration] it was, 'Let's work everything out before it gets to Ronald Reagan.' "

Although the cabinet and the staff both apparently appropriated Reagan's powers to decide (not necessarily without his approval), the cabinet was more successful in doing so routinely. The cabinet had an arena in which to air differences, one which encouraged them to bridge differences. The staff had no such device and had to work out conflict informally among themselves, aware that Reagan never would. This was not always possible, and in the case of the ideologues in the Office of Program Development versus the managerially minded supporters of Meese, the only choice was the disbandment of OPD and resignation for several of its members.

The second limitation of Reagan's routinized management style was its failure to generate ideas or to foster innovation.[19] Ideas were not central to Reagan's philosophy of limited, efficient government and when strong ideas were introduced they often fell prey to the system. New ways of doing things and new programs had to be massaged into form by the decision-making procedures, and they had to stand up to the rigors of the mini-memo process. Someone could not just come up with an idea and test it out; it had to be subjected to research and to the comments of the cabinet and the senior staff who sat around the edge of the room and made observations. While this did not allow frivolous or half-baked ideas to come to fruition, it also meant the death of unproved but potentially sound ideas. It was also frustrating to people who had come to government hoping to put their ideas into practice. One cabinet officer who worked on a massive and lengthy welfare reform program saw what he believed to be important reforms subject to unnecessary analyses and considerations. "There were simply too many technicians and too many policy guides."

Because the Reagan administration was not founded on a strong set of substantive ideas, thinking up ideas actually had to be construed as an organizational function and to be assigned to a particular group. OPD, whose job it was to generate conservative ideas that could be put into practice, was *too* ideological and was finally disbanded, as we described earlier. Part-way through the second term, a year after OPD was gone, the top members of the administration decided that they needed to come up with ideas to focus the remaining years in office so as to avoid a lame duck administration. The entire top level of government, the cabinet and the staff, went off to the board room of a Sacramento bank for a brainstorming session the day after Thanksgiving in 1971. "We were concerned that if we didn't continue to stimulate the administration, we would let people get into a rut," said one of the participants. Interstingly, Reagan did not attend the meeting where the agenda for his remaining three years in office was hammered out.

Task forces were also an important producer of ideas in the Reagan administration.[20] A group of experts, often from both the government and industry, would be assembled to examine major problem areas of government and to offer recommendations. They functioned much like presidential commissions and were instrumental in making sweeping recommendations for change in the areas of health and welfare. But task forces, effective as they were, focused on how to fix problems, not on challenging the basic arrangements or premises of government. They were reform devices, not agents of a conservative revolution.

A final, ironic consequence of the structured Reagan administration was that it worked well to systematize government. Many of the management reforms and experienced executives that the Reagan administration brought to Sacramento in fact made government run better and deliver services more effectively. While the budget more than doubled from $4.6 billion to $10.2 billion, in large part due to inflation, the number of state workers did not grow appreciably. But neither did California government shrink and allow private citizens to handle their own affairs. Instead, government entrenched itself in many ways as a strong, effective force in California society.

GOVERNOR BROWN

Philosophy

Where Pat Brown had a New Deal belief in the efficacy of government to cure the problems of California, Reagan feared the power of big government to undermine social relations. Jerry Brown, in contrast to both of them, was not convinced that government had the magnitude of power that his father approved, and that Reagan disliked. A frequent theme in interviews with Brown was his belief that much government action was ceremonial or insignificant, given the truly important issues of the day. For example, when running for governor he told an *L.A. Times* reporter, "I've been in government all my life and I'm not bemused by it. I read *Commentary* and *The Public Interest* and, like them, I take a somewhat jaundiced view of the ability of government to perform."[21] Two years later, when he was governor, he said, "I think it's important to realize that you don't just change the world with a new tax or a new bill or a new regulation. . . . Holding out the promise that a bill with a few million dollars, or a few hundred million dollars, is going to profoundly alter family structure, the relationship of various groups in the society, is not just true."[22]

Although not impressed by the administrative possibilities of government activity, Brown believed government office to be an important forum for articulating ideas, and thought that political organization could be a useful incubator for innovation and social change. "That's the most important part of the political process—placing ideas in the public domain. I see my role as identifying ideas that are on the margin and bringing them into the mainstream in a way that people can grapple with. . . . The persuasive power of government is the power of ideas to influence the culture, influence the thinking, which then will shape the response that society makes to external and internal challenge."[23]

Both Reagan and Brown saw government primarily as a process, rather than a set of programs.[24] Reagan, however, believed the significant process to be managerial, while Brown saw it to be in the generation and testing of ideas. Brown's belief in government as a cultural force led him beyond the narrow special interest concerns of traditional politics. Brown tried seriously to divine such diverse things as the proper role of technology in an environmentally sensitive world and the proper place of art in society. Brown worked hard to foster relations with the Mexican governor of Baja California, seeing the regional interests of the two states surpassing political bounds. He was interested in the exploration of space, not just because it was good for the California high-technology industry, but because it promised new possibilities for human endeavor. Brown's sponsorship of such media events as "Space Day"[25] and "Whale Day," were dismissed by critics as mere symbolism, but Brown took symbols seriously and believed that government could use them to focus attention. Brown used state government as a forum and test site for a wide-ranging agenda of cultural propositions.

Accordingly, Brown's philosophy was as difficult to discern as Reagan's was simple. Its substance was highly eclectic and borrowed heavily from *Small Is Beautiful* economist E.F. Schumaker, as well as assorted eastern and western religious and social thinkers, including St. Ignatious Loyola and Zen teacher Suzuki-roshi.[26] Brown's education in a Jesuit seminary gave him contact with an unusually broad spectrum of philosophies, which he used to test the received wisdom of mainstream politics. Although reducing Brown's interests to a coherent philosophy is elusive, he consistently sought new answers to the increasing tension between the environment and an advanced industrial society. He supported environmentally sensitive solutions to such mundane problems as sewage treatment, and was a continuing and vocal critic of nuclear energy. Brown believed people do best in small-scale social organizations where they can experience psychological and physical security. Although he opposed the death penalty, he was extremely tough on crime; his measures doubled the number of incarcerated felons, overcrowding California's prison system. He believed, too, that citizens should find government approachable and that government should reflect the composition of the citizenry. He carried out this last conviction through his political appointments.[27] "Without a doubt, the biggest change Brown brought to California government was an end to white male domination of virtually all positions of power. Of 5,680 appointments made by the governor through mid-April [1982], 1,367 were to women, 412 to blacks, 517 to Chicanos, 255 to Asians, and 44 to Native Americans."[28] Although some were not experienced managers, their appointments made a statement Brown felt it important to make, as several people said. Unusual for a Democrat, Brown was a fiscal conservative who "out-Reaganed Reagan,"[29] perhaps because of his belief in the limited possibilities of government to solve problems.

Brown's image among some of his detractors as capricious and irresponsible fails to credit him with looking beyond simple solutions

to complex problems, or for the personal energy Brown put into issues he thought important. His failure to articulate his concerns through
the existing structure of government was *deliberate,* and while philosophically consistent with his activist beliefs, assured that many of his
intriguing ideas would never find a lasting place in government.

Management Practices

Brown's philosophy did not fall within the confines of party politics
or any other ideology; it was a highly personal working out of ideas
and an unfinished product. His view of government organization flowed
from this: he saw the executive branch, more than anything else, as
a support for his highly personalized probing, and as a showcase for
innovation. Because these functions defied systematization, his use of
subordinates was as untraditional as Reagan's was stereotyped.

Personalized Decision Making: The day after Brown was elected
governor, he appointed two people to his staff, Gray Davis, who became the first chief of staff, and Anthony Kline, who for six years was
his legal affairs secretary. In chapter 1 we described Kline's recollec-
tion of a briefing by Meese during the transition period, and how ill-
suited the formal Reagan arrangements were for Brown's purposes.
Because Brown was interested in how his subordinates could help *him*
debate issues, he studiously avoided creating routines that would constrain his prerogatives.

Indeed, Brown's first management effort on assuming office was
wildly unorganized. Soon after the inauguration Brown called "cabinet" meetings that his top staff and cabinet officers would attend in
the evenings. As many as twenty people would sit around the room
from seven in the evening until two or three o'clock in the morning
debating ideas, "Then there would be a post mortem after that." According to one cabinet officer, "They were really policy-forming sessions. We'd take an issue—it didn't matter if it was a big issue or a
small issue—and [Brown] would spend hours on it and everybody would
express their opinion and argue about it." The meetings did not have
formal agendas, and did not produce decisions, but served to bring
attention to issues that people thought important. "There were a broad

range of brilliant discussions, they were some of the best discussions in the world." These meetings were conducted nightly for weeks and described by participants as "ordeals." Eventually they were ended at midnight, and then held only two or three nights a week. After about six months they stopped completely, later to be revived as monthly luncheon meetings for the few cabinet officers.

Although the meetings were not designed to make decisions, participants found them useful ways to learn how each other viewed issues, and to hear the governor's philosophy. Brown used them as a debating society that would poke holes in his thinking or lead him to view issues in ways he had not considered. While Reagan sat at his cabinet meetings watching from the sidelines, Brown was the center of the storm, pushing, probing, arguing, testing. More than anything, the meetings were stages for Brown.

Eventually, however, Brown found the meetings less useful and cabinet officers started to rebel; they were being pulled into the management demands of their agencies and did not want to spend hours in philosophical discussion. Brown increasingly turned to a more limited circle of top advisors on whom he relied to help him in his decision making. Mostly, but not entirely, they were members of his top staff. Brown, however, would bring in all sorts of people to his discussions when he felt they had a worthwhile opinion. Because Brown reasoned that ideas, not the maintenance of a systematic organization, was primary, he felt justified in ignoring bureaucratic protocol. For example, he frequently telephoned people at the lower levels of the bureaucracy to get information that had not been filtered up the hierarchy. One aide recalled a Saturday afternoon when they were debating the merits of a bill to subsidize home mortgages for low-income veterans. Brown telephoned the budget analyst working on the program to get his opinions. "He was out cutting the back lawn [when he was called to the phone]. This young man must have been all of 24, 25 years old, just starting out in the department and here he is confronted by the Governor, cold turkey." He and Brown debated over the phone, and then the Governor made up his mind.

Brown, particularly during his first term, did much of his own research. According to his staff, Brown distrusted the formalized memoranda on which Reagan relied. "That's not Jerry Brown's style at all, because I think he feels, perhaps correctly, that the governor then becomes dependent upon the quality of the information that he gets, indeed on the sensibilities and values of those close around him," said a close aide. Many of his appointees and staff characterized Brown as an extremely inquisitive person who took great intellectual pleasure in considering the ramifications of issues and programs. One gave as a humorous example Brown's research on a bill to allow the sale of green turtle meat in California. A state senator was supporting the legislation and there was no notable opposition to it. When the bill arrived on the Governor's desk for his signature, a staff member included a ten-year-old *National Geographic* article on green turtles in the bill's file. "The Governor saw it, and a little squib describing the author as the world's leading expert on green turtles. Turns out he was a professor emeritus at the University of Florida. The Governor spent about an hour on the phone with the professor on three different occasions. I would say that the professor's views were almost entirely responsible for the vetoing of the bill." According to the aide, the Governor's veto message, which he wrote himself (as he frequently did in his first term), was so well thought out that it was reproduced in its entirety on the editorial page of the *Los Angeles Times*. Although this was not a significant bill, Brown's research on it was typical of many other decisions that faced him.

Research, of course, was only part of the decision-making process. When a number of ideas had been proposed Brown liked to test them through argument. The function of his top advisors was to participate in this decision-making process with him by advancing new theories, arguing opposing viewpoints, and simply allowing the Governor to articulate his views before an audience. One of his appointees in the Department of Health said, "Even when he asks my advice on malpractice he argues with me. I was just part of his research." A Cabinet officer said, "He likes arguing. He likes you to tell him 'Jerry, that is a lot of bullshit, you don't want to do that,' or 'you don't understand that.' " Another person said that Brown was argumentative to provoke responses to his ideas in order to "test" them.

Another characteristic of Brown's management style was his willingness to let an issue reach a crisis point before making a decision. It frequently frustrated the staff who were left holding off legislators and interest groups, but Brown felt that it exposed hidden interests that came out at the last moment. Brown, unlike Reagan, did not mind conflict and felt it could be put to use in defining the best action.

Brown's cabinet members were often called into this decision-making process, but never as a body. "That's not to say that cabinet members didn't have strong voices," said one of them. "But as an entity, the cabinet in the Brown administration never decided anything." With time the demands of their agencies and departments pulled them into administrative matters, and they only saw the Governor when he called or when they needed his approval. One cabinet officer estimated that Brown attended only about one fourth of their monthly meetings.

The staff, aside from the few closest advisors, also established routines with time. Despite Brown's lack of interest in management, in fact there were many activities in the Governor's Office that needed to be managed: appointments, legislative analysis, clemency appeals, press relations, correspondence, and so forth. Many of these routine activities came to be the province of Brown's "second circle" of aides, people who reported to his top advisors and were not normally part of the Governor's deliberations.

Two other factors led to the increasing routinization of the Brown administration (although it never achieved the systematic character of the Reagan administration).[30] First, the nature of issues changed. When Brown first assumed office the state had a large surplus and a tax schedule that promised even more. Although financially conservative, Brown spent his first years in office confident that he could fund most any project he wanted; hence, the early preoccupation with debating alternatives for California. With the passage of Proposition 13 in 1978, however, taxes from real property declined dramatically.[31] The state began distributing funds to local governments to prevent the collapse of education systems and other vital services. Brown's second term in office was overwhelmingly concerned with financial matters and he fought desperately to hold off tax increases his last three years in office. Brown began to rely on people with traditional financial skills, and was forced into less esoteric concerns.

The other forces for routinization were Brown's second and third chiefs of staff. Gray Davis, the first chief of staff, was often described as much like Brown, an idea man first, and an administrator only reluctantly.[32] Where Clark and Meese had run the staff organization for Reagan, Davis acted more as a coordinator of the Brown staff. Davis's primary role was that of trusted advisor and, like Brown, he minimized the importance of memos and regular meetings. When Brown ran for a second term Davis left to run the campaign. Brown uncharacteristically appointed a businessman, Richard Silberman, to the chief of staff position. Silberman began instituting traditional management practices that many agreed made the office run more smoothly, and there was speculation as to whether or not Davis would return to his old position. The day after the election, however, Davis was back as chief of staff. Brown appointed Silberman as Director of Finance, certainly the most important appointive post after the passage of Proposition 13. Davis later left the administration to run for office, and B.T. Collins assumed the job for the last two years of Brown's term.

Collins, a Republican, was a surprising choice for the chief of staff post, but proved to be a perfect complement to the Governor. Collins was a former Green Beret and given to barking orders in a friendly way. He freely let loose obscenities in front of Brown, who was notoriously prudish. Collins was outgoing and warm, where Brown was uncomfortable with intimacies. Collins was eminently quotable and, despite one embarrassing interview with the *Los Angeles Times*, typically got good press for the Governor.[33] He was also skillful at wheedling support for the Governor's programs. But more importantly, Collins was happy to perform administrative work and see that the office ran efficiently; he was not an intellectual and did not care to debate ideas. He said to a *Wall Street Journal* reporter, "Everybody things Jerry Brown is a flake, but he's just so far ahead of his time. His mind is so full of ideas it's like a dump truck. So he handles the issues and I handle the people."[34]

Program Offices: Reagan's primary vehicle for making important changes in the state government was the task forces. Brown, however, encouraged the proliferation of small organizational units as a means for generating ideas and for nurturing them to fruition, as well as to give more than symbolic support for some of his propositions. Program offices attached to the Office of the Governor were staffed with exampt positions, just like the personal staff, and were typically filled by Brown with advocates and policy analysts. The Office of Planning and Research (OPR), which had never been important during the Reagan administration, became a center for special projects and studies, particularly those relating to the environment. OPR, which numbered about one hundred people, itself gave birth to other offices. The Office of Appropriate Technology, the brainchild of unconventional architect Sim Van der Ryn, promoted such ideas as building designs that used less energy, solar energy systems, a heating and cooling system powered by woodchips, and a composting toilet. Among the other organizational units that Brown established, sponsored through legislation, or gave new prominence, were the Office of Citizen Initiative and Volunteer Action, the Office of Criminal Justice Planning, the California Arts Council, the Agricultural Labor Relations Board, and the California Conservation Corps.[35] Each of these, in some way, was responsible for taking ideas compatible with Brown's philosophy, developing them into programs, and either implementing them or placing them into the appropriate department in the executive branch. The theory was to debate ideas within these protective enclaves, elaborate them, and then gain support for them among the interested governmental and private parties.

Advantages of Limited Routines

Jerry Brown's management practices purposely undermined the routinization of government in several ways and supported his interest in challenging conventional wisdom. First, his appointment of known innovators and advocates helped to assure that his staff and appointees would not easily become captives of the bureaucracy. They came to office with strong commitments of their own, not just the commitment to efficiency in government typical of Reagan appointees. Second, Brown never made strong distinctions between cabinet officers, the staff, and even some of the top civil servants. Anyone with a good idea, anyone with useful information, was important to Brown. He purposely blurred role distinctions so as to liberate people from traditional obligations. Third, Brown's eschewing of routine kept his subordinates responsive, both to him and to his ideas; many of them adopted his distaste for routine in their own work arenas. Brown personalized the organization, making it help him debate ideas first, and attend to business only secondly. [36]

This release of the organization from an obligation to perform routinely was in some respects successful. The Brown administration was clearly one of the most untraditional political administrations American government has ever seen. Although often criticized for his unorthodox methods, Brown was a governor whose creative ideas frequently upset cozy political alliances and challenged long-held assumptions. Political analyst Ed Salzman's summing-up of the Brown incumbency is apt. "The voters may not like him, but they find him thoroughly fascinating." [37]

Disadvantages of Brown's Management Practices

Brown's pushing against the inclinations of a functionally organized structure had its limits, and they were not inconsiderable. Ignoring routine, selecting people for their ideas rather than their administrative abilities, and a weak cabinet all had unintended consequences.

The loose organization in the Governor's Office, while it fostered innovative decisions, was chaotic and disrupted the work of those trying to respond to requests from groups outside. While Brown was debating the three or four issues that were of interest to him (one person said he wore mental "blinders" so he could focus intently) all other issues were in limbo. For those others in government who were concerned with meeting deadlines and accomplishing the substantial routine business of government, Brown's intellectual retreat was frustrating. Eventually, those outside the intimate circle of advisors began to appropriate power simply to respond to the demands of their jobs. The second circle of staff members, especially, became powerful people by default.

Because Brown reserved the right to make decisions and did not need his cabinet as a forum, they never became powerful, either as a body, or as individuals. The Reagan cabinet met to exercise power, but the Brown cabinet met only to exchange information among themselves. Their subordinates, the directors of the departments, knew that cabinet officers were not influential and were known to ignore or repudiate agency directives. Some of the conflict between agency secretaries and department directors were carried out publicly in the Sacramento papers to the great embarrassment of the Brown administration. For example, the agency secretary for Health and Welfare repeatedly tried to place his choices on the staffs of his department directors, against their will. The feuding that ensued was subject to much publicity, and in the end, the State Personnel Board refused to notify the secretary when vacancies occured. The unity of purpose, the solid front that Reagan maintained, was never true of the Brown administration.

Brown's selection of bright, interesting thinkers was a boon to many lackluster units of government, but they were more than occasionally administrative disasters.[38] For example, Brown's first selection to head the state's mammoth Department of Health was both a lawyer and physician (to farmworker leader Cesar Chavez, among others), and had a reputation as a "free thinker." Brown called him "an excellent human being who symbolizes the kind of philosophy I like to see in government."[39] But after the federal government threatened to hold up $25 million in health benefits because the department was not complying with its reporting requirements, as well as reports of widespread administrative bungling, Brown put a long-term government official as second in command to unblock the administrative channels. Finally, the Governor replaced the director with a CEA from the Department of Finance. The *Sacramento Bee* said of the ousted director, "His three-year tenure was wracked with scandals not of his own making, but which verified another earlier statement he made. He called himself 'a lousy administrator, but a very fine physician.' "[40]

The state architect, Sim Van der Ryn, resigned with the general agreement that his ability to innovate was not matched by administrative skills. In an article entitled "Architect Failed Bureaucracy Test," the *Sacramento Bee* quoted an associate of Van der Ryn's, "Sim is a great idea person, but he doesn't know how to implement them. . . .

Everybody knew he didn't have administrative ability."[41] Likewise Brown's Director of Parks and Recreation, a man who built his own homestead cabin, lived off the land, and considered permitting nude beaches in state parks, was criticized for failing to keep up the state's land acquisition program. He quit as a result of repeated criticism from legislators, but was finally coaxed back by Brown. The Governor, however, appointed a Finance Department CEA to manage the acquisitions program.

The spotty management record of the Brown administration had an ironic twist. The ideas that flowed from every corner of the administration often failed to find a place in government because no one was concerned with governing or was qualified to govern. One of Brown's cabinet members stated this poignantly, "One of the weaknesses of this administration is that there are lots of ideas, pocketfuls of ideas. What we don't have are people who can carry out these ideas, put them in place, make them work, get departments to do them, make effective legislation. We have ideas that fall. You know, they die on the floor of the legislature; they die in the departments; they die in the streets. Wherever they die, you don't get them done. What's the point in having them?"

REAGAN *vs.* BROWN

The sixteen years that this study spans is a relatively brief period in the developmental history of California government. During this time there were few important structural changes that distinguished the Brown administration from the Reagan administration; both governors managed essentially the same organization. Although it is not our intent in this comparison to declare either Reagan or Brown the "better" governor of the state, it is appropriate to assess the impact of their very different styles on the conduct of government and their relative effectiveness in achieving self-defined ends.

In 1966 Reagan would appear to have been an exceedingly weak candidate for the managerial aspects of governing. Reagan not only had never held public office, his only executive position had been President of Hollywood's Screen Actor's Guild, hardly a place to get experience for a demanding management post. And, in fact, California government was one of the largest and most complex organizations in the world. The thought of Reagan, a political and executive amateur, running the largest state prompted the *New York Times* to editorialize a month before the election, "Mr. Reagan belongs in the studios in Hollywood, gracing the movie and television screens he knows so well. Californians will, we trust, understand where reality ends and fantasy begins."[42] Californians, of course (and fourteen years later, New Yorkers), elected Mr. Reagan to office with an overwhelming mandate. Considering his ill-preparedness for office, Reagan's eight years as governor left behind a surprisingly strong record of accomplishment. He put together a competent, if politically narrow, group of administrators who largely worked well together. His programs were not of revolutionary proportions—many dealt with administrative reforms and budget trimming—but they were usually well-researched and thoughtful expressions of a pro-business philosophy. His success in getting approval for his legislative proposals was extraordinary despite having had to face Democratic majorities in the state legislature for two terms. Reagan, incredibly, had only one veto override in eight years.

Jerry Brown came to office surrounded by far higher expectations. Although only 36 years old at the time of his election, Brown had more apparent qualifications for high office. He was a lawyer and had spent four years as California Secretary of State. Like the governorship, the Secretary of State post is a statewide elective office. It is not an important position, being largely concerned with maintaining documents of incorporation and enforcing election laws, but Brown used the office in new and imaginative ways. While the country was going through a post-Watergate distrust of political officials, Brown forged a "clean up politics" campaign using the Secretary of State's powers to control elections as a basis of operation. He authored Proposition 9, a campaign reform proposal to limit campaign spending and to make lobbyists' activities publicly accountable. Brown ran for governor and campaigned for Proposition 9 at the same time, developing a crusader image at precisely the opportune moment.

Unlike Reagan, who followed party doctrine, Brown was saying new and interesting things about government. He turned his inquisitive mind to questioning all sorts of long-accepted relationships between government and society. His political education under his father had not locked him into traditional patterns. Writers were hailing Brown as the first truly new politician in decades. A few months after his election as governor, the *Los Angeles Times* reported that "Brown is being closely watched in Democratic statehouses and in Washington for a possible model for a post-New Deal Democratic politics." Brown created excitement among Democrats and Republicans alike because he seemed to have a genuinely new approach to government.

Although the assessments of Jerry Brown's eight years as governor are just beginning to come in, many indicate that Brown has been a disappointment, given his high promise. His administration never developed the unity of effort or sense of mission that marked Reagan's years in office. Brown's questioning of government's purpose did not become a coherent philosophy, much less a program; it remained a series of interesting questions. Without an integrating theme many of Brown's appointees were left to create their own agendas. Some were successful, but frequent battles with constituents and legislators often gave the impression of an administration in disarray.

Why, against strong odds, was Ronald Reagan an effective governor, and Jerry Brown, who ran essentially the same organization, a disappointment? Some attribute the difference of outcome to the nature of what Reagan and Brown attempted. Reagan always understood politics as the art of the possible, while Brown dreamed of greater transformations. Reagan's chances of success were supposedly better because he attempted less. Another analysis locates the difference of outcomes within the two men. Reagan, in this view, was simply the more astute, more able executive. Brown, despite his obviously quick mind, was at best a poor administrator, and at worst a gadfly indulging in political highjinks.

While there is perhaps some truth to some of these views, our analysis leads to another conclusion: *The most consequential difference between Reagan and Brown was their orientation to organization.* Reagan saw government primarily as an administrative structure that had to be mobilized while Brown saw it as an impediment to be overcome. Reagan tried (through his extensive delegations, never personally) to accept the state bureaucracy on its own terms while making it more efficient, more stylized, and more responsive to his essentially managerial political goals. He always used the bureaucracy in ways consistent with its structure and, if anything, sharpened such structural attributes as role differentiation, communication-channels, and chains of command. Not incidently, Reagan was a master at the use of the symbols of office. He performed the role of the governor, with all of its pomp and ceremony, in ways that certified his leadership.

Brown, in contrast, did not accept the bounds of the organization. He constantly fought the fetters of structure by ignoring procedures, by failing to give routine assistance to administrators with routine problems, and by repeatedly using his subordinates in unorthodox ways. A much harder working governor than Reagan, Brown's failure to take on at least some of the trappings of office, and to act "gubernatorial" as his role demanded, ironically left open to question his capacity to govern. Brown's most notable accomplishment as governor—bravely holding off taxes during a recession—was a result of his one consistent mastery of the government apparatus, the budgetary system. But for the most part, Brown failed to develop the administrative tools for implementing a new approach to government and his successes were uneven. In the end, by fighting the system, Brown paralyzed government. It could not operate, because of its inherent organizational qualities, in the novel ways to which Brown aspired.

THE LIMITS OF ADMINISTRATIVE ORGANIZATION

Our assessment of these two administrations has consequences that go beyond the impact of Reagan and Brown as individuals, and beyond the political bounds of California. These two cases, quite different examples of political philosophy and management orientation, together suggest the limits of possibility for executive government action today. Government is more than simply the arena in which policies are debated and in which political personalities clash. The social structure of government—the arena itself—is an active and influential participant in the political process. The organization of government that has developed over the last hundred years influences the type of leaders who will be successful, constrains the policies that can be considered, and even restricts the nature of social change that will be implemented.

The impact of bureaucratic organization in the political sphere has been an important theme in sociology, largely due to the writings of Max Weber. Weber, who wrote at the turn of the century, was concerned with the growth of large bureaucratic structures and predicted that they would defy control by the citizens they were intended to serve. In particular, Weber saw the bureaucratic officialdom and the elected representatives of the public locked in a contest for control over the organization, a contest which he believed the officials were well equipped to win.

> The power position of a fully developed bureaucracy is always great, under normal conditions overtowering. The political "master" always finds himself, vis-à-vis the trained official, in the position of a dilettante facing the expert.[43]

Weber recognized that although the elected leadership had *formal* authority over the organization, in fact, they were amateurs when faced with the organizational skills of bureaucratic officials. Bureaucratic administration, according to Weber, is based on "domination through knowledge,"[44] rather than through the force of a leader's personality or the traditional right to rule, such as some monarchs possess. With knowledge about the organization and its procedures critical to getting things done, bureaucratic officials are in a clearly superior position to the politicians who arrive for a relatively brief four-to-eight-year term in office.

This power of knowledge derives largely from the structural characteristics of bureaucracy. As the organization grows in size and complexity, as has been the case in California, work is increasingly divided and specialized. No governor or department director could hope to match the power of expertise wielded by career officials; appointees can barely oversee their departments' activities, much less master their legalistic intricacies. And because the officialdom shares a like structural location in government they begin to develop, just as the personal staff or the cabinet, a distinct orientation to action. They develop a vision of themselves as a group apart having interests separate from the governor and his aides. Although not powerful as individuals, career officials have the strength of numbers.

While the power of bureaucratic experts is formidable and may appear to political leaders to be decisive, governors and presidents have acquired their own array of organizational weapons not foreseen by Weber. The proliferation of independent boards and agencies at the turn of the century, as shown in figure 1 of chapter 3, led to what Herbert Kaufman described as "the formation of highly independent islands of decision-making occupied by officials who went about their business without much reference to each other or to other organs of government,"[45] including the executive. These islands of authority could not respond adequately to the increasing social demands on government. The result was support for control centralized in the executive.

This control has been granted in a number of ways, including the power of the purse expressed as an executive budget, increased appointive powers, and the right, within limits, to reorganize the executive branch. It has also been expressed as tolerance for a growing corps of personal aides and the creation of the CEA in California and the Senior Executive Service in the federal government. Each of these administrative concessions has increased the control of the "political master" over the government organization.

In fact, however, there has been something of a seesaw of power between the executive leadership and the bureaucratic officialdom. While the formal powers of the leadership have grown, not only relative to the bureaucracy but also to the legislature, career officials have strengthened their position, too. Members of the permanent administration are increasingly professionalized, have developed powerful links to constituent groups, and are unionizing at a rate faster than any other segment of the workforce. The battle for control has been neither won nor lost, but remains in dynamic tension.[46]

The real consequences for the public of this organizational push-pull do not lie in which group currently or eventually assumes dominance, however. Rather, the ascendant party in the battle for control is indisputably the organization itself, the arena. Viewed historically, the one clear progression has been the increasing subordination of political substance, process, and actors to organizational norms and procedures.

The influence of organization that we have emphasized most in this study has been the organization's power to shape the commitments and views of actors. The individuals who joined California state government at the invitation of Ronald Reagan were not particularly like the people whom Jerry Brown appointed in experience, political beliefs, or personal style. Yet, after some months in office, the orientations to action and organizational views of the Brown administrative appointees were in significant ways akin to those of the Reagan administration. Reagan cabinet officers viewed the personal staff in much the same way as Brown cabinet officers, that is, as often inexperienced and politicized interlopers. Reagan administrators tried as hard to divine and live by their governor's philosophy as did Brown administrators. Both sets were drawn into the concerns of the bureaus they managed, often becoming their champions to the chagrin of the personal staff. And, importantly, appointees of both governors were far more like *each other* in their understanding of and participation in government's processes, than they were like the personal staffs in their own administrations.

Clearly, these men and women of government were shaped by the places they assumed in the organizational structure. They stepped into social roles that both prompted and constrained them, though not in a deterministic or scriptlike way. As individuals they demonstrated a range of responses to their roles, some never embracing the role emotionally, and some even violating the role's norms. But most, we have argued, accommodated themselves to their position in government because it was expected of them by those they met, and because they wanted the power to do a good job. Having power in organizations is a matter of acting predictably, not in a self-defined way, but in support of publicly understood role obligations. To become a powerful staff person, one must always put the well-being of the governor first; to be a powerful CEA, one must cultivate a reputation for professionalism. The most cynical, most self-interested actor in government, as well as the most selfless, soon comes to understand that the only way to achieve one's ends and be effective with others, is to be obedient to one's position. Maintaining the bounds of a role, cynically or sincerely, is the only way an individual can sustain relationships with a multitude of others. It is the only way that complex administration is possible.

There is an apparent dilemma at work here. In order to achieve one's ends, be they personal or ideological, an actor must assume a role that limits the means for realizing ends and even limits the ends that are considered appropriate. Moreover, the assumption of a role transforms, often subtly, the ends one chooses to pursue. As people become insiders, skilled in the routines of government, they quite reasonably do that which it is possible to do within the organization, transforming their outsider intentions into organizational possibilities.

For some, particularly ideologues, this is difficult. They must subordinate their ideals to organizational processes, watching as others with different agenda and different obligations chip away at their principles. Most actors, however, readily orient themselves to the organization. Government, especially for those at the policy-making levels we studied, is an exciting, even exhilarating world. The issues are important, the actors committed and powerful, and the work itself of interest. Few can resist the seduction of power politics—or would want to—and are drawn, emotionally and behaviorally, into accepting government on its own terms.

In practice, this means adopting the values, vocabulary, and routines of the organization. It means accepting the structure of reality that is government, and reproducing that reality through actions that accord with it. Goals, for example, must be amenable to bureaucratic technique. Ideas and ideals must be couched in the often arcane language of policy professionals, must be "actionable" in ways suited to the organization, and justifiable according to the institutionalized value structure of economic analysis. Activity must accord with bureaucratic requirements and statutory procedure. Failure to conform with hierarchical processes renders an act incomprehensible, even deviant. Government, like all social systems, cannot tolerate deviance; social life is smooth and continuous only if participants uphold public norms.

Government, we are suggesting, creates an internal morality, a set of internally coherent ethical standards by which action and actors are judged.[47] The three loyalties analyzed in earlier chapters are extended examples of the sort of moral precepts that underlie modern government; their power to channel action is substantial, if not overwhelming. While these standards are public and commonsensical to members of government and to people who interact with it frequently, to outsiders government may appear a foreign terrain of alien rituals and language.

The extensive repertoire of insider knowledge that is now required to participate in the political process of institutionalized government has meant a growth industry for certain types of insiders. Lobbyists and professionalized political action groups become the representatives of citizen concerns. The staffs of legislators learn the system as apprentices, then run for office themselves, citing their experience and contacts in government. The CEAs are useful to appointees precisely because they know the ropes. The necessity of inside knowledge favors insiders who interact in ways only they fully understand.

Certainly, bureaucrats have been accused of speaking bureaucratese and adhering to seemingly inane organizational requirements, but it is no less true that appointees and even the chief executive must shape their activities in terms of administrative organization. No one, not even the governor, can remain an outsider untainted by an organizational view and refusing to play by organizational rules.[48] Government only operates in terms of itself and defies even powerful challenges to bureaucratic life-as-usual.

Today's life-as-usual rests on norms that have been in the making for decades. When government organized hierarchically in response to Progressive-era reforms, an organizational logic of development was set in motion: increasing size meant increasing specialization, which in turn meant the need for greater expertise and management skill. In government, as in other management arenas, this has meant the increasing reliance on professionals, experts, and technicians. Such people are the logical consequence of a bureaucratic society: they operate according to rules they bring with them to the organization, internalized rules that are reinforced by an organization that values professionalism.

Professionals in government apply procedural standards and intellectual formulas to judge political claims and program alternatives. Program evaluation focuses on the correctness of political action according to objective criteria that may be applied routinely, case after case; policy analysis evaluates the efficacy of means, not ends. Egon Bittner, in an address entitled "Technique and the Conduct of Life," reminds us that the use of professional codes to guide analysis, rather than "standards of propriety," is an historically recent phenomenon, one that he finds "remarkable."

> [The existence of professional codes] attests that among ourselves it is nec-
> essary to consult two unrelated bodies of information before deciding what
> to do. *Whether* one should build a bridge across the river, and *how* one
> should build it belongs to two different departments of the mind, so to speak,
> departments that are not even on speaking terms with one another.[49]

Hierarchical government, in its reliance on professionals, focuses on the "how" of political action. It is beyond the capabilities of modern government to consider in any significant way the "whether" of ethical implications and value judgments.

In theory, of course, it is the role of the elected official at the top to carry the agenda of value propositions to government; the administrative apparatus exists only to implement these values as programs. In fact, however, it is the value of objective rationality inherent in professional codes and many organizational norms that directs the political process. Only political propositions that assume the importance of efficiency and correct technique can be administered.

Given this, Ronald Reagan's agenda of streamlined government was readily accommodated by California's professionally sophisticated executive branch. The meshing of Reagan's political purposes with the organization's capabilities does not suggest that what he accomplished was without difficulty or management skill, for it was not. But Reagan only had to refine further the structural tendencies of the organization that he found. He merely emphasized such things as the separation of roles that already existed. Despite his arguments for a more "businesslike" government, the structure was amenable to his philosophical and managerial bent.

Not so with Jerry Brown. Brown found an organization designed to smother the very thing he valued: innovation. The "role clarity" perfected by Meese, could only prevent the kind of cross-fertilization of ideas Brown so fervently wanted. Brown constantly had to strain against the structure to achieve his purposes. To an amazing extent, particularly in his first term, he was able to realize many of the attributes of what organization theorists call "organic" or "postbureaucratic" forms of structure,[50] forms characterized by fluid organization charts, low specialization, and little formalized behavior or routines. The lack of standardization, and a normative structure that promoted ideas rather than routines, had to be instituted by Brown personally and in opposition to the organization that he found.

But Brown was never able to extend this nonroutine form beyond a relatively small circle of advisors. The larger structure of government, including Brown's appointees, were embedded in bureaucratic procedures and functional specializations. Brown could institutionalize neither the products nor the process of innovation necessary to sustaining a nontraditional approach to government. He failed to recognize that the institution of executive power is more powerful than any incumbent governor. Even the chief executive could not hope to best it.

Nor did Brown recognize that a major source of the executive's influence today lies in his role as the manager of government. To reject this role, as Brown clearly did, was to divorce himself from the others who held organizational power in the name of the Governor—the cabinet, the staff, and the CEAs. Brown upset government, less for the substance of his policies or because he was capricious—he was consistent, given his philosophy—but because the state's hierarchy and Brown's innovative, substantively-oriented style were inherently antagonistic. Reagan proved that modern government, when it is well-managed, can produce exactly what its reformers of the 1920s intended, organizational unity. In contrast, Brown demonstrated that bureaucratic government can never support innovation, whether in furtherance of radical or conservative ends.

APPENDIX:
A NOTE ON INTERVIEW
METHODOLOGY

BECAUSE OUR INTERVIEW TECHNIQUES depart from standard survey methodology, this note supplies supplementary information on various aspects of our data collection and analysis.

SAMPLING

The purpose of interviewing was to reconstruct the Reagan and Brown executive organizations in order to understand their exercise of executive authority. Therefore, our sample resembles more that used in an oral history than that in a social science survey. We did not randomly draw our interviewees from the total population of Reagan and Brown appointees, but rather selected people to interview who had observed and had worked with the two governors or their top appointees. We chose people who had knowledge of specific aspects of the executive branch, such as the routines in the Governor's Office, of specific trouble spots, such as the former Department of Health, or of specific incidents. Many individuals interviewed were suggested by earlier informants who told us to see a particular individual if we wanted to know more about an event or policy in which we expressed interest. In some ways this resembles a "snowball" sample, but our decision about selecting informants was always based on their ability to answer our research questions, not on any attempt to randomize our interviews. We did, however, attempt to balance the interviews between the two administrations.

Our sample included ten women in staff positions, six of whom served in high staff roles (four Brown and two Reagan) and five women in appointee positions (all Brown). Because we decided to make most of our informants' responses anonymous, we felt it best to report all of the interview data without regard to sex. We have reported the responses of women in such a way as to make the sex of the speaker ambiguous. Sex did not have any significant influence on the results of this study and to reveal the informant as a woman would in most cases identify the individual.

Table 1
Distribution of Interviews by Position and Administration

	Brown	Reagan	Total
Personal Staff	20	25	45
Administrative Appointees	18	16	34
CEAs [1]	18		18
Others [2]	13		13
			110

---

[1] All CEAs interviewed worked in both administrations.
[2] Includes three lobbyists, five professional and clerical workers in the Governor's Office that worked for both Reagan and Brown, one former governor, and four civil servants who were not CEAs.

INTERVIEWS AND INTERVIEWING

The interview schedule went through two stages. The first round of interviews were directed towards gaining knowledge of staff and appointee organization, procedures, and roles. The interviews were open-ended and tailored to fit a particular informant's position, but each covered topics in four main areas:

1) The organization of the Governor's Office
2) The role played by appointees in the conduct of the state government

3) The relations among staff members, administrative appointees, and civil servants
4) The characteristics one looks for in an appointee.

When questioning individuals about these areas we would ask them to compare their own position with what they observed was required by other positions. In this round of interviews we were soliciting information about structure and organization rather than about any succession of events, although within each area of questioning we asked about changes during the administration. These early interviews, which numbered about twenty, were planned for about an hour's duration and typically lasted an hour and a half.

Once we were familiar with each governor's organization and the key figures and events in each administration, we began the second round of interviewing. We abandoned our more-or-less standardized coverage of topic areas for a chronological approach tailored to each person's experience in state government. This required that we do some research on the events each individual took part in or had observed. By focusing on specific issues, controversies, and decisions we encouraged our informants to reconstruct past events, project themselves into the processes of government, and reflect on their performance and the performance of others. We were familiar enough with the different positions that were taken in regard to each event to solicit information about why some people did one thing and others did something else. We encouraged people to reflect back on themselves, on their own motives, and on the possible motives of others.

Obviously we were not seeking standardized statements; rather we were talking with individuals whose perspectives, from the viewpoint of historical reconstruction, were crucial. Only they could tell us why something happened as it did, and they, as individuals, saw their role as important and responded to our interview with this recognition.

We had very few refusals, partly because respondents recognized that only they could give answers to the kind of questions we were asking. Although scheduling interviews with tremendously busy people is often very difficult, and sometimes impossible, only five people refused our request for an interview. Four of these individuals were close aides to Brown, who was then Governor, and considered such interviews inappropriate given Brown's position and presidential aspirations. In addition to these five refusals we had difficulty in completing interviews with several other individuals, a fact caused by the busy schedules and active lives of people who serve or have served in government.

The people we interviewed were generally very cooperative, in part because they wanted to "tell their side" when they knew we had heard about the other side, as we suggested in the text of this book. Some were genuinely interested in seeing that people have a better view of how government operates, particularly when they believed that the public unfairly criticizes the people who work in government. We kept notes about the setting of each of our interviews and our impressions about whether or not our informants were reluctant or uncertain about their responses. We used this information to guide us in our analysis, especially when we had conflicting reports of events. Most interviews, however, we judged to be candid and honest appraisals of situations from the participants' points of view. For example, many people were self-critical and mentioned how they might have acted differently in some instances. The second round of interviews also lasted around an hour and a half. Of the 110 interviews we completed with different people, 21 lasted over two hours. Of the 21, 7 lasted over three hours, and 2 of these lasted six hours.

CODING AND DATA ANALYSIS

We established coding categories based on the organization of the executive appointees and on particular topical areas of interest. With the exception of three people who preferred not to be taped, all interviews were recorded. Occasionally a person would request that the tape recorder be turned off in order to assure the confidentiality of a particular statement, after which the tape recorder would be turned back on (we promised confidentiality to all CEAs and to anyone who made it a condition of the interview). Although we made notes on the untaped interviews as well as the unrecorded statements, we have only quoted statements in this book that can be verified by our tapes.

All interviews were assigned a code number. Recorded interviews were transcribed and proofread for accuracy. The proofed transcription was duplicated; one copy was retained as a master copy and the other was filed into the coding categories. Because many statements concerned issues that spanned categories, they were cross-referenced. The file was arranged to facilitate our comparative methodology; statements could be identified by administration, by position, and by individual (by looking up the code number). It was possible, for example, to compare statements about how decisions are made in the Governor's Office between Brown's staff and Reagan's staff, or between staff people and appointees.

We analyzed the data by using both the file in which the interviews were broken apart and the whole interviews. An analysis of the internal logic and structural sources of each type of loyalty came from reading and rereading all of the interviews of people holding the same position. Our understandings came initially from sharing our interview experiences and impressions with each other and then checking back with the transcriptions. Once we began to suspect the framework in which responses were being made, we were able to formulate an interpretation that we could systematically test by reviewing our file system. In addition, our understanding came in part from the information that one can only gain by personally interviewing informants. Transcriptions, although they accurately replicate the spoken word, omit the pauses and reluctant responses, as well as the emotion that suggests another dimension of meaning. By sharing our impressions of such factors we were able to see subjective similarities of response, both the emotional and those devoid of emotion, and to understand how these qualified the data in the transcripts.

Our general intent was to seek historical reconstructions. Historical or autobiographical reconstructions are, of course, a selective perception of reality and contain both factual information as well as justifications and interpretations. Typically, the researcher tries to account for the personal biases inherent in the data by holding constant factors such as class, sex, age, position, and other individual variables that might lead the informant to skew the account one way or another, particularly when it differs from accounts by other informants. Our original intent in studying government was to do precisely that.

But as we came to realize, *it is also possible to hold the "facts" constant, and look at the biases.* This study has not concerned itself only with what took place in the Reagan and Brown administrations, but also with the subjective frameworks, the systematic biases, that people used to view events. We have been concerned with what those frameworks are, how they operate, their structural origins, and their consequences for action in government.

NOTES

CHAPTER ONE. EXECUTIVE ORGANIZATION

1. The press covering the Reagan presidency have often reported that Meese lacks organizational abilities. During Reagan's governorship, the press took quite the opposite view of Meese. For example, Ed Salzman, the influential editor of *California Journal*, even thought that Meese, who "has shown an incredible capacity for calmly keeping the complex machinery of government running smoothly" during Reagan's term in office, would make a "terrific administrator . . . of some massive and complex agency of state government" for Jerry Brown's administration (vol. 5, December 1974, p. 398).

2. The chart to which Klein refers is actually an organizational chart of the executive branch before the 1919 reorganization. For a similar discussion of this reorganization see chapter 3.

3. When developed academically, this view of organization stresses leadership over other organizational variables. In the literature on the presidency, this perspective is particularly prominent in discussions equating a president's personal qualities with the rest of his administration, as has been done with particular vigor with the Kennedy and Nixon terms in office. Perhaps the most sophisticated treatment of this theme in reference to political institutions is found in James MacGregor Burns, *Leadership* (New York: Harper and Row, 1978). In organization theory, leadership is a key variable in such classic works as Chester I. Barnard, *The Functions of the Executive* (Cambridge, Mass: Harvard University Press, 1938).

4. The view of administration as being separate from politics came to prominence in the United States during the last decades of the nineteenth century. A particularly insightful history of the attempt to bureaucratize government and to distinguish government from politics is Martin J. Schiesl's, *The Politics of Efficiency* (Berkeley: University of California Press, 1977).

5. For discussions of Weber's approach to historical analysis, see Guenther Roth and Wolfgang Schluchter, *Max Weber's Vision of History* (Berkeley: University of California Press, 1979); and Wolfgang Schluchter, *The Rise of Western Rationalism: Max Weber's Developmental History* (Berkeley: University of California Press, 1981).

6. For our preliminary statement on this problem see Gary G. Hamilton and Nicole Woolsey Biggart, "Making the Dilettante an Expert: Personal Staffs in Public

Bureaucracies," *Journal of Applied Behavioral Sciences* 16, no. 2 (May 1980):192–210.

7. For discussions of the use of a Weberian perspective in organizational studies, see Charles Perrow, *Complex Organizations: A Critical Essay*, 2nd ed. (Glenview, Ill.: Scott, Foresman, 1979).

8. We want to emphasize three theorists whose work we have found particularly important in this regard: Ralph H. Turner's, "The Role and the Person," *American Journal of Sociology* 84 (July 1978):1–23; "The Real Self: From Institution to Impulse," *American Journal of Sociology* 81 (March 1976):989–1016; Howard S. Becker, "Art as Collective Action," *American Sociological Review* 39 (December 1974):767–76; and Erving Goffman, whose many works, starting with *The Presentation of Self in Everyday Life* (Garden City, New York: Doubleday Anchor, 1959), have been particularly important.

9. We should note that we do not treat the two administrations as independent cases that occur in the same setting. Quite the contrary, they are sequential cases; Reagan's administration, through establishing organizational ideas and procedures, directly influenced what occurred in Jerry Brown's terms in office.

10. For a discussion of this strategy in historical sociology, see Theda Skocpol and Margaret Somers, "The Uses of Comparative History in Macrosocial Inquiry" *Comparative Studies in Society and History* 22 (April 1980):174–97; and Reinhard Bendix, *Nation-Building and Citizenship* (Berkeley: University of California Press, 1977).

11. For a discussion of quasi-experimental analysis, see Thomas Cook and Donald T. Campbell, *Quasi-Experimentation* (Chicago: Rand McNally College Publishing, 1979). We should note that our analysis certainly differs from the field studies discussed by Cook and Campbell, but we have followed the logic of this approach to structure the collection and analysis of our data.

CHAPTER TWO. THE GOVERNOR'S PERSONAL STAFF

1. Until the 1957/58 fiscal year the state budget listed the people on the payroll of the Governor's Office. By law, the California governor must prepare and submit the budget to the legislature every session. This list is found in *Budget of the State of California for the 83rd and 84th Fiscal Years, July 1, 1931 to June 30, 1933* (Sacramento: State Printing Office), p. 10.

2. Ibid.

3. Ibid. Some information on the administration of James Rolph, Jr., is found in H. Brett Melendy and Benjamin F. Gilbert, *The Governors of California* (Georgetown, Calif.: The Talisman Press, 1965), pp. 363–78.

4. *Budget for the 83rd and 84th Fiscal Years*, p. 10. The practice of borrowing was not, however, discontinued, but rather became the standard practice of every governor since Rolph, even though some governors have tried to eliminate the practice. For an article on Reagan's efforts, see *The Sacramento Bee*, December 15, 1972, p. A14.

5. Also included in the Governor's Office were the Governor's Wellness Council,

the Office of Appropriate Technology, and others. Since Earl Warren's administration, each governor has added or subtracted separately organized units from the Governor's Office budget. The governor retains management control over these units even though they are not located in the Office itself.

6. The Agency Plan, adopted in 1961, placed the offices of the agency secretaries under the control of the governor and their personnel on the Governor's Office payroll. This placement was in keeping with the recommendation made by the organizing committee that the agency secretaries be "an extension of the governor's personality and authority." (The Governor's Committee on Organization of State Government, *The Agency Plan for California* [Sacramento: State Printing Office, 1959], p. 12.) In their inception, then, agency secretaries were to have been organized according to the same principles as are personal staff aides. As chapters 3 and 4 show, however, agency secretaries always acted as administrative appointees, and never as staff aides.

7. *Governor's Budget for 1980–81* (Sacramento: State Printing Office, 1980), Legislative, Judicial, Executive Section, p. 18.

8. During Brown's term the official number of positions shrank to 82. But Brown did not reduce the actual members of his staff. As the Legislative Analyst to the Joint Legislative Budget Committee reported, "this reduction has been achieved by transferring staff and related costs of one activity to a new budget item entitled 'Office for Citizen Initiative and Voluntary Action.' " *California Legislature Analysis of the Budget Bill for the Fiscal Year July 1, 1978 to June 30, 1980*, p. 17.

9. The present Governor's Office, located in the east end annex of the Capitol building, was first occupied by Earl Warren in October 1951. This space was designed in 1947 and construction began in 1949, all during Warren's terms in office. The same suites have been used since that time for the governors' aides, although the space in recent administrations has been further partitioned to accommodate more offices.

10. This overflow has several consequences. First, the closest aides to the governor are usually the ones remaining in the Governor's Office; these aides certainly have the most immediate access to the governor. There are rare exceptions to this generalization: one of the directors of the Office of Planning and Research was reputedly one of Brown's closest aides. Second, the overflow also isolated the special projects the governor would take on from routine politics in the Governor's Office. This tended to increase the ideological visibility, but in the long run also to decrease the practical significance of these projects.

11. An adequate history of the Governor's Office remains to be done. For some information on the development of the office, see Nicole Woolsey Biggart, "The Magic Circle" (Ph.D. Dissertation, Department of Sociology, University of California, Berkeley, 1981). For the Governor's Office under Earl Warren, see James R. Bell, "The Executive Office of California Governor under Earl Warren, 1943–1953." (Ph.D. dissertation, University of California, Berkeley, 1956). Additional historical information on the office before and during the Warren administration is found in a report prepared by the Department of Finance, "Organization and Staffing of the Gov-

ernor's Office," dated March 26, 1947. This report is found in the State of California Archives.

12. Studies of the Office of the President and of presidential aides are extensive and offer a similar, but more complex view of the executive role of personal staffs. Among the best of these are Patrick Anderson, *The President's Men* (Garden City, N.Y.: Doubleday, 1968); Larry Berman, "Johnson and the White House Staff," in Robert A. Divine (ed.), *Exploring the Johnson Years* (Austin: University of Texas Press, 1981), pp. 187–213; Thomas E. Cronin, *The State of the Presidency* (Boston: Little, Brown, 1975); Stephen Hess, *Organizing the Presidency* (Washington, D.C.: Brookings, 1976); Richard E. Neustadt, "Approaches to Staffing the Presidency," *The American Political Science Review* 57, no. 4 (December 1963):855–63; Lester G. Seligman, "Presidential Leadership: The Inner Circle and Institutionalization," in Aaron Wildavsky (ed.), *The Presidency* (Boston: Little, Brown, 1969), pp. 632–45; Richard Tanner Johnson, *Managing the White House* (New York: Harper and Row, 1974). Studies on gubernatorial staff are not extensive. The best of these include Ronald D. Michaelson, *Gubernatorial Staffing—Problems and Issues: The Ogilvie Experience* (DeKalb, Ill.: Center for Government Studies, Northern Illinois University, 1974); Coleman B. Ransome, Jr., *The Office of Governor in the United States* (University, Alabama: University of Alabama Press, 1956); Donald P. Sprengel, *Gubernatorial Staffs: Functional and Political Profiles* (Iowa City: University of Iowa Press, 1969); Martha Wagner Weinberg, *Managing the State* (Cambridge, Mass.: MIT Press, 1977); Alan J. Wyner, "Staffing the Governor's Office," *Public Administration Review* 30, no. 1 (January/February 1970):17–24.

13. For a detailed description of the functions of staff aides, see Sprengel, *Gubernatorial Staffs*.

14. There is some indication of this view at the presidential level, with the journalists' and academics' use of feudal and kingly metaphors to describe staff activity. See our comments on this in "Making the Dilettante an Expert," *Journal of Applied Behavioral Science* 16, no. 2 (May 1980):192–210.

15. For Warren's role in developing California's gubernatorial staffs, see James Bell, "The Executive Office." Considerable information on this has recently become available with the University of California's Oral History Project on the Warren Years.

16. For information on the Warren governorship, see Richard B. Harvey, *Earl Warren, Governor of California* (New York: Exposition Press, 1969); Royce D. Delmatier, Clarence F. McIntosh, and Earl G. Waters, *The Rumble of California Politics, 1948–1970* (New York: John Wiley, 1970), pp. 300–27; and James Bell, "The Executive Office." For background information on the California economy and growth of state government, see Gerald D. Nash, *State Government and Economic Development: A History of Administrative Policies in California, 1849–1933* (Berkeley: University of California Press, 1964).

17. For management ideas current in Warren's time as adapted to public administration see Barry Dean Karl, *Executive Reorganization and Reform in the New Deal* (Cambridge, Mass.: Harvard University Press, 1963). Also see A. E. Buck, *The Reorganization of State Governments in the United States* (New York: Columbia Uni-

versity Press, 1938); Kirk H. Porter, *State Administration* (New York: F. S. Crofts, 1938); and John C. Bollens, *Administrative Reorganization in the States Since 1939* (Berkeley: Bureau of Public Administration, University of California, 1947).

18. Department of Finance Report, "Organization and Staffing of the Governor's Office," pp. 3–8.

19. Ibid., pp. 4–5.

20. *State of California Budget for the Fiscal Year July 1, 1954 to June 30, 1955* (Sacramento: State Printing Office, 1954) p. 29.

21. For more on Warren's innovations in the Governor's Office, see James Bell, "The Executive Office."

22. In 1953, the Governor's Office suite contained 56 authorized positions. If we discount borrowing and overflow into other units on the Governor's budget, then the Governor's Office that Reagan took over added only 31 positions, this in comparison with the considerably larger growth occurring in other sectors of state government, including other unit increases in the governor's budget.

23. *State of California Support and Local Assistance, 1967* (Sacramento: State Printing Office, 1967).

24. Ibid., p. 18–34.

25. *State of California Governor's Budget, 1976–77,* p. 16–35.

26. Warren, of course, was an innovator in this regard, but only insofar as he built upon the management ideas of his day, which included ideas about the formation of a staff. One of the important forces in disseminating the ideas about staffs among public administrators was the Brownlow report: Louis Brownlow, *President's Committee on Administrative Management: Report with Special Studies* (Washington D.C.: U.S. Government Printing Office, 1937).

27. For a good introduction to the sociological analysis of organizations, see W. Richard Scott, *Organizations: Rational, Natural and Open Systems* (Englewood Cliffs, N.J.: Prentice-Hall, 1981). Following Scott, we see the development of executive organization as an example of nonevolutionary change, an example of an open system developing in response to environmental and internal pressures.

28. Our finding that personal loyalty is the defining feature of the staff role is in agreement with the conclusions of earlier studies. Wyner in "Staffing the Governor's Office," p. 18, states "The crux [of a governor's staffing his office] revolves about the necessity for intense staff loyalty to the governor." Sprengel, *Gubernatorial Staffs,* building on Wyner's article, finds considerable organizational differences among the arrangement of gubernatorial staffs, but finds a "uniformity in normative constructs" (p. 58). He states that among the staffs he studied, "comments indicated the possible existence of universal norms and a common work paradigm. These norms included personal loyalty to the governor, hard work and long hours, and personal anonymity; the common paradigm concerned the awareness that staff decisions should be calculated for their probable impact upon the governor's image." This finding at the gubernatorial level is matched by a similar finding at the presidential level. See references in note 11, as well as Hamilton and Biggart, "Making the Dilettante an Expert."

29. This merger of the person and role is often viewed as having a charismatic component. At the federal level Garry Wills offers a penetrating view of charismatic force in the Kennedy presidency in *The Kennedy Imprisonment* (New York: Atlantic-Little Brown, 1982), suggesting that Kennedy, as well as his close aides, were the "prisoners of charisma." It is important to note, however, that charisma is an overworked but analytically a very useful term. See Reinhard Bendix's "Charismatic Leadership" in Reinhard Bendix and Guenther Roth, *Scholarship and Partisanship* (Berkeley: University of California Press, 1971), pp. 170–87. Also see Max Weber's important distinction between personal and office charisma in *Economy and Society* (New York: Bedminster Press, 1968) pp. 1139–41. Office charisma particularly applies to American elected officials. Also see Edward A. Shils's discussion of charisma in *Center and Periphery* (Chicago: University of Chicago Press, 1975).

30. Some useful insights on the dilemma of role identities can be obtained from George J. McCall and J. L. Simmons, *Identities and Interaction* (New York: Free Press, 1978).

31. We should emphasize that feelings of personal devotion did not arise because Reagan and Brown solicited this kind of affection. On the contrary, both have been described as uncomfortable with intimate interpersonal relations. This fact is well known for Brown, but is also true for Reagan. According to one of Reagan's personal secretaries, "There was always a distance between the governor and his staff. He did not wish to be anyone's buddy. No one could say that they really knew the Reagans. After the working day, the blinds were drawn and a veil of privacy separated the Governor from his public life." Kathy Randall Davis, *But What's He Really Like?* (Menlo Park: Pacific Coast Publishers, 1970), p. 36.

32. Our analysis differs somewhat from other studies of executive staffs in that we find that the normative components of roles, such as personal loyalty for the staff role, derive from the role obligations, including the authority that is a part of those obligations, and from the active but conditional participation of individuals pursuing goals. This viewpoint is extended in chapter 6. For a similar treatment to ours, see Rosabeth Moss Kanter, "Commitment and Social Organization: A Study of Commitment Mechanisms in Utopian Communities," *American Sociological Review* 33, no. 4 (August 1968):499–517.

33. In fact, there is every reason to think that public statements, such as those we received in our interviews, differ from private beliefs. For an analysis of such statements, see Marvin Scott and Stanford Lyman, "Accounts," *American Sociological Review* 33, no. 1 (February 1968), pp. 46–62.

34. Charles Perrow discusses the rationale for the selection of people who will develop ties of loyalty to people in power in *Complex Organizations* (Glenview, Ill: Scott, Foresman, 1972), p. 15. See Lewis Coser, *Greedy Institutions* (New York: Free Press, 1974), for historical examples of political staff recruitment strategies. Good discussions of recruitment strategies for gubernatorial staffs are found in Michaelson, *Gubernatorial Staffing*; Sprengel, *Gubernatorial Staffs*; and Wyner, "Staffing the Governor's Office."

35. This same recruitment pattern was followed by former Massachusetts Governor Francis Sargent. "Sargent relied exclusively on men whom he already knew and with whom he had previously worked to fill the major positions in his office . . . these people were to remain the key actors in the Sargent staff," Weinberg, *Managing the State*, p. 17. Sprengel's study, like ours, shows that personal friends are not the most common source of staff members. His survey (*Gubernatorial Staffs*, p. 27) revealed that only about 20 percent of staff members were personal or family friends. He does not distinguish between initial appointments and those made later in the administration. Our study shows most friends were appointed early and later appointments were mainly people with whom the governors had little previous association.

36. These early appointments and their connections to Brown are listed in the following series of articles: "The Team that Jerry Built," *The Sacramento Bee*, January 26, 1975, p. 1; Bruce Keppel, "New Faces of 1975," *California Journal* 6, no. 1 (January 1975):19–20; Bruce Keppel, "The New Executives" *California Journal* 6, no. 2 (February 1975):51–53; Francis Carney, "The Riddle of Governor Jerry Brown," *Ramparts* 13, no. 7 (April 1975).

37. Reagan's difficulties in staffing his first administration are described by Lou Cannon in *Ronnie and Jesse* (Garden City, N.Y.: Doubleday, 1969) pp. 131–37.

38. Original staff members in both administrations claimed that the character of the staff organization changed as replacements dominated the organization. Not having proven themselves as long-term friends or as campaign stalwarts, their loyalty was open to question.

39. For example, a previous friendship with the governor often made it more difficult for the friend to subordinate himself to the governor, and hence more difficult to simulate an attachment of personal loyalty. Equality, as opposed to subordination, is the mark of friendship.

40. See Lewis Coser's insightful analysis in *Greedy Organizations* (New York: Free Press, 1974) for some historical material on organizations that require undivided commitments.

41. Some differences existed in the pattern of staff marriages between the two administrations. Reagan's aides were more often married and remained that way throughout the administration. Reagan, we were told numerous times, strongly favored stable marriages and encouraged his staff aides to devote time to their families. In truth, most worked long hours and spouses stoically accepted these conditions, according to a number of informants. Brown, being single and a night worker, did not attend to matters of his aides' marriages, and many of Brown's aides were single or divorced. But this difference should not be overemphasized, because the number of adult single and divorced persons have increased in the population as a whole.

42. Several of Brown's close advisors, such as Tom Quinn, supposedly refused staff positions because they desired greater independence and a sense of individual accomplishment. See chapter 3, p. 79, for a statement by another such advisor who opted for an administrative position.

43. See chapter 6, p. 166 for a statement by a Reagan appointee that brings out this contrast between staff aides and appointees in terms of the physical closeness to the governor.

44. For a detailed description of the spatial arrangement in the Governor's Office, see T. A. Quinn and Ed Salzman, *California Public Administration* (Sacramento: California Journal Press, 1978), pp. 9–12.

45. As discussed in chapter 1, Brown simply adopted Reagan's staff organization more or less intact, even though the two staffs differed considerably in terms of their internal procedures.

46. A similar feeling seems to exist among presidential aides. For some insights on the isolation of the presidential aides from others in the executive branch see Hugh Sidey, "The White House Staff vs. the Cabinet: An Interview with Bill Moyers," in Charles Peters and John Rothchild (eds.), *Inside the System* (New York: Praeger, 1973), pp. 38–50; also Cronin, *State of the Presidency*, 153–75.

47. Unlike other major gubernatorial appointees, staff aides do not have to go through Senate review. In this regard, staff aides differ from administrative appointees, a point that is expanded in chapters 3 and 4.

48. As described in chapter 7, some differences existed between the two administrations in terms of the routinization of staff duties during the term of the governor. Edwin Meese, Reagan's Executive Assistant, tried to formalize the Office positions, making exact titles and job classifications for each. Brown's Office positions remained flexible nearly to the end of his term, allowing Brown to call upon people in different positions for advice on the same issues.

49. These responsibilities have been discussed in numerous books. For example, see James R. Bell and Thomas Ashley, *Executives in California Government* (Belmont, Calif.: Dickenson, 1967), pp. 66–77.

50. Partly because of the difference in Reagan's and Brown's approaches in organizing their administrations most special projects in Brown's terms were supervised by the Governor's Office (e.g., Office of Planning and Research and Office of Appropriate Technology). In Reagan's terms special projects were more often housed in executive departments.

51. According to our interviews the transition between Pat Brown and Reagan was acrimonious, which prompted Reagan to allocate considerable resources to the transition from his administration to Jerry Brown's. Though smooth, the transition to Brown's administration did not lessen the chaos of his first year in office.

52. Most discussions of staff members do not elaborate on the power of staff members; to us, the authority embodied in roles is a central feature creating the norms that characterize the role. In this sense vicarious authority and personal loyalty are complementary aspects of the same role requirement. See chapter 6 for an extended discussion of power and roles.

53. A Brown aide expanded on this theme as follows: "You don't want others to separate the Governor's authority from a staff member's authority. To do so would demystify the process and many staffers don't want outsiders to know how close or

distant the relationship is between a staffer and a governor. Remember, when all relationships are clear, you can't bluff!"

54. The problems associated with access are endemic to executive government. For historical material, see Coser, *Greedy Organizations*. For the presidential level, the following comment by Bill Moyers represents standard wisdom:

> There are two main sources of power . . . in Washington. One is information. The other is access to the President. The White House staff now has information more quickly, or just as quickly, as the Secretary of State or the Secretary of Defense, and they certainly have physical access to the President more readily than the Cabinet Secretaries do. This tends to give the initiative to the White House staff operation. ("White House Staff vs. the Cabinet," p. 42.)

55. For details on these staff arrangements, see chapter 7.

56. A number of informants mentioned the gossipy "Capitolscope," a feature in the Sunday *Sacramento Bee*, as one place to look for this kind of information.

57. Although similar splits occurred in both administrations, they were resolved in different ways. With Reagan, the split was resolved in favor of those adopting a managerial perspective on running the Governor's Office. With Brown, the split was resolved in favor of those adopting a political perspective, in particular in favor of the top workers in Brown's presidential campaign, some of whom joined Brown's staff after the bid for the presidency.

58. Departure in protest is rare in American politics, but when it occurs it is typically among administrative appointees, rarely among personal staff members. See E. Weisband and T. Franck, *Resignation in Protest* (New York: Grossman, 1975). Hirschman's notion of the price of "exit," or departure may suggest the reason: staff members typically have greater personal investment and fewer alternatives than appointees. Albert O. Hirschman, *Exit, Voice, and Loyalty* (Cambridge: Harvard University Press, 1970).

59. The concept "vocabulary of motive" is one first used by C. Wright Mills, "Situated Actions and Vocabularies of Motive," *American Sociological Review* 5 (December 1940):904–13.

60. Several individuals told us about these alumni meetings. It seems that former top staff aides to Governor Reagan organized these alumni meetings in order to keep alive the "esprit de corps" of the administration, as well as to maintain an organization for Reagan's future political ambitions.

61. Books such as John Dean's *Blind Ambition* (New York: Simon and Schuster, 1976) and Jeb Stuart Magruder's *An American Life* (New York: Atheneum, 1974) do little to protest policies and are almost exclusively personal statements. We suggest that Hirschman's notion of "voice," or protest, in *Exit, Voice and Loyalty* operates very differently depending on who is activating it, and that is a direct consequence of the type of loyalty involved.

62. For the distinction between the role and the person, see Ralph H. Turner, "The Role and the Person," *American Journal of Sociology* 84, no. 1 (July 1978):1–23. The distinction is an important one, because the central component of the staff

role, as well as other roles, is that the role implies a self. Adopting this self-in-role, as we suggest in chapter 6, helps to legitimate the exercise of vicarious authority. But adopting this self-in-role often conflicts sharply with one's personal conception of oneself, hence causing a personal dilemma.

63. It is important to stress that the dilemma is, in some sense, unavoidable, and that neither Brown nor Reagan could have acted so as to prevent their staff members from feeling its force. The dilemma arises because of the contradictions between assuming a staff role, which includes exercising the authority of the governor, and maintaining a sense of individual autonomy and self-determination that Americans are taught to have.

64. Only in the last year of Brown's administration, after B. T. Collins became chief-of-staff, did Brown begin to attend office parties, which supposedly happened at Collins' insistence.

65. The term "stereotype," is used after the fashion of Weber (*Economy and Society*, pp. 1038–42), who discusses the process of "typification" of official positions as a form of decentralization in patrimonial empires.

CHAPTER THREE. THE GOVERNOR'S ADMINISTRATORS

1. *California Blue Book or State Roster 1911* (Sacramento, California: Friend W. Richardson, Superintendent of State Printing, 1913), pp. 34, 47.

2. For a general survey of political reforms during this era, see Martin J. Schiesl, *The Politics of Efficiency* (Berkeley: University of California Press, 1977).

3. W. W. Mather, *Administrative Reorganization in California* (Ontario, California: Board of Trustees of Chaffey Junior College, 1929), pp. 42–46, gives a summary of this trend.

4. See David P. Barrows, "Reorganization of State Administration in California," *California Law Review* 3 (1915):91–102, for an excellent discussion of, as well as of the distinction between, boards and commissions.

5. As Mather, *Administrative Reorganization*, pp. 21–28, shows, from 1890 California governors grew increasingly aware that they lacked control over appointees for whose actions the public held the governors accountable.

6. Ibid., p. 43.

7. Cited in ibid., p. 24.

8. Ibid., p. 43.

9. This is the official number of statutory agencies, as computed by the State Department of Finance in figure 3.1, "Organization of Executive Branch of Government of State of California as of January 1, 1919," Department of Finance, *Organization Charts*, 1929. The incongruity between the 112 figure and the total given by Mather, which is 135, results from the fact that about 25 of the agencies were either disbanded or were altered before 1919. Mather, *Administrative Reorganization*, p. 43. An earlier and similar organization chart is found in the *Report of the Committee on Efficiency and Economy of California to Governor William D. Stephens* (Sacramento, California: California State Printing Office, 1919).

10. This number was constructed from information contained in *California Blue Book 1911* and in Elsey Hurt, *California State Government: An Outline of its Administrative Organization from 1850 to 1936.* (Sacramento, Calif.: Supervisor of Documents, 1936); and John Richard Sutton, *Civil Government in California* (New York: American Book Company, 1914).

11. Spencer Olin in *California's Prodigal Sons* (Berkeley: University of California Press, 1968) contends that Hiram Johnson, Governor of California during the Progressive era (1911–1917), had little to do with either the preparation or passage of the package of Progressive legislation that went through the legislature in 1911. For an earlier and slightly broader survey of the Progressive era in California, see George E. Mowry, *The California Progressives* (Chicago: Quadrangle Books, 1951).

12. Hurt, *California State Government*, p. 121.

13. Ibid., p. 79.

14. Barrows ("Reorganization," pp. 95–96) discusses the bureau concept and its early use in California.

15. Ibid., p. 96. See chapter 6 for a discussion of the administrative ideas of the day.

16. Ibid.

17. Ibid., p. 92.

18. Ibid., p. 100.

19. Ibid., p. 101.

20. Ibid., p. 99.

21. *Report of the Committee on Efficiency and Economy of California to Governor William D. Stephens* (Sacramento, Calif.: California State Printing Office, 1919).

22. Ibid., p. 23. See p. xx for a discussion of the organizational principles that this committee saw as most important.

23. Ibid., p. 22.

24. Mather, *Administrative Reorganization*, p. 47–56.

25. Hurt, *California State Government*.

26. *California State Government, A Guide to Its Organization and Function*, p. 6.

27. *Report to the Governor on Reorganization of State Government by the Task Forces* (Sacramento, Calif.: State Printing Office, 1959), p. 3.

28. Ibid., p. 4.

29. Ibid., p. 5.

30. Personal interviews.

31. *Report to the Governor*, p. 12. It is important to note that in this report the agency secretary was envisioned to be "an extension of the Governor's personality and authority." As this chapter shows, this vision did not materialize. Agency secretaries came to be administrative appointees, like department directors, and not part of the governor's personal staff organization, as originally planned.

32. Barrows, "Reorganization," p. 101.

33. Allegiance is often associated with patriotism in the sense that both are terms for loyalty to symbols and philosophy; see Morton Grodzins, *The Loyal and the Dis-*

loyal (Cleveland: World, 1966) and John H. Schaar, *Loyalty in America* (Berkeley: University of California Press, 1957). In the case of patriotism, loyalty is to national symbols and a political philosophy. It is because of this connotation that allegiance is the appropriate term to describe the loyalty of administrative appointees to chief executives.

34. This conclusion is similar to the conclusions most scholars reach about Cabinet officers at the federal level. Most such studies of the presidency make a sharp distinction between the staff and cabinet personnel. In these studies, such as in Cronin's excellent book, *The State of the Presidency*, there is a recognition that the staff role differs from the cabinet role. Moreover, there is a recognition that staff aides and some particularly close cabinet officials "may be selected primarily on the basis of personal loyalty to the president" (Cronin, p. 197). There is not, however, the explicit recognition that cabinet level officials are equally selected for their loyalty to the president, and that their loyalty is qualitatively of a different type. But implicitly, at least, many scholars of the presidency see the cabinet ethos as being one of team play intermixed with independence and stature. This parallels our discussion of allegiance. Consider, for instance, the comment of Richard F. Fenno, Jr., *The President's Cabinet* (Cambridge, Mass.: Harvard University Press, 1959), p. 35, "Historically, an emphasis on the Cabinet is frequently associated with a set of attitudes and beliefs which minimizes strong executive leadership. Individuals of the persuasion are apt to accent 'the men around me,' 'the best minds,' or 'the Team' to the relative detraction of the presidential office." For other studies on the federal staff/cabinet differences, see Hess, *Organizing the Presidency*; Sidey, "White House Staff vs. the Cabinet"; and Hugh Heclo, *A Government of Strangers* (Washington, D.C.: Brookings Institution, 1977).

35. For discussions of appointee recruitment at the federal level, see Marver H. Bernstein, *The Job of the Federal Executive* (Washington, D.C.: The Brookings Institution, 1958); Dean E. Mann, *The Assistant Secretaries* (Washington, D.C.: The Brookings Institution 1965); Heclo, *A Government of Strangers*; Laurin L. Henry, "The Presidency, Executive Staffing, and the Federal Bureaucracy," in Aaron Wildavsky, *The Presidency* (Boston: Little, Brown, 1969), p. 529–57. At the gubernatorial level, the literature on recruitment of administrative managers is not large or very insightful. For a short discussion, see Martha Wagner Weinberg, *Managing The State*, p. 35–37.

36. The recruitment is cloaked in a formality that partially disguises the impossibility of actually finding the "best" qualified people for the jobs. Murray Edelman's comments, as usual, are right to the point: "Although there is obviously no systematic canvass of all the available talent in selecting people for elective or appointive posts, and although a large fraction of the talent is systematically rejected for reasons other than their qualifications, the impression is assiduously cultivated and apparently widely accepted that the candidates under active consideration represent the carefully winnowed pick of the crop" (*The Symbolic Uses of Politics*, p. 88).

37. In the following discussion of the appointment procedures used by the two

governors, we only analyze the selection of administrative appointees. Selection of judges and members of boards and commissions are also a task of the Governor's Office, but are not handled in the same way or with the same criteria in mind. We should also mention a difference between Reagan's and Brown's aides in charge of appointments, including the aides on the recruitment task force that each appointed during their transition into office. With Reagan, the appointments sections was headed by one of Reagan's campaign chairmen, Tom Reed, who was publicly known as a "politico," a person more interested in politics than in administration. Unlike Reagan, however, Brown appointed Carlotta Mellon to head his appointments section. Mellon, a novice in politics, was an academic, a professor of history and women's studies at Pomona College, before her appointment to the Governor's Office. Similarly the recruitment task force was made up of people with little or no experience in party politics.

38. It should be noted that many of Brown's appointments to administrative positions became known for their lack of administrative ability, and this was also true for Brown's first director of the Department of Health services, Jerome Lackner; his lack of skill in this regard provided the substance of numerous newspaper articles. For instance, see the page one articles of the *Sacramento Bee*, March 24 and 25, 1978. Brown's second director, Beverlee Myers, supposedly had better managerial skills. See chapter 7 for a further discussion of this point.

39. Both administrations tried to "balance" their appointments, but the definition of a balanced set of appointments differed greatly. To Reagan's aides a balanced set of appointments tended toward evenness in northern/southern, urban/rural, private/public, conservative/moderate dimensions. Some women and some minorities showed up on Reagan's roster, but very few in comparison with Brown's. To Brown and his aides, a balanced set included very few businessmen and -women but did include many people with a range of political views, as well as women and minorities.

40. Edelman, *Symbolic Uses of Politics*, p. 88, makes an acute and largely accurate observation about the selection for expertise: "That a man is conspicuous is what makes him a potential candidate for high public office. Nor does it much matter for what reason he has become conspicuous so long as his achievements are generally regarded as respectable."

41. For more information on Reagan's political philosophy, see chapter 7.

42. For more information on Brown's political philosophy, see chapter 7.

43. This outline is found in chapter 7, pp. 184–85.

44. Reagan, of course, appointed Republican Party regulars to many posts, but he did not know many of these individuals before their appointment and he insisted that these individuals be qualified to manage specific executive units. More important, Reagan's appointments show no evidence of clientage in the sense that William Nelson ("Officeholding and Powerwielding," *Law and Society Review* 10, no. 2 [Winter 1976]:187–233) shows was the case earlier in the United States system of government.

45. Appointee separation from the President is a theme of several discussions of Cabinet officials. See Fenno, *The President's Cabinet*; Cronin, *The State of the Presidency*; and Hess, *Organizing the Presidency*, for their comments on this point.

46. See chapter 7 for further discussion of Reagan's cabinet system.

47. For similar comments made in reference to the President see Cronin, *The State of the Presidency*, pp. 183–88.

CHAPTER FOUR. THE GOVERNOR'S ADMINISTRATIONS (CONTINUED)

1. For some statements about the authority of cabinet level officers, see Fenno, *The President's Cabinet* (Cambridge, Mass.: Harvard University Press, 1959).

2. A distinction between power and authority is found in chapter 6. In general, we find that authority is embodied in the role and that one's power within an administration is conditioned by one's role performance.

3. The phrase "captured by the bureaucracy" or "captured appointee" is a cliché, and there has been little research to uncover its exact meaning and significance. Our finding is that appointees must, to some degree, be captured by the bureaucracy if they are to succeed in their jobs. This is the same conclusion that Fenno, *The President's Cabinet*, p. 232, reached:

> His very position as head of one executive establishment among several carries with it certain attitudes and organizational necessities non-presidential in character. He inherits an immense bureaucratic structure with its own traditions, its own *raison d'être*, and its own operating methods. None of these depend on him, nor will he be able to alter them very significantly. He cannot help but become a part of this particular organization, supporting its vested interests, concerned for its *esprit de corps*, and speaking for it in all of its conflicts.

4. The distinction between authority and influence or persuasion is a fairly common one. See for instance Herbert Simon's discussion of this in *Administrative Behavior* (New York: Free Press, 1945), pp. 126–28. For a more recent and very good discussion of this, see Sanford M. Dornbusch and W. Richard Scott, *Evaluation and the Exercise of Authority* (San Francisco: Jossey-Bass, 1975). Our approach differs from theirs in our emphasis that both the ability to command and the requirement to persuade are part of the appointees' role obligation and hence are aspects of their legitimized or authorized power. At a more general level, then, the powers of command and the powers of persuasion are not as distinct as many treatments would suggest, but are usually, we would argue, aspects of role-related conduct.

5. Cronin's comment about this point at the federal level is accurate at the state level as well. Quoting a former subcabinet official, he writes:

> One basic problem lies in the fact that domestic cabinet members are so rarely with the president that when they do have a chance to see him, they have to advocate and plug the departmental program in an almost emotional style, trying to make a plea for expanded appropriation or some new departmental proposal. (*The State of the Presidency*, pp. 198–99.)

6. Fenno's *The President's Cabinet*, p. 248, in regard to federal level cabinet officials, makes this same point very nicely:

As a group the Cabinet draws its life breath from the President, but as individuals the Cabinet members are by no means so dependent on him. In many instances, we are presented with the paradox that in order for the Cabinet member to be of real help to the President in one of his leadership roles, the member must have non-presidential "public" prestige, party following, legislative support, or roots of influence in his department. And in any case, the problems of his own success and survival will encourage him to consolidate his own nexus of power and will compel him to operate with some degree of independence from the President.

In a similar vein, Hugh Heclo, *A Government of Strangers* (Washington, D.C.: Brookings Institution, 1977), p. 97, cites an unsuccessful Nixon attempt to garner personal loyalty from his appointees.

The Nixon administration eventually went further than any other in trying to clarify the lines of allegiance by placing White House loyalists in key department positions. Yet well before the Watergate controversy began weakening the administration, experience was beginning to show why some division rather than a monopoly of loyalties has usually been found to be more satisfactory. . . . One of Nixon's aides responsible for these placements expressed the inevitable dilemma of overcentralization: "I didn't think this would be much of a problem but it was. For the guy to be worth controlling, he has to know what is going on in his department. If he knows what's going on there, he's less likely to be amenable to social control."

7. On the interplay between symbols, conflict, and cooperation in an administrative setting, see Murray Edelman's insightful treatment in *The Symbolic Uses of Politics*, chapter 3.

8. Other spheres also allow the governor to exert controls over appointee behavior, such as through the State Personnel Board, whose members the governor appoints. But no other spheres offer the governor such direct control as finance and legislation.

9. The Department of Finance is a control agency within state government. The governor has fairly open access to the Department of Finance because he appoints the director, because the Department has cabinet status, and because it is the only department or agency office located in the same building as the Governor's Office. Nonetheless, the Department of Finance is a distinct force within state government, quite separate from the governor's authority, and is staffed by highly professionalized career civil servants. The same is true for the federal level. See Larry Berman's excellent study, *The Office of Management and Budget and the Presidency, 1921–1974* (Princeton: Princeton University Press, 1979). Also see footnote 13 below.

10. In contrast to the federal level, state-level administrative appointees do not have an open access to the legislature because of the Governor's control over the budget and legislative package. For the federal level, see David B. Truman, "Presidential Executives or Congressional Executives?" in Aaron Wildavsky (ed.), *The Presidency* (Boston: Little, Brown, 1969), pp. 486–91.

11. At the federal level, Cronin (*The State of the Presidency*, pp. 198–99) calls this obligation of appointees to battle for their department "advocacy conflicts."

12. See chapter 7 for our comments about Reagan's dislike of open conflict among his appointees and staff members. Therefore, most such conflicts occurred without Reagan's full knowledge that something was happening.

13. One of Brown's former staff aides explained the role of Finance in state government as follows:

> [Don't] confuse Finance with the Administration. It's really a separate force with its own powerful myths. It's a bit like the Administration, but it's not. It's a bit like career civil service, but it's not. My Church politics aren't terrific, but I'd liken Finance to the Jesuits. They're part of the Administration/Church, but they don't work directly for the Governor/Pope. Instead they work for the Director of Finance/Director General. . . . The recurring tension between agency secretaries and Finance is like the conflict between the Curia and the Jesuits. Why? Because Finance (and the Jesuits) have their own code-within-a-code. Highly trained and professional, each group really answers to its own norms. Finance battles the departments who want to get more money, and it battles the Governor and his staff who are looking for political gain. Fought by both groups, Finance turns inward, and . . . rewards its faithful "number-crunchers" with slow advancement through the hierarchy. . . . Finance is its own team, just like the Jesuits.

14. See Cronin's very similar conclusions regarding staff views of cabinet officials and vice versa (*The State of the Presidency*, chapters 6 and 7).

15. News about some of these conflicts reached the California press. For the struggle to control the state drug program see the *Sacramento Bee*, April 10, 1976, p. C16. For a struggle over which unit could stipulate state policy with regard to the proposal of Dow Chemical to locate a plant in California, see *Los Angeles Times*, January 26, 1977, p. 1. For a bureaucratic feud over the rights to hire personnel, see *Sacramento Union*, January 7, 1980, p. 1, and *Sacramento Union*, July 16, 1981. For a jurisdictional squabble between agency secretary and department director, see *Sacramento Bee*, August 21, 1982.

16. For details, see the *Sacramento Union*, January 30, 1979, and especially *Sacramento Union*, March 25, 1979. Also *Sacramento Union*, August 31, 1981, p. 1.

17. Brown's first Director of Finance was Roy Bell, a career civil servant who had served in the Department of Finance for 32 years before his appointment. After Proposition 13, a property tax reduction amendment, was approved by voters, and the state surplus began to be given to local governments, Bell came under attack as being unable to make the political decisions required by Brown. Brown demoted Bell in 1978 and replaced him first with Richard Silberman and later Mary Ann Graves, both outsiders to Finance before their appointments.

18. On resignations from public life, see Edward Weisband and Thomas M. Franck, *Resignation in Protest* (New York: Grossman, 1975).

19. Resignation in protest is rare in American politics. This in part is explained by Weisband and Franck (*Resignation in Protest*, p. 113), who compare the U.S. and Great Britain, where resignations in protest are not only more frequent, but have a prescribed ritual. "Parliament does not forgive a member who resigns high office, except when he does so for weighty reasons of principle. Thus, whereas the American cabinet member will deliberately overlook policy differences in stating that his resignation is for personal reasons, the British cabinet member will tend to overlook personal aspects of a resignation to stress policy differences." For some additional

discussion of loyalty and resignation, see Albert O. Hirschman's, *Exit Voice and Loyalty* (Cambridge, Mass.: Harvard University Press, 1970).

20. The most publicized firing of an appointee occurred in 1978, when Brown dismissed Dr. Jerome Lackner as Director of the State Department of Health in part for his lack of administrative ability. In Lackner's final press conference held with Brown, Lackner explained some of the differences he had had with Brown, and remarked "Although I love the governor dearly, there have been times . . . when I have had the impulse to swiftly juxtapose the dorsum of my distal right extremity into the posterior spheroidicities encasing the gubernatorial ischial tuberosities," *Sacramento Bee*, March 27, 1978, p. A8.

21. James D. Lorenz, *The Man on the White Horse* (Boston: Houghton Mifflin, 1978).

22. Ibid., p. 174.

23. Ibid., p. 218.

24. See chapter 6 for an extended discussion of role performances.

25. The same sort of frustration is evident among those at the federal level whom Cronin calls outer-cabinet members: "The blunt advice of a former Nixon labor secretary to those who come after him was 'nobody is going to appreciate what you do and you are going to get shafted from all sides.' " (*The State of the Presidency*, p. 198).

CHAPTER FIVE. THE GOVERNOR'S EXPERTS: HIGHER CIVIL SERVANTS

1. Much has been written about how modern industrial societies are increasingly being populated by technocrats. Technocrats are specialists with highly particularized skills who are knowledgeable in a restricted sphere. Experts, in contrast, have broader skills that may be applied in a variety of situations by a variety of clients. See Anthony Downs, *Inside Bureaucracy* (Boston: Little, Brown, 1967) for a discussion of specialists in bureaus.

2. The word "divine" is used intentionally to describe the work of experts. Expert consultants predate bureaucratic organization and in the premodern world were often called shamans, priests, witch doctors, astrologers, oracles, or simply wise men. But whatever their title, leaders used their superior knowledge to determine a course of action, such as going to war, or for finding the source of a failed plan. Modern consultants, whether in-house or outside, still play the role of the impersonal dispenser of knowledge, often with briefing rituals as elaborate as a medicine man's.

3. For discussions of professionalism see, for example, Anselm Strauss, *Professions, Work and Careers* (San Francisco: The Sociology Press, 1971); Wilbert E. Moore, *The Professions: Roles and Rules* (New York: Russell Sage, 1970); and Julius A. Roth, Sheryl K. Ruzek, and Arlene K. Daniels, "Current State of the Sociology of Occupations," *The Sociological Quarterly* 14 (1973):309–33.

4. The CEA is an example of what Whyte calls a "social invention," a new role or organizational structure devised to meet felt needs. William Foote Whyte, "Social

Inventions for Solving Human Problems," *American Sociological Review* 47 (1982):1–13.

5. John F. Fisher and Robert J. Erickson, "California's Career Executive Assignment," *Public Personnel Review* 23 (1964):82–86; Lloyd D. Musolf, "California's Career Executive Assignment: A Perilous but Necessary Voyage," *Public Personnel Review* 23 (1964):87–89.

6. Greg King, *Deliver Us From Evil: A Public History of California's Civil Service System* (Sacramento: State Office of Planning and Research, 1979).

7. California State Government was paralleling similar developments in the federal government. See Paul P. Van Riper's comprehensive work *History of the United States Civil Service* (Evanston, Ill.: Row, Peterson, 1958).

8. John Birkenstock, Ronald Kurtz, and Steven Phillips, "Career Executive Assignments—Report on a California Innovation," *Public Personnel Management* 4 (May–June 1975):151–55.

9. U.S. Commission on Organization of the Executive Branch of the Government, Personnel Policy Committee (Washington, D.C.: U.S. Government Printing Office, 1949).

10. A Brookings Institution study renewed interest in alternative federal personnel systems in the 1960s. David T. Stanley, *The Higher Civil Service* (Washington, D.C.: Brookings Institution, 1964). For a recent description of the work of members of the SES, see Loretta R. Flanders, "Senior Executive Service and Mid-Managers' Job Profiles," report of the U.S. Office of Personnel Management, Washington, D.C., March 1981.

11. The rationale and anticipated functioning of the CEA program is outlined in a letter dated December 20, 1963, from the State Personnel Board to Governor Brown, Sr. and to the legislature (Government Documents, Shields Library, University of California, Davis). The Board saw this new role as a response to the "Managerial crisis brought on by multiplying complexities in all of our functions and enterprises." See also Bruce Hackett, *Higher Civil Servants in California* (Berkeley and Davis: Institute of Governmental Studies and Institute of Governmental Affairs, 1969).

12. The CEA differs in some respects from the federal Senior Executive System. In California certain jobs carry CEA ranks; in Washington, SES employees carry their own rank to the job. No CEA may come from outside the government service; the SES system permits the recruiting of a limited number of non-civil servants to SES ranks.

13. Four other state governments have developed senior executive systems; Minnesota, Oregon, Wisconsin, and Iowa. See Arthur L. Finkle, Herbert Hall, and Sophia S. Min, "Senior Executive Service: The State of the Art," *Public Personnel Management* 10 (Fall 1981):299–305.

14. Marc Bloch, *Feudal Society* (Chicago: University of Chicago Press, 1961), p. 147.

15. *Feudal Society*, p. 146.

16. *Economy and Society*, p. 959.

17. Impersonality should not be confused with neutrality. CEAs often performed

highly political activities; they did not, however, initiate them or make political decisions.

18. The ethics of political neutrality and bureaucratic expertise have given rise to what is often described as intransigence in American bureaucracies, and the CEAs and the SES are responses to this. But in Communist China, where political loyalty to the party is required of *all* government workers, the crisis is one of competence, not loyalty. See Ezra Vogel, "Cadres, Bureaucracy, and Political Power," in *Communist China*, Doak Barnet (New York: Columbia University Press, 1967).

19. State Personnel Board report of June 30, 1978, submitted by Board President William R. Gianelli to the Senate Finance Committee and the Assembly Ways and Means Committee.

20. Senior Executive Service employees in the federal government are also used frequently as liaisons to other agencies and the Congress. Rudi Klauss, Darleen Fisher, Loretta Flanders, Lisa Carlson, Martin Griffith, and Mary Hoyer, "Senior Executive Service Competencies," report of the U.S. Office of Personnel Management, Washington, D.C., July 1981.

21. A leader cannot disregard his experts with impunity, however. "When the expert has effectively performed his task of pointing out the necessary ways and means, there is generally only one logical and admissible solution. The politician will then find himself obliged to choose between the technician's solution, which is the only reasonable one, and other solutions, which he can indeed try out at his own peril but which are not reasonable." Jacques Ellul, *The Technological Society* (New York: Vintage, 1964), pp. 258–59.

22. This "objectivity" could be a managerial liability at times. The most rational plan can fail in government for not having considered adequately the political dimension. The politician must always infuse political aims into expert advice. Experts can argue choices on technical grounds, but action for a political leader must in the end be evaluated for its ability for further goals, and for its philosophic and moral content. Guy Beneviste, in *The Politics of Expertise* (San Francisco: Boyd and Fraser, 1977), pp. 3–4, recounts Georges Pompidou's fear of experts when he was prime minister of France, a post surrounded by the experts of the French bureaucracy. "He said there were three ways for a politician to ruin his career: chasing women, gambling, and trusting experts. The first, he said, was the most pleasant and the second the quickest, but trusting experts was the surest."

23. Lloyd Musolf, p. 89.

CHAPTER SIX. POWER AND ROLE PERFORMANCES

1. In our use of the term here, "developmental" does not connote evolutionism in the sense that change follows predictable and inevitable courses or stages of being. We use developmental in the sense that Weber used "rationalization." Here changes are products of human doing and represent the systematization of human conduct and belief with reference to some facet of life. A developmental sequence, such as the executive changes described in this chapter, represent, in analytical terms, a se-

ries of efforts to systematize conduct with reference to a consistent, though changing, set of practices, beliefs, and problems. For some excellent attempts to develop the Weberian concept of rationalization, as well as a notion of developmental change, see Guenther Roth and Wolfgang Schluchter, *Max Weber's Vision of History* (Berkeley: University of California Press, 1979) and Wolfgang Schluchter, *The Rise of Western Rationalism* (Berkeley: University of California Press, 1981). For a fine analysis of the meanings of rationalization in Weber's writing, see Stephen Kalberg, "Max Weber's Types of Rationality: Cornerstones for the Analysis of Rationalization Processes in History," *American Journal of Sociology* 85 (March 5, 1980):1145–79.

2. Many students of American government have noted the antimonarchical attitudes of most of the authors of federal and state constitutions. Strongly expressed in the documents upon which early executive government was based, this antimonarchical bias led to a separation of powers, to a rudimentary and often to no idea of executive departments, and to a powerful legitimizing myth that governmental authority resided in the people. For some works on the distrust of executive power and on the centrality of the idea of the people, see Joseph E. Kallenbach, *The American Chief Executive: The Presidency and the Governorship* (New York: Harper and Row, 1966); R. R. Palmer, *The Age of Democratic Revolution* (Princeton: Princeton University Press, 1959); Seymour Martin Lipset, *The First New Nation* (New York: Basic Books, 1963); Garry Wills, *Inventing America* (New York: Vintage Books, 1979). Also see additional references below in note 6.

3. There have been two constitutional conventions in California's past, the first in 1849 and the second in 1878–79. For an analysis of the first convention, see Woodrow James Hansen, *The Search for Authority in California* (Oakland, California: Biobook, 1960), and for analysis of the second, see Carl Brent Swisher, *Motivation and Political Technique in the California Constitutional Convention, 1878–79.* (New York: Da Capo Press, 1969). The 1878–79 convention employed stenographers and the record is collected in three volumes, *Debates and Proceedings of the Constitutional Convention of the State of California* (Sacramento: State Office, 1880).

4. This definition of organization is the one found in *The Compact Edition of the Oxford English Dictionary* (New York: Oxford University Press, 1971), p. 1008. The OED lists the first use of organization with this meaning as 1816. A similar meaning ("construction in which parts are so disposed as to be subservient to each other") is found in Samuel Johnson's *A Dictionary of the English Language* (1827 edition), which derives from Glanville's and Locke's seventeenth-century use of the term. In all these usages, however, organization is not a thing in its own right, but rather always refers to something else being constructed so that the parts relate to one another as well as to the whole. Only in the middle portion of the nineteenth century was organization used as a general term to identify a group of people in systematic association with one another. The OED (p. 2008) records Herbert Spencer, in 1873 in *The Study of Sociology*, as the first to use the term to mean "an organized body, system, or society." Recently, students of Social Darwinism and of the Progressive era have found the growth of organizations to be one of the most important developments of the era. In particular, see Alfred D. Chandler, Jr.'s monumental work

on the topic: *The Visible Hand, The Managerial Revolution in American Business* (Cambridge, Mass.: Harvard University Press, 1977). Chandler's study documents the growth of complex business organization. See references in footnote 11, for the growth of complex organization in government.

5. The 1849 Constitution, as amended in 1862, contains 3 different uses of the term organization. The counties, the militia and the Legislature were said to be organized or in a state of organization. For example, with reference to the Legislature, the 1949 Constitution states in Article 12, Section 9, "If this Constitution shall be ratified by the people of California, the Legislature shall assemble at the seat of government on the fifteenth day of December next, and in order to complete the organization of that body the Senate shall elect a President pro tempore. . . ." This usage of organization as well as the others in the 1849 constitution means more the act of being brought together than a systematic whole. In the 1879 constitution, organization retains the earlier meaning in most uses of the term, which occurs 5 times, but in at least one reference (Article 9, Section 9) the more modern usage of the term appears: "The University of California shall constitute a public trust, and it's organization and government shall be perpetually continued in the form and character prescribed by the Organic Act. . . ."

6. A number of scholars have analyzed governors and state constitutions and have uniformly concluded that in early state governments, in contrast to the federal, executive power was always weak and often split among elected officers. In addition to the references in note 2 above, see Leslie Lipson, *The American Governor: From Figurehead to Leader* (Chicago: University of Chicago Press, 1939) and Larry Sabato, *Goodbye to Good-time Charlie* (Lexington, Mass.: Lexington Books, 1978), chapter 1.

7. These are Lieutenant Governor, Secretary of State, Controller, Treasurer, Attorney General, Surveyor General, Superintendent of Public Instruction, plus four members to the State Board of Equalization.

8. See Barrow's discussion of these divisions in executive power in "Reorganization of State Administration in California," *California Law Review* 3, no. 2 (January 1915), pp. 94–95.

9. *Constitution of the State of California*, Article V, Sections 5–13.

10. Ibid., Article V, Section 1.

11. Martin J. Schiesl, *The Politics of Efficiency* (Berkeley: University of California Press, 1977). On the same point also see Robert Wiebe, *The Search for Order, 1877–1920* (New York: Hill and Wang, 1967) and Barry Dean Karl, *Executive Reorganization in the New Deal: The Genesis of Administrative Management 1900–1939* (Cambridge, Mass.: Harvard University Press, 1963).

12. W. W. Mather, *Administrative Reorganization in California* (Ontario, California: Chaffey Junior College, 1929), pp. 22–23.

13. Cited by Mather, ibid., p. 26.

14. Cited by Mather, ibid., pp. 26–27.

15. Before the rise of modern bureaucratic organization, centralized political authority was conceived of in terms of a ruling personage, in Weber's terms, of a pa-

trimonial or charismatic ruler. Administration, meaning an arrangement of staff positions, a governing apparatus, was never explicitly unified. Nor was it conceived this way. Rather the apparatus was a systematic assignment of authority that followed the maxim "divide and rule." See Weber's discussion of patrimonial and charismatic domination in *Economy and Society* (New York: Bedminster Press, 1968), chapters 12–15. Also see Reinhard Bendix, *Kings or People* (Berkeley: University of California Press, 1978).

16. For greater development of this idea, see Schiesl, *Politics of Efficiency*; Wiebe, *Search for Order*; and Louis Galambos, "The Emerging Organizational Synthesis in Modern American History," *Business History Review* 44, no. 3 (Autumn 1970), pp. 279–90.

17. An elaboration of this point is found in Gary Hamilton and John Sutton, "The Common Law and Social Reform: The Rise of Administrative Justice in the U.S., 1880–1920" (unpublished paper presented at the 1982 Annual Meeting of the Law and Society Association, Toronto, Canada).

18. Earlier attempts at executive reorganization did not succeed in recasting the structure of state government but did certainly strengthen the governor's authority. Some discussion of the earlier attempts, as well as the 1919 reorganization, is found in Mather, *Administrative Reorganization*; James R. Bell and Earl L. Darrah, *State Executive Reorganization* (Berkeley: University of California Press, 1961; and Gerald D. Nash, *State Government and Economic Development* (Berkeley: University of California Press, 1964).

19. *Report of the Committee on Efficiency and Economy of California* (Sacramento: California State Printing Office, 1919), p. 22.

20. Ibid., p. 23.

21. After 1919, the movement towards a unified executive organization proceeded slowly but surely. See Mather's complaint and recommendation on this score (*Administrative Reorganization*, chapters 8 and 9).

22. Bell and Darrah, *State Executive Reorganization*.

23. *Report to the Governor on Reorganization of State Government* (Sacramento: State Printing Office, 1959), p. 14.

24. Ibid.

25. Ibid., p. 39.

26. For a description and analysis of the amendment, see "Organization of the Executive Branch," *California Legislature Assembly Interim Committee on Government Organization* vol. 12, no. 12 (1967).

27. California Legislature, *Assembly Committee Report on Executive Reorganization Plans 1 and 2 of 1970*, p. 3.

28. Many recent works on power and authority do not distinguish in qualitative terms a typology of power. Some important exceptions include Sanford M. Dornbusch and W. Richard Scott, *Evaluation and the Exercise of Authority* (San Francisco: Jossey-Bass, 1975) and Dennis Wrong, *Power, Its Forms, Bases and Uses* (New York: Harper & Row, 1979). Others make a distinction among the sources or bases of power, such as J. R. French, Jr. and B. H. Raven in "The Bases of Social Power,"

in D. Cartwright (ed.) *Studies in Social Power* (Ann Arbor: University of Michigan Press, 1959) and Amitai Etzioni, *A Comparative Analysis of Complex Organizations* (New York: Free Press of Glencoe, 1961). But these distinctions differ somewhat from ours. We argue that power of one over the other takes its justification from role relations. Thus qualitatively different role relations imply different types of power. In this regard, our argument harkens back to Weber's typology of domination in *Economy and Society*. The same sort of argument, as well as a similar Weberian foundation, is also present in Herbert Goldhamer and Edward A. Shils, "Types of Power and Status," *The American Journal of Sociology* 45, no. 2 (September 1939):171–82.

29. Important academic definitions of the distinction between the two terms include Richard Emerson, "Power-dependence Relations," *American Sociological Review* 27 (February 1962):31–40; James March, "The Power of Power" in David Easton (ed.), *Varieties of Political Theory* (Englewood Cliffs: Prentice-Hall, 1966), pp. 39–70; Terry N. Clark, "The Concept of Power" in Terry N. Clark (ed.) *Community Structure and Decision Making* (San Francisco: Chandler, 1968); Dennis Wrong, "Some Problems in Defining Social Power," *American Journal of Sociology* 73 (May 1968):673–81. Dornbusch and Scott, in *Evaluation*, survey most of the theoretical literature and thoughtfully draw their own conclusion that power in organizations exists in an atmosphere of performance and evaluation, a conclusion we reach as well.

30. Our definitions and analysis are based on an interpretation of interview material, the summary of which follows. But a number of power theorists have made a similar point that power implies a scope. See, for example, Wrong, "Some Problems" and *Types of Social Power*, and Samuel B. Bacharach and Edward J. Lawler, *Power and Politics in Organizations* (San Francisco: Jossey-Bass, 1980). Fewer theorists identify a style of action as a defining quality of power. Exceptions include David Bell, *Power, Influence and Authority* (New York: Oxford University Press, 1975); Stewart Clegg, *The Theory of Power and Organization* (London: Routledge and Kegan Paul, 1979); and most to the point, Darwin L. Thomas, David D. Franks, and James M. Calonico, "Role-taking and Power in Social Psychology," *American Sociological Review* 37, no. 5 (October 1973):605–14. For a more in-depth and more theoretical analysis of power defined in terms of roles, see Gary Hamilton and Nicole Biggart, "The Power of Obedience" (unpublished paper presented at the 1982 Annual Meeting of the Society for the Study of Symbolic Interaction, San Francisco).

31. Our analysis suggests that authority implies an organized system of control that is logically integrated in terms of legitimizing principles. In this regard, we draw upon Weber's sociology of domination found in *Economy and Society*. Also see references in note 34.

32. In the most common usage power means, quite simply, the ability to control another person's behavior despite their resistance. This is Weber's definition as well (*Economy and Society*, p. 53) and is also the basis of Robert Dahl's and Richard Emerson's well-known behaviorist definitions, found respectively in "The Concept of Power," *Behavioral Science* 2 (July 1957):201–15; and "Power-dependence Relations."

33. Our interviews show that people clearly attribute power to individuals so that, for example, they can discuss the differences in power between two individuals who had occupied the same position. They attribute the differences to a person's style, which we here term role performance. The following are several quotations that illustrate the awareness of role performances. Said one appointee about two individuals who had been Brown's chief-of-staff, "A lot depends on the personal style of the individual. [One person] is more organized in terms of time and in terms of meeting agendas and calendars; and [the other person] is more oriented toward making sure there's a full discussion of the issue. No matter who goes in there, whether it's [one] or [the other] or somebody else, there's a personal style that's going to involve that job." In comparing Reagan's legislative aide with Brown's, a lobbyist noted, "Every administration has a sort of spokesperson who is supposed to fill that role. But you'll get personality differences. Some people will feel more comfortable dealing with [Brown's aide] than they did dealing with [Reagan's aide]. That is not a formal or structural difference [between administrations], but it is a matter of personality." A CEA makes this point more generally: "I don't care if it's [the Governor's] Office or any office, but the personal style of the individuals running it is going to characterize the method of operation. I don't think there's anything unique in that. Whether it's a governor's office or any agency office or a director's office or any government or any private industry office, as a matter of fact, the characteristics of the man or the woman making the decisions are decisive [in how those jobs are done.]" References to the academic literature on role performances and power are found in note 35.

34. The people we interviewed made the distinction between role legitimacy and personal legitimacy in their evaluations of one or the other, as the following quote shows. One CEA noted in reference to department directors in general, "I don't think there's any question in the bureaucracy that a director has a legitimate role . . . but [civil servants] are always going to have opinions as to how effective an individual is in that role." A similar distinction between role and personal legitimacy is found occasionally in the literature on power, but most frequently and in line with Weber (*Economy and Society*, pp. 953–54) legitimacy is a term used only in reference to the structure of authority. This exclusive emphasis on role and structural legitimacy is characteristic of most organizational theorists. See, for instance, W. Richard Scott, *Organizations* (Englewood Cliffs, N.J.: Prentice-Hall, 1981), pp. 279–81, who in another connection links power, performance, and evaluation (ibid., pp. 283–86; also Dornbusch and Scott, *Evaluation*). A few theorists, however, see legitimacy to be primarily a function of performance and less so of structure, such as George J. McCall and J. L. Simmons, *Identities and Interactions* (New York: The Free Press, 1978), pp. 69–73, 92–100.

35. This conclusion of our analysis differs somewhat from the more conventional view that power depends upon resources and upon position in a network. For extremes on these views, see Karen Cook, "Exchange and Power in Networks of Interorganizational Relations," *Sociological Quarterly* 18, no. 1 (Winter 1977):62–82 and Ronald S. Burt, "Power in a Social Typology," in Roland J. Liebert and Allen W. Imershein, *Power, Paradigms, and Community Research* (Beverly Hills, Calif.: Sage,

1977), pp. 251–334. While we agree resources and positioning are important in matters of power calculations and attributions, we find that role and role performances are the beginning premises of calculations and attributions concerning power. In this regard, we find most useful the interactionist literature on power, which is not extensive. In particular, see Thomas et al., "Role-taking and Power in Social Psychology"; Mary F. Rogers, "Instrumental and Infra-Resources: The Bases of Power," *American Journal of Sociology* 79, (May 1974):1418–33; Mary F. Rogers, "Goffman and Power," *The American Sociologist* 12 (April 1977):88–95; Mary F. Rogers, "Goffman on Power, Hierarchy and Status" in Jason Ditton (ed.), *The View From Goffman* (New York: St. Martins Press, 1980); V. Lee Hamilton "Who is Responsible? Towards a Social Psychology of Responsibility Attribution," *Social Psychology* 41, no. 4 (December 1978):316–28; Thomas Scheff, "Negotiating Reality: Notes on Power in the Assessment of Responsibility," *Social Problems* 16 (Summer 1968):3–17; Edwin M. Schur, *The Politics of Deviance* (Englewood Cliffs, N.J.: Prentice-Hall, 1980). Also helpful are the structuralist and phenomenological treatments of power, such as those of David Bell, *Power, Influence and Authority*; Stewart Clegg, *The Theory of Power and Organization*; and Graeme Salaman and Kenneth Thompson (eds.), *Control and Ideology in Organizations* (Cambridge, Mass.: MIT Press, 1980).

36. "Interaction Ritual" is a term taken from Erving Goffman's book of that same name (Garden City, N.Y.: Anchor Books, 1964). Goffman's essays in this book, in particular "On Face-work" and "The Nature of Deference and Demeanor," are brilliant interpretations of organizational behavior that have been too little used by organizational theorists. The thrust of Goffman's analysis is to argue that in society "the person becomes a kind of construct, built up not from inner psychic propensities but from moral rules that are impressed upon him from without" (p. 45). These moral rules require the ritualized enactment of a social order and of people in that order: "Deference and demeanor practices must be institutionalized so that the individual will be able to project a viable, sacred self and stay in the game on a proper ritual basis" (p. 91). Randall Collins in "On the Microfoundations of Macrosociology," *American Journal of Sociology* 86, no. 5 (March 1981):984–1014, has used Goffman's work and the term "interaction ritual" to criticize role theory on the basis that value, norms, roles, and situation are "dubious constructions," because they never can be "fully defined" in interaction (p. 991). Although we agree with Goffman's main ideas, we disagree with Collins' excessive ethnomethodological bent. Our point of view is that interaction rituals in state government enforce the self-in-role and support the moral basis of that self. To be sure, such rituals are based upon tacit understandings about how roles and role identities should be established. But that such tacit knowledge exists, we argue, supports also the validity of role theory, both in action and in academic practice. For pertinent examples of role theory, see McCall and Simmons, *Identities and Interactions*; Ralph Turner, "The Real Self: From Institution to Impulse," *American Journal of Sociology* 84, no. 1 (July 1978):1–23; Sheldon Stryker, *Symbolic Interactionism* (Menlo Park, Ca.: Benjamin/Cummings, 1980).

37. For further discussion of this relation between obedience and power, see Hamilton and Biggart, "The Power of Obedience."

38. One of the important differences between our findings and those of most power theorists is the notion that power, however defined, should be viewed within a continuous stream of action and that one's exertion of control over another is seldom a single act disconnected with other acts in the past or planned actions in the future. Hence, effective power cannot be measured in terms of specific outcomes, cannot be isolated in the solitary act, and cannot be ripped out of an institutionalized context and only viewed in the abstract. Instead we find that the analysis of power always involves calculations made in an ongoing social setting with regard to repetitiveness, to a temporal spread, and with regard to qualitative distinctions made in that setting, such as those concerning roles.

39. A useful orientation to power and evaluation is found in Dornbusch and Scott, *Evaluation and the Exercise of Authority.*

40. On the concept of "loose coupling," see Karl Weick, "Educational Organizations as Loosely Coupled Systems, *Administrative Science Quarterly* 21 (1976):1–19.

41. For an excellent, though largely descriptive account of the California Legislature in action, see Michael J. Bevier, *Politics Backstage* (Philadelphia: Temple University Press, 1979), as well as Eugene Bardach's more analytic treatment in *The Skill Factor in Politics: Repealing the Mental Commitment Laws in California* (Berkeley: University of California Press, 1972).

42. This is not to say that all routines are equivalent. Clearly they are not. For example, the routines established for making decisions about signing legislative bills differed greatly between the two administrations. Reagan's Cabinet, meeting in lengthy sessions, would debate whether Reagan should sign or veto bills. Brown's legislative aides met with Brown, wherever he was or was going, in order to get the decisions on time. The point is that both administrations gradually created routines to handle the task of signing bills, because they had to get the job done.

43. Most decision-making literature assumes a model of economic rationality at its basis, although economic rationality may be "bounded" by constraints, such as time, money, or cognitive skills. We argue in this chapter, however, that organizational decision making is based on multiple models of *substantive* rationality that are differentiated by roles. Role-based value orientations are critical factors in such decision-making processes as setting goals, analyzing the appropriateness of alternatives, and gaining support for decisions. Decision making typically involves moral as well as economic calculations.

44. Many organization theorists have argued recently that goals in most organizations are seldom distinct and unambiguous and that they are often justifying accounts of past actions. See W. Richard Scott's (*Organization*, pp. 260–90) useful summary of these ideas. While we agree with this conclusion, we also note that people in state government must work in the contexts of ubiquitous goals. It is the nature of the political enterprise to have continuous discussions about goals.

45. For a good statement on account behavior, see Marvin Scott and Stanford Lyman, "Accounts," *American Sociological Review* 33 (December 1968):46–62.

46. This conclusion accords with a line of analysis taken by the pragmatist philosopher, George Herbert Mead, who, in 1924 in an article entitled "The Genesis of the Self and Social Control" (*The International Journal of Ethics* 35, p. 274), wrote the following:

> The human individual is a self only insofar as he takes the attitude of another toward himself. Insofar as this attitude is that of a number of others, and insofar as he can assume the organized attitudes of a number that are co-operating in a common activity, he takes the attitudes of the group toward himself, and in taking this or these attitudes he is defining the object of the group, that which defines and controls the response. Social control, then, will depend upon the degree to which the individual does assume the attitudes of those in the group who are involved with him in his social activities.

Later interactionists—Erving Goffman, George McCall, Ralph Turner, and others— have widened the appreciation of Mead's insights, but have not substantially changed them.

47. The conflict that this person is referring to has been nicely analyzed by Dale Everett Carter, *When Governors Change: The Case of Mental Hygiene* (Davis, Calif.: Institute of Governmental Affairs, University of California, Research Report No. 2, 1968).

48. Some organizational theorists assume that organization goals, and decisions more generally, can be objectively evaluated when, for instance, cost-benefit analysis is applied. Others are less optimistic. Simon (*Administrative Behavior*) and Lindblom ("Muddling Through") point to the limitations in making a fully objective decision, but first these limitations in the lack of information and of time, as well as the existence of obstructive values. Our view differs slightly from that of most organizational theorists in that we see objectivity and subjectivity, rationality and irrationality as being operating factors in making decisions but being defined entirely within conduct in settings. Objectivity is relative to settings and to thinkers but insofar as individuals share a common activity and establish common objects and symbols as a means to conduct that activity, then people have access to the organized attitudes of another's role. Therefore, they can evaluate another's objectivity in making decisions, which is a fact known to and hence a source of control upon the person making decisions. For some discussion of this sort of interpretation, see Salaman and Thompson, *Control and Ideology in Organizations*, sections 3 and 4.

49. The organization literature usually refers to strategies as organizational means to accomplish goals. See Scott's discussion in *Organization*, pp. 260–90. We use the term strategy to emphasize the strategic nature of calculated interaction that often occurs prior to goals but in anticipation of them. For some useful ideas about the analysis of strategies, see John Lofland, "Interactist Imagery and Analytic Interruptus," in Tomotsu Shibutani (ed.), *Human Nature and Collective Behavior* (Englewood Cliffs, N.J.: Prentice-Hall, 1970), pp. 35–45. For some case insight into strategies in California government, see Bardach, *Skill Factor*.

50. This is true generally rather than in this one case. See David L. Miller's discussion in *George Herbert Mead: Self, Language and the World* (Chicago: University of Chicago Press, 1973), p. 34. Writes Miller, "In order to solve problems and make adjustments by the aid of the symbolic process or by thinking, one must be conscious of alternative possible ways of responding towards and manipulating distant objects, physical objects."

51. One CEA told what happened when one did not do one's homework: "Usually what destroys almost any legislative hearing [is when] some assemblyman or senator says, 'When are you going to build my project?' And if you don't say, 'Tomorrow,' then all you do is go off on a project [discussion]." We found that people in government use their knowledge of the commitments of others to stop, short-circuit, or solicit their actions. As one Brown department director put it, "You have to be able to read people, situations, and know when you do, and when you don't."

52. The following example shows the perceived importance of building and maintaining a network. Sacramento, like Washington and other capital cities, has its share of "watering holes" where lobbyists, staff members, reporters and other people with an interest in government's actions meet on an informal basis. In the clublike atmosphere of the Brass Rail, acquaintances are made, information passed, and alliances created. One of Reagan's legislative aides spoke at length of his work day and that of his two fellow legislative aides. "Our typical day would go until the bars closed: two o'clock in the morning. But the rest of the staff was not subjected to that. [One of the aides], it might interest you, never drank anything but orange juice. I think the guy was a Mormon. He never touched liquor, and yet it was part of his job to be out there. Nobody ever told me or even suggested that I do it, but after all, I had been there a long time and I knew that if you wanted to get your job done, you'd better be out there with them."

53. For some useful ways to conceptualize bargaining and negotiation, see Samuel B. Bacharach and Edward J. Lawler, *Bargaining: Power, Tactics and Outcomes* (San Francisco: Jossey-Bass, 1981); Anselm L. Strauss, *Negotiations* (San Francisco: Jossey-Bass, 1978); and Robert Day and JoAnn V. Day, "A Review of the Current State of Negotiated Order Theory: An Appreciation and a Critique," *The Sociological Quarterly* 18 (1977):128–44. The Strauss view of negotiation is an insightful and useful extension of symbolic interactionism, but differs slightly from our own in a number of ways. The most important difference is our emphasis on the priority of structure and power in an individual's working out of his role relations and obligations. Structure establishes the parameters of negotiations; similar negotiations reoccur in similar structural settings.

54. State workers recognized the ubiquity of these conflicts, as well as their inevitability. They saw these conflicts as part of their jobs, and came to accept them as "natural." Said one Brown department head appointee about the conflict between appointees and civil servants, "I think that's just natural that as the relationship (between appointees and bureaucrats) continues and you [the appointee] start with your reforms and then you start getting the pressure of people who are affected beneath

by these changes, then the problems start and the frustrations build. The frustration level gets higher and then the senior civil servants and the appointees tend to lock horns on some of these issues and how to deal with these problems that have cropped up. I just think it's a natural process, and we have to work at it." Of the continuous conflict between the Department of Finance and other units in the executive branch, one Finance appointee said, "This conflict [between Finance and other departments] goes on; it is never really solved. It always continues—this conflict over who has the power to make budgetary decisions." Of the tension between appointees and the governor's staff, many stated that it was built into government. "That's a natural conflict," said one Reagan aide, "There's no way in the world you can avoid it."

55. Our interpretation here has benefitted from the work of Salaman and Thompson (*Control and Ideology*, section 4), as well as from the phenomenological work of Clegg *(The Theory of Power and Organization)*, and Peter Manning "Rules in Organizational Contexts" *Sociological Quarterly* 18, no. 1 (Winter 1977):46–63; "Rules, Colleagues and Situationally Justified Action," in Ralph Blankenship (ed.), *Colleagues in Organizations* (New York: John Wiley, 1977). We differ from their interpretation primarily in our emphasis upon the priority of rules and organizational structure, and in this regard we accept the more Weberian position that justifications of power only exist within an organized structure of domination.

56. Some important work has recently appeared on the emotional and ethical, as opposed to the economically rational, basis of organizational behavior. See Theodore Kemper, *A Social Interactional Theory of Emotions* (New York: John Wiley, 1978); Susan Schott, "Emotion and Social Life," *American Journal of Sociology* 84, no. 6 (May 1979):1317–34; Arlie R. Hochschild "Emotion Work, Feeling Rules, and Social Structure," *American Journal of Sociology* 85, no. 3 (November 1979):551–74; and Randall Collins, "On the Microfoundations of Macrosociology."

CHAPTER SEVEN. EXECUTIVE STRATEGIES AND THE STRUCTURE OF GOVERNMENT

1. Larry Sabato, "Goodbye to Good-Time Charlie" (Lexington, Mass.: D. C. Heath, 1978).

2. J. Oliver Williams, "Changing Perspectives on the American Governor," in Begle and Williams (eds.), *The American Governor in Behavioral Perspective* (New York: Harper and Row, 1972), pp. 1–6.

3. Jack Langguth, "Political Fun and Games in California," *New York Times Magazine*, October 16, 1966, pp. 27–28.

4. Pat Brown's philosophy is stated obliquely in his books about his successor: *Reagan, The Political Chameleon* (New York: Praeger, 1976); and *Reagan and Reality: The Two Californias* (New York: Praeger, 1970).

5. Tom Wicker, "Reagan Shuns Image of Goldwater in Coast Race," *New York Times*, June 1, 1966, p. 38.

6. This document, a copy of which we received from the Hoover Institution Archives (Stanford University), was mentioned frequently in interviews by Reagan ap-

pointees, particularly department directors who had less contact with the governor than cabinet officers. The Hoover Institution document does not indicate the author or distributor.

7. This analysis of Reagan's orientation is confirmed by his repeated confrontations with conservative ideologues, during both his gubernatorial and presidential incumbencies.

8. John C. Waugh, "Reagan, Warren Eras Contrasted," *Christian Science Monitor*, July 11, 1968.

9. An earlier analysis of the Reagan management style and structure, which is elaborated here, is Nicole Woolsey Biggart, "Management Style as Strategic Interaction: The Case of Governor Ronald Reagan," *Journal of Applied Behavioral Science* 17:291–308. For an excellent analysis of Reagan's biography as it has influenced his managerial orientation see Lou Cannon, *Reagan* (New York: Putnam, 1983).

10. Meese was one of the few top advisors to Reagan who was not part of either of his gubernatorial campaign efforts. Meese was a deputy attorney general in Alameda County (Oakland) when he was suggested for the Extraditions and Clemency Secretary position in the Governor's office (later retitled Legislative Affairs Secretary). His lack of campaign credentials, some interviewees suggested, was an important source of his later confrontation with Reagan political advisors. A good biography of Meese's career as an aide is Herb Michelson's "Meese: Old-Fashioned, Self-Effacing Reagan Aide," *Sacramento Bee*, August 10, 1980, p. A1.

11. An article in the *California Journal*, June 1970, pp. 151–53, described Clark's actions to open up the cabinet. "This effort to involve the operating departments and other constitutional officers in the decisions of the administration is a conscious reaction to the tight-knit circle that surrounded Battaglia and alienated those who were outside it." The article also describes the workings of the cabinet under Clark, and its later refinement under Meese.

12. In an interview with the *California Journal*, June 1970, pp. 156–58, Meese described his functions as chief of staff as having four components: finding the right people for positions, setting priorities, promoting communications within the staff, and keeping the Governor informed. It is clear that Meese saw his role as that of a facilitator, not a policy planner. This, of course, was in keeping with the managerial orientation of the Reagan administration.

13. In fact, the members of OPD cultivated an image of themselves as a group apart. For example, they all started to wear Mickey Mouse watches as a symbol of their group spirit. According to our interviews, this annoyed some members of the Governor's Office and served to alienate the OPD further.

14. Bell and Darrah, *Executive Reorganization*, p. 53.

15. W. Richard Scott makes the same point about formalized organizational processes generally. "Formalization also serves to objectify the structure—to make the definitions of roles and relationships appear to be both objective and external to the participating factors. These qualities contribute substantially to the efficacy of these systems in controlling behavior" (*Organizations*, p. 61).

16. Reagan's Secretary of Resources cited, as a humorous example, the only time

that the Governor bypassed him in a decision affecting his agency. California was considering a state duck stamp on hunting licenses, the proceeds of which would go to Ducks Unlimited, a Canadian organization. The Department of Fish and Game was "violently opposed" to the tax and Livermore prepared a "meticulous cabinet issue memo" in opposition. But before he could present it to the cabinet, the Governor approved the program. Livermore later heard that entertainer Bing Crosby had called the Governor urging his support, and Reagan had agreed. Livermore recalled that "then we had a duck dinner, and everybody laughed at me."

17. Reagan, largely at the request of Nancy Reagan, decided to vacate the old Governor's Mansion because it was drafty and lacked the stateliness required of the Governor's position. With money raised from wealthy Republican backers, the Reagans moved to a more suitable house. At the same time, Reagan initiated the legislation for a more modern Governor's Mansion. This mansion was finished by the 1974 election, when Governor-elect Jerry Brown refused to occupy the building. This incident has been admirably interpreted by Joan Didion in *The White Album*.

18. In his classic work about the movement of government from personal rule to impersonal organization, Sheldon Wolin, *Politics and Vision* (Boston: Little, Brown, 1960), p. 383, discusses how the formal structuring of government makes experience and skill unnecessary. "Organization, by simplifying and routinizing procedures, eliminates the need for surpassing talent. It is predicated on 'average' human beings."

19. A recent study of theater companies demonstrates how routinization and formalization in the form of "role clarity" actually inhibits innovation. See R. A. Goodman and L. P. Goodman, "Some Management Issues in Temporary Systems: A Study of Professional Development and Manpower," *Administrative Science Quarterly* 21:494–501. Jerald Hage and Michael Aiken, "Program Change and Organizational Properties," *American Journal of Sociology* 72, no. 5, pp. 503–19, found that the adoption of new programs is negatively correlated with formalization because people in standardized settings have little time or support for innovation.

20. See *California Journal*, July 1, 1973, pp. 123–27, for a description of the working of the Reagan Task Forces on Health. These task forces were typical of the type favored by Reagan.

21. David S. Broder, "Candidate Brown—A Politician of the '70's?" *Los Angeles Times*, May 9, 1974, section 2, p. 7.

22. Robert Pack, *Jerry Brown: Philosopher Prince* (New York: Stein and Day, 1978).

23. Orville Schell, *Brown* (New York: Random House, 1978), p. 3.

24. Douglas L. Hallett, " 'New Progressivism' Links Brown Reagan," *Los Angeles Times*, October 19, 1975, found Reagan and Brown to be linked philosophically to the extent that they both opposed the program-orientation of the previous three decades of government. "Ronald Reagan and now Jerry Brown have begun an equally fundamental—and potentially equal [sic] influential—revolt against the New Deal liberalism their fathers served, respectively, as a minor WPA official and California chief executive." Our conclusion differs insofar as we see Reagan distrustful of government, and Brown with little confidence in the powers of government, rather than the two sharing similar beliefs.

25. Joseph Lelyveld, "Jerry Brown's Space Program," *New York Times Magazine*, July 17, 1977.

26. An intriguing selection of Brown's philosophical statements is to be found in *Thoughts* (San Francisco: City Lights, 1976).

27. Brown's nontraditional appointments to government posts were given considerable attention by the press. See, for example, Nancy Friedman, "Brown and Women: How Affirmative the Action," *California Journal*, September 1975, pp. 311–12; Lee Fremstad, "The Team That Jerry Built," *Sacramento Bee*, January 26, 1975, p. A-1; Bruce Keppel, "Brown and the Youthful New Spirits," *California Journal*, January 1975, pp. 19–20, and "The New Executives," *California Journal*, February 1975, pp. 51–53; Nancy Skelton, "Percy Pinkney . . . From the Streets of SF to the Governor's Office," *Sacramento Bee*, November 9, 1975, p. S1; Charles Buxton, " 'Old Girls' Network," *California Journal*, January 1980, pp. 37–39. In contrast, Reagan's record of appointing few women and minorities was discussed in Jennifer Jennings, "Are Qualified Females Available for Executive Posts in Sacramento?" *California Journal*, March 1974, pp. 84–85.

28. Ed Salzman, "Judging Jerry," *California Journal*, June 1982, pp. 189–94.

29. In an article about Brown's first budget, Ed Salzman, "The Shape of Brown's First Budget, *California Journal*, February 1975, pp. 55–57, the author called Brown "reminiscent of Reagan" (p. 55). The following year Salzman wrote in "Brown's Second Budget," *California Journal*, February 1976, pp. 57–58, "In case any doubt remained, Governor Brown proved with his second state budget that he really is a skinflint" (p. 57). The article is accompanied by a cartoon showing the Governor's Office entrance as a vault door enscribed "Jack Benny, Financial Consultant."

30. There was a third, more general force for routinization. Highly fluid structures have a tendency to develop patterns with age as people develop routines to avoid uncertainties and to protect their interests. "It is difficult to keep any structure in that dynamic state for long periods of time—to keep behaviors from formalizing and to ensure a steady flow of truly innovative, ad hoc products." Henry Mintzberg, *The Structuring of Organizations* (Englewood Cliffs, N.J.: Prentice-Hall, 1979), p. 455.

31. Although Brown did not support Proposition 13, he did support an alternative tax-reduction proposal.

32. An interview and brief political biography of Davis appears in Henry Abramson, "The Gray Side of Brown," *Sacramento Union*, October 28, 1979, p. C1.

33. Collins also received good press in his earlier jobs as Brown's Legislative aide and as head of the California Conservation Corps. For example, a *Sacramento* magazine article said "his detractors have dubbed him the Brown court jester, but B. T. Collins' blend of blarney and iron discipline has turned the CCC into one of the biggest successes of the governor's administration." Betty Johannsen, "B. T. Collins's Private War," *Sacramento*, June 1981, pp. 53–57.

34. Carrie Dolan, "Brash B. T. Collins Handles the People for the Brown Camp," *Wall Street nal*, July 19, 1982, p. 1.

35. Some program offices that were established by Reagan were given new missions and visibility by Brown. For example, Brown's Office of Criminal Justice Plan-

ning was established by Reagan as the California Commission on Criminal Justice, and the California Arts Commission became Brown's California Arts Council; the California Conservation Corps had its origins in the California Ecology Corps. The CEC was founded by Reagan as a means of providing alternative public service for young men seeking exemption from military duty. See Orville Schell, *Brown* (New York: Random House, 1978) for insightful descriptions of The California Arts Council, the Office of Appropriate Technology, and the California Conservation Corps.

36. Brown fostered what Cohen, March, and Olsen called the "garbage-can" model of decision making. In this model, ideas, solutions, and participants flow in and out of the decision-making process and become associated as much by serendipity as by rational criteria. In the Brown administration this was a deliberate process fostered by the Governor, who believed better decisions come from the nonrestrictive juxta-position of choices and issues. Garbage-can decision making also accorded with the populist, nonhierarchial norms of the 1960s and early 1970s. Like all decision-making systems, it rests on political ideas about who may participate in decisions, the allowable forms of participation, and who has ultimate authority to decide. Michael D. Cohen, James G. March, and Johan P. Olsen, "A Garbage Can Model of Organizational Choice," *Administrative Science Quarterly* 17:1–25.

37. Ed Salzman, "Judging Jerry," p. 194.

38. Ironically, one of the Brown appointees that was indisputably an administrator, Taketsugu Takei, a former public defender and career public official, was subject to criticism *because* he was an administrator. His appointment to head the Department of Consumer Affairs was criticized by consumer advocates because he did not have activist credentials. Ed Salzman, "The Administrator and the Activists," *California Journal*, April 1975, p. 118.

39. "Procunier, Lackner—State's Odd Couple," *Sacramento Bee*, October 11, 1976, section A, p. 3.

40. Jim Lewis, "Reports: Brown Fires Lackner," *Sacramento Bee*, March 24, 1978, p. 1.

41. Jeff Raimundo, "Architect Failed Bureaucracy Test," *Sacramento Bee*, September 10, 1978, section A, p. 1.

42. "Man *vs.* Image," *New York Times*, October 6, 1966, p. 28.

43. Max Weber, *Economy and Society*, p. 991.

44. Ibid., p. 225.

45. Herbert Kaufman, "Emerging Conflicts in the Doctrines of Public Administration." *American Political Science Review* 50 (1956):1062.

46. For a more detailed statement about the modern resolution of the tension between the executive and bureaucracy, see Hamilton and Biggart, "Making the Dilettante an Expert: Personal Staffs in Public Bureaucracies."

47. The idea of organizations as a moral order has been argued by a number of organization theorists, the most influential of which is Philip Selznick. See *Leadership in Administration* (New York: Harper and Row, 1957).

48. The most recent prominent example of this was Jimmy Carter's first years as President. Carter campaigned as an outsider, promising not to make political deals

with Congress and other government actors. True to his word, his first months in office were marked by poor congressional relations and legislative stalemates.

49. This was the presidential address to the Society for the Study of Social Problems, San Francisco, September 1982, reprinted in *Social Problems* 30:258.

50. T. Burns and G. M. Stalker, *The Management of Innovation* (London: Tavistock, 1966); Warren G. Bennis, *Changing Organizations* (New York: McGraw-Hill, 1966).

INDEX